Nassau William Senior, M. C. M. Simpson

Conversations with distinguished Persons during the Second Empire, from 1860 to 1863

Vol. II

Nassau William Senior, M. C. M. Simpson

Conversations with distinguished Persons during the Second Empire, from 1860 to 1863
Vol. II

ISBN/EAN: 9783337166519

Printed in Europe, USA, Canada, Australia, Japan

Cover: Foto ©ninafisch / pixelio.de

More available books at **www.hansebooks.com**

CONVERSATIONS

WITH

DISTINGUISHED PERSONS

DURING THE SECOND EMPIRE

FROM 1860 TO 1863.

BY THE LATE

NASSAU WILLIAM SENIOR

MASTER IN CHANCERY, PROFESSOR OF POLITICAL ECONOMY,
MEMBRE CORRESPONDANT DE L'INSTITUT DE FRANCE, ETC.
AUTHOR OF
'CONVERSATIONS WITH M. THIERS, M. GUIZOT, ETC.'
'A TREATISE ON POLITICAL ECONOMY,' 'BIOGRAPHICAL SKETCHES,' 'ESSAYS ON FICTION,'
'HISTORICAL AND PHILOSOPHICAL ESSAYS,'
'JOURNALS KEPT IN TURKEY AND GREECE,' 'JOURNALS KEPT IN IRELAND,'
'JOURNALS KEPT IN FRANCE AND ITALY,'
'CORRESPONDENCE AND CONVERSATIONS WITH ALEXIS DE TOCQUEVILLE,' ETC.

EDITED BY HIS DAUGHTER

M. C. M. SIMPSON.

IN TWO VOLUMES.
VOL. II.

LONDON:
HURST AND BLACKETT, PUBLISHERS,
13 GREAT MARLBOROUGH STREET.
1880.

CONTENTS

TO

THE SECOND VOLUME.

1862.

Saturday, March 8th.

CONVERSATION WITH HOTZE.

	PAGE
Causes of the rupture between North and South America	3
Superiority of the South	4
Aggressions of the South	4
Estimate of the two armies	5
The poor Whites	5
Pecuniary resources of the South	7
No Unionist party in the South	7
Probable terms of accommodation	9
The North will regain its preponderance	9
The South has less political ambition	10
Meeting at the Institute	10
Claims of Vuitry	11
Speech of Guizot	11

Tuesday, March 11th.

CONVERSATION WITH D. E. F.

Apartments in Paris	13
The garrets are schools of vice	13
General Charras' History of the Campaign of 1815	14

CONTENTS.

	PAGE
The Italian Republicans	15
Objects of the Provvidemento Society	16
Assassins seldom succeed	16
Because they will not sacrifice their own lives	17
Louis Napoleon fears the Italian dagger	17
This will induce him to withdraw from Rome	17
Clerical party weak in the army and in Paris	18
Rattazzi and Ricasoli	18
Naples hates Northern Italy	19

Wednesday, March 12th.

Visit to the Corps Législatif	19
Speech of Billault	19
Ministers *sans portefeuille*	19
The Senate is inaccessible	20

Thursday, March 13th.

| Dinner with Prince Napoleon | 20 |

CONVERSATION WITH THE PRINCE, PIETRI, X, Y, W, PETINET, R, AND MADAME DE ———.

The French want '*caractère*'	21
They hate their superiors	21
The peasant hates the priest	21
He tolerates the préfet	22
The *ouvrier* hates his *patron* and the *Bourgeois*	22
The *Bourgeois* hates everybody	23
No aristocracy except official aristocracy	23
No possibility of liberty except in religion	24
Religious tolerance arises from disbelief	24
France is less illiberal than she was in 1852	25
The press should be absolutely free	25
The system of *avertissement*	26
Probable return of opposition members to the Chamber	27
The Emperor's compliment to Thiers	27
The French should evacuate Rome	28
Savoy would rather be French than Piedmontese	29

CONTENTS.

CONVERSATION WITH MADAME DE CIRCOURT.
Madame Mohl's book on Madame Récamier . . . 29
Idolatry of Chateaubriand 30
Character of Madame de Chateaubriand . . . 30
Augustin Thierry 30
Lavergne is anxious about the Mexican expedition . 31

CONVERSATION WITH A. B. C.
He is even more alarmed than Lavergne . . 32
Emperor's motives for making the war . . . 33
He wishes to dazzle 33
He likes his actions to be unexpected 33
His blunders in 1859 33
Probability of the crown being offered to Maximilian . 34
England would be perfectly satisfied 34

CONVERSATION WITH GUTIERREZ DE ESTRADA.
The Spaniards have made the expedition unpopular 35
Our interference absolutely necessary . . . 35
He prays for Maximilian 35

CONVERSATION WITH BARON GROS.
Barbarities of the Taepings 36
French conquests in Cochin China . . . 36
England is glad of French distant conquests . . 36

Saturday, March 15th.
CONVERSATION WITH MADAME CORNU.
Louis Napoleon's delight in his *Cæsar* 36
Prince Napoleon has no designs on Naples . . . 37
He cannot bear to leave Paris 37
The Campana collection 38
Antonelli accuses him falsely 38
Weakness of Pio Nono 39
Rival bidders for the collection 39

	PAGE
Abominable treatment of Campana	39
Madame A——'s exhibition	40

EVENING AT MRS. DIGBY'S.
Gérard the lion-killer 41

Sunday, March 16*th.*
Sermon of the Père Félix	42
Three insurrections of *la raison contre la foi* . . .	42
The first was Protestantism in the 15th century . .	42
The second against the Supernatural in the 18th century	42
The third is pure Scepticism in the 19th century . .	43
This last will fail as that of the 18th has failed . .	44
He used the word *foi* in different senses . . .	44

CONVERSATION WITH A. B. C. AND CORCELLE.
The debates have been mischievous to Louis Napoleon .	45
His policy cannot bear discussion	45
Speech of Billault	45
Folly of the Opposition to Palikao's pension . . .	46
Anomalous position of the Assembly	47
Celui-ci must obtain some military success . . .	47
His desire for power is insatiable	48
He would like to be head of the Gallican Church . .	48
Frenchmen always wish to be with the majority . .	49
The peasant likes his curé	49
The peasantry and bourgeoisie the only religious parties	49

Monday, March 17*th.*
CONVERSATION WITH LASTEYRIE.
Passion for political *égalité* in France	50
There is little social *égalité*	50
In London there is much more	50
The difference is shown in marriage	51
Tocqueville's candidature in 1837 . . .	51

CONTENTS.

CONVERSATION WITH CIRCOURT.
 Aristocratic character of Parisian society . . . 52
 Noble families in France 52
 Marriage between a bourgeoise and a noble . . . 53
 Noble young ladies will not marry *roturiers* . . . 55

Friday, March 21st.
CONVERSATION WITH CORNELLIS DE WITT.
 Position of the Emperor has deteriorated . . . 55
 His Italian campaign 55
 The Austrian army ill commanded 56
 The peace not such as he wished 56
 Three causes of distress 56
 Unpopularity of Commercial Treaty 57
 Sense of political insecurity 57
 A conspiracy discovered 57
 The Emperor cannot depend on the army . . . 58
 They despise his military talent 59
 Distant expeditions unpopular 59
 Financial deficits 59
 Speech of the Marquis de Pierre 60
 Chances of war with England 61

Saturday, March 22nd.
CONVERSATION WITH LASTEYRIE.
 Politics of the Marquis de Pierre 62
 General *malaise* 62
 The new taxes must be withdrawn 63
 The Palikao business 63
 Emperor's quarrel with the Society of St. Vincent de
  Paul 63
 Dulness of ecclesiastics 64
 Their ignorance . . . . 64·

CONVERSATION WITH CIRCOURT.
 Ignorance of the Père Lacordaire 65

CONTENTS.

Sunday, March 23rd.

CONVERSATION WITH SAY.

	PAGE
Louis Napoleon has lost strength	66
Difficulty of imposing new taxes	66
His possible successors	66
He will fall by some unforeseen blow	67

Monday, March 24th.

CONVERSATION WITH HORE AND CIRCOURT.

The *Gloire* and the *Warrior*	67
Paris never safe from an *émeute*	68
French princes right in joining the Federal army	68
Influence of the Prince de Joinville over President Lincoln	69
Extent of a peasant's vocabulary	70
Conversation in the Faubourg St. Germain	70
Conversation of two Turks	70

CONVERSATION WITH D. E. F.

The Imperial throne is shaking	71
D. E. F. thinks so for the first time since 1854	71
Can be saved only by a successful war	71
The army does not respect him	72
He is unpopular in the *ateliers*	72
The *bourgeois* has no more belief than the *ouvrier*	73
Who are the people that fill the churches?	73
Unpopularity of the clerical party overthrew the Restoration and Louis Philippe	73
Hypocrisy of Louis Philippe's and Louis Napoleon's Governments	73
Nothing irritates the French so much	74
The Père Gratry's *conférences*	74

DINNER AT KERGORLAY'S.

Dayton's opinion of the chances of reunion of the States	75

CONTENTS.　　　　　　　xi

Tuesday, March 25th.
CONVERSATION WITH SLIDELL.
The French sympathise with the North . . . 76
There is no Unionist party in the South . . . 76
England ought to have recognised the South . . 77
Threat of Mr. Seward 77
International law influences constitutional governments 77
Distress in English manufacturing counties . . . 78
Europe will not intervene in America 78
Obstinacy of North and South 78
Whether the South would abolish slavery . . . 79
Impossible in that climate 79
Coloured agriculturists must be slaves 79
Condition of the British West Indian Islands . . 80
Separation of slave families a myth 80
Emancipation in Louisiana 80
Doubling of slave population 81

CONVERSATION WITH LAVERGNE.
Louis Napoleon behaved well in the *Trent* affair . . 81
He is playing the part of a constitutional king . . 81
Palikao letter 81
His behaviour to the Corps Législatif 82
France does not wish for constitutional government . 83
There is no Bonapartist party 83
The First Napoleon is forgotten 83
Who the Bonapartists are 84

CONVERSATION WITH JOBEZ.
The First Napoleon is forgotten 84
Success under universal suffrage depends on notoriety . 85

CONVERSATION WITH ST. HILAIRE.
There is no Bonapartist party 86
The dynasty will fall 86
Louis Napoleon is a Fatalist 86
Financial difficulties 87

CONTENTS.

DINNER AT MASSON'S.
CONVERSATION WITH MASSON, DUVERGIER, LANJUINAIS, BUFFET, AND CORCELLE.

	PAGE
The nominees of the Emperor his fiercest opponents	88
Morny's unsent letter	89
Importance of the opposition	90
Emperor has promised not to dissolve	90
Persigny declares he will influence the elections	90
The new constitutional machine will not work	91
Inconsistency of Billault's speech	92
Impolicy of offending the Pope	92

Friday, March 28th.
Madame Duchâtel's concert 92

CONVERSATION WITH DUMON AND CORCELLE.

Louis Napoleon is despised	93
Unpopularity of the Commercial Treaty	93
The salt-tax a heavy burden	94
Story of the Emperor at the railway station	94
Obsequiousness of Fleury	95

Sunday, March 30th.
CONVERSATION WITH M. J.

Portrait of the Emperor's charger	95
The barricades in 1832	96
The army will fail to support Louis Napoleon	97

Tuesday, April 1st.
CONVERSATION WITH AUGUSTE CHEVALIER.

Weakness of the dynasty	97
Gradual growth of the change	97
Courses open to Louis Napoleon in 1852	87
He chose to be despotic	98
The nation was sick of parliamentary government	98
Success made him confident	98

CONTENTS. xiii

	PAGE
He resolved to unmuzzle the Chambers	98
He invented *ministres sans portefeuille*	98
The parliamentary campaign ended in defeat	99
Mistakes of Baroche	99
Advantages of the Opposition	100
He must drift into parliamentary government	100
He will prefer to make a *coup d'état*	100
France seems to be without leaders	100
There are three organized bodies: the Army, the Church, and the Secret Societies	101
MacMahon the most popular man in France	101
Changarnier is forgotten	102
Importance of the secret societies	102
The foreign relations of France are going from bad to worse	103
Louis Napoleon managed them well up to 1855	103
They were managed by Drouyn de Lhuys	103
Since that time the Emperor has made enemies of everybody	103
He is a Creole, a Corsican, and a Dutchman	104
He is calm in the presence of danger	104
Lavalette's and Goyon's instructions are opposed to each other	105

Wednesday, April 2nd.
CONVERSATION WITH RENCONTRE.

The *ouvriers* are all Republicans	105
They are not Socialists	106
They are all Italians and Unitarians	106
They do not listen to the clergy	106
Increased expense of living	107
Lodgings have become insufficient	107
Wages have risen very little	108
Story of the shoemaker's son	108
Simon collects money to obtain a substitute	108

Saturday, April 5th.
DINNER AT MADAME ANISSON'S.

Madame Anisson objects to the English luncheon	109
A day for morning reception is worse	110
English downs and commons	110
The village green unknown in France	110

CONVERSATION WITH THIERS.

Louis Napoleon's reign as an absolute monarch is over	111
The remnant of liberty has destroyed it	111
His domestic policy is as mischievous as his foreign policy	111
Will he silence the tribunes?	112
His next step must be parliamentary government	112
Il sait reculer	112
Obstinate in his ends, not in his means	112
Europe should intervene in Mexico	113
The interference of France alone is Quixotic	113
The Emperor would not tolerate a Bourbon in Mexico	113
The Mexicans proposed Maximilian	114

Monday, April 7th.
CONVERSATION WITH MADAME CORNU.

Louis Napoleon's character changed by his brother's death	114
He believes that he has a mission	114
He worships his son	115
Constitutionalism more favourable to his dynasty than despotism	115
He will sacrifice anything to preserve his dynasty	115
Readiness to confess mistakes	116
He delights in astonishing and thinks himself inspired	116
His suppressed fits of passion	116
Endeavours to conceal his expression	117
He thinks himself like Hernani	117
Adoration of his child	118
Relations with Prince Napoleon	118

CONTENTS. xv

	PAGE
His *entourage*	118
His prestige is sinking	119
Probability of a reconciliation between him and Madame Cornu	119

CONVERSATION WITH MONTALEMBERT AND SIMON.

Italian unity will be followed by German unity	120
Interview between Montalembert and the Emperor	120
The French, not the English, require passports in France	121
Humiliation of this law	121
Arrest and imprisonment of Veuillemont	121
Difficulty of getting servants in Paris	122
Their garrets are uninhabitable	122
Conversion of Lacordaire	123
Success as a preacher slow	124
His liberalism	124
Rashness of Montalembert	125
Louis Napoleon is afraid of him	125
Ignorance of Lacordaire	125
His imagination, quickness, force, and facility	126
His moral excellencies	126
His disinterestedness and modesty	127
Sacrifice of his will	127
And of his life	127

April 8th.
CONVERSATION WITH CORBON AND SIMON.

History of Corbon	128
There is no Bonapartist party	128
The army get disheartened	128
Means of resisting an *émeute* improved	129
So are the means of making an *émeute*	129
The Republicans are enthusiastically Italian and Anti-papists	129
A fair day's work ought to ensure a fair day's wages	129
The Imperial *régime* supported by fear of a free press	130
Even that danger is overlooked	130

BREAKFAST AT SENIOR'S.
CONVERSATION WITH HOTZE AND SLIDELL, CORCELLE, DUVERGIER, AND LANJUINAIS.

No fear of the negroes being emancipated	130
The negro was not intended for freedom	131
He does not wish for emancipation	131
It would be followed by the destruction of both races	131
Cruel treatment of slaves is illegal	132
Yet a black must not give evidence against a white	132
Europe will become neutral and acknowledge the South	133
The South will retire before the North until its independence is acknowledged	133
Fate of the Border States	134
Lincoln is not an Abolitionist	134
The South will remain a Republic	134
The North will sink into despotism and anarchy	134
New Orleans and all the Southern ports will be free	135

DINNER AT MR. DAYTON'S.
CONVERSATION WITH WEED, BIGELOW, DAYTON, AND DOREMUS.

They see the beginning of the end	136
Slaves will cease to have political value	136
New Fugitive Slave law	137
No interference with the municipal laws of the South	137
The North will assume the Southern debt on its reunion with the South	137
Emancipation of the slaves the last weapon	138
How to deal with emancipated slaves and poor whites	138
The English do not want them in Jamaica	139
They would die of hunger in Central America	139
The South to be treated as William the Conqueror treated England	140
The slave-owners will be ruined	140
How to deal with the slaves in the Border States	141
France, but not the Emperor, sympathises with the North	141

CONTENTS.   xvii

	PAGE
Story of Mr. Seward and the Duke of Newcastle	142
Dr. Doremus' improvement in gunpowder	144

April 9th.
CONVERSATION WITH MOHL AND RENAN.
Dr. Cureton's edition of St. Matthew 148
Genesis contains fragments older than Moses . . 149
Difference between Hebrew poetry and Hebrew prose . 149
Age of the book of Job 149
About the time of Homer 150
Superior theology of the Semitic race 150
Despair of Job 151
There is no argument in Job 153
Impatience of Job 154
Age of the Song of Solomon 154
Exaggerations in the book of Kings 155
Interpretation of the Song of Solomon 155
The heroine a Shulamite girl, taken to Solomon's seraglio 156
It is a picture of real love 157
Its appreciation of natural beauty . . 157

Comparison of Renan's translation with the English version 158

CONVERSATION WITH DUFAURE AND DUVERGIER.
Bill for the amendment of criminal law . . 160
It favours summary conviction for political offences 160
Story of M. de Flers 160
Mr. Senior liable to imprisonment . . 161

Thursday, April 10th.
CONVERSATION WITH THE DUC DE BROGLIE AND DUMON.
The government is a despotism collapsing . 162
Fould a bad Minister of Finance . . . 162
Imperialist pieces hissed at the theatres . . 163

VOL. II.   *b*

CONTENTS.

Friday, April 11th.
BREAKFAST AT SENIOR'S.
CONVERSATION WITH CHANGARNIER, GUIZOT, ARRIVABENE, AND CIRCOURT.

	PAGE
Critical position of the Federals in America	164
Difficulties of the march to Richmond	164
Lacordaire on the power of space	165
Fortifications of Antwerp	166
Fortifications of Paris	167
Prince Napoleon refused the crown of Naples	167
Power of amalgamation in an army	168
Conduct of the United States towards Mexico	168
France favours the North on the supposition that the North is opposed to England	169
America is the enemy of all Europe	169
Negotiations with the United States	170
Negotiations with England	170
Lord Palmerston perfectly honest	170
Not much honesty in the House of Commons	170
Peel wore two masks	170

CONVERSATION WITH FÉNÉLON AND CHEVALIER.

Fénélon thinks ill of the Federal cause	171
Wretched state of South America	172
No roads, shops, or manufactures	172
Tenacity and endurance of the South	172
Wastes its strength in uncombined operations	172
MacClellan's army is not yet a good one	173
It wants officers and traditions	173
France would easily beat in a war on the Rhine	174

April 12th.

Guizot's praise of his English friends	174
No jealousy between the distinguished men of letters	174

CONVERSATION WITH THIERS AND DUVERGIER.
 The liberty remaining in the Government is making it
  cease to be despotic 175
 The Emperor has irritated every class 175
 The clerical party by forsaking the Pope . . . 175
 The manufacturers by the Treaty 176
 The fund-holders by the deficit 176
 The lovers of peace by his senseless wars . . . 176
 Austria has not taken the place of Russia . . . 176
 France finds Imperialism a failure . . . 176
 To yield ill is fatal to a despot 176
 In the Palikao affair he yielded ill 177
 He must give up his ministers 177
 Fould the worst of them 177
 Absurdity of the *ministres sans portefeuille* . . . 177
 Only by these means can he prolong his dynasty . . 178
 Palmerston believes in Italian unity 178
 Scarcely any Frenchman does so 178
 Victor Hugo's *Misérables* 178
 Michelet and Victor Hugo 179

April 12th.
CONVERSATION WITH PRINCE NAPOLEON.
 He agrees with Lord Palmerston 179
 Rome must become united to Italy 179
 The Pope's death would be a great misfortune . . 179
 His probable successor 180

1863.

Sunday, March 29th.
CONVERSATION WITH LAVERGNE.
 Paris is asleep 183
 The Legitimists are forgotten, the Orleanists despair,
  and the Bonapartists have ceased to exist . . 184
 No love for the Imperial dynasty 184

	PAGE
The Empire has wantonly destroyed its prestige	184
Unpopularity of the Mexican war	185
The officers are *désillusionnés*	185
Celui-ci remains because the *Rouges* are feared	186
Expenses of an Opposition candidate	186
A Government candidate has neither trouble nor expense	186
The Government will not tolerate an opposition	187

Thursday, April 2nd.
CONVERSATION WITH LANJUINAIS.

Mr. Senior's article too severe on the French	188
Their abject submission is founded on fear of revolution	188
The Bonapartist threaten a general *sans-culotterie*	188
The *prolétaires*, the bourgeoisie, and the army	188
Any two can crush the third	189
The army is proprietary and anti-revolutionist	189
The *Garde* is the blind instrument of the Empire	190
The mob is Socialistic	190
The Emperor may combine the two	190
Centralisation a network of espionage and coercion	190
The Constitution not to be touched	191
The Emperor would willingly improve it	191
He knows that only constitutional dynasties are safe	191
Between him and freedom rolls a sea of blood	191
Liberty of the press would sweep him away in three months	191
The ministers would become contemptible	191
As soon as the people joined the bourgeoisie, the army would join them and turn against him	192

Friday, April 3rd.
CONVERSATION WITH PRINCE NAPOLEON.

English have no active sympathy with Poland	192
The French cannot forget that the Poles have fought with them	193
English policy is founded on reason, French on sentiment	193

CONTENTS. xxi

	PAGE
England cannot help admiring the self-devotion of the Poles	193
Or detesting the barbarity of Russia	193
Baseness of Prussia	194
Austria fears to give up her share of the spoil	194
England folds her arms	195
The French tell the Poles to rely on the Czar	195
That was an insult of Billault's	195
France will do something great	195
France does not wish for war	195
But she is always ready to sacrifice herself	195
English statesmen	195
Character of Lord Palmerston	196
The English like commonplaces	196
Treatment of servants in England and in France	197

Saturday, April 4th.
CONVERSATION WITH D. E. F.

Split in the Liberal party	197
Principles of Ollivier	197
His ideas are impracticable	197
Consequences of the death of Louis Napoleon	198

Sunday, April 5th.
CONVERSATION WITH MADAME CORNU.

Her reconciliation with the Emperor	198
Scene at the Tuileries	199
She sees him now frequently	200
Charming manners of the Empress	200
Comparison between Louis Napoleon and his cousin	201
Emperor disapproved of his Polish speech	202
Emperor's delight in the *Cæsar*	202
He is longing to be a member of the Academy	203

CONVERSATION WITH CORCELLE.
Guizot's opinion that the Emperor should be received with open arms by the Academy 203

CONTENTS.

	PAGE
Corcelle calls on Lamartine by mistake	204
Letters on both sides	205
They are reconciled	206
Lamartine's lavish expenditure	206

Monday, April 6th.
DINNER AT DROUYN' DE LHUYS.
CONVERSATION WITH ROUHER AND HERBET.

The French owe free-trade to the Emperor	207
Hard work of French officials	207
Magnificence of the Hôtel des Affaires Etrangères	208

Friday, April 10th.
CONVERSATION WITH MONTALEMBERT AND CARNÉ.

Why England is cold to Poland	208
Likelihood of a general war	208
France would begin by taking the Rhine	209
The Mexican war a God-send to Europe	209
Until 1804, absolute power was forgotten in Europe	210
The Roman Emperors are beginning to be admired	210
Universal suffrage will prevail everywhere	210
Candidates for the Academy	211

CONVERSATION WITH THIERS.

The Opposition will gain members in the new Chamber	211
Ought Thiers to be a candidate?	212
Thiers dislikes systematic opposition	212
He likes the prospect of power	212
Preference of a literary life	213

Saturday, April 11th.
CONVERSATION WITH ARCHBISHOP BONNECHOSE.

The Commercial Treaty and American war have ruined France	213
The French deeply wounded by the language of Lord Palmerston	214
A war with England would be enthusiastically welcomed	214

PARTY AT THE EMBASSY.
  The ministers of North and South America equally angry
    with England 214

Sunday, April 14th.
CONVERSATION WITH CIRCOURT.
  The conscription in Poland a Polish act . . . 215
  A new levy had become necessary 215
  Falstaff's method of recruiting 215
  The practice in Russia 216
  Wielopolski suggests that the recruits should be taken
    from towns 216
  He took none from the upper classes 216
  Montalembert is wrong in supposing them all unwilling . 217
  Wielopolski acted as Cavaignac did in 1848, and Louis
    Napoleon in 1852 217
  He made soldiers of dangerous persons 217
  They made exiles and prisoners 217
  Continental recruits are always unwilling . . . 217
  Why this recruitment was specially disliked . . . 218
  Few peasants joined in the insurrection . . . 218
  The *petite noblesse* in Poland 218
  Russian Government is not unpopular with the lower
    classes 219
  No Poles in the Duchy of Posen 219
  There are really 780,000 219
  The Germans buy out the Poles 220
  Statistics of Poland 220
  How the Poles got into Russia 217
  They introduced serfdom 221
  Mischievous and turbulent character of the Poles . . 221
  They are consequently always ill-treated . . . 222
  The Mexican war has saved France from a great
    danger 222
  Mexico will become another Algeria 223
  Neither wars nor colonies pay their expenses . . 223

	PAGE
England the object of general dislike and calumny .	223
Russia will fight to the knife	224

Monday, April 13th.
CONVERSATION WITH DROUYN DE LHUYS.

Europe is full of burning questions . .	225
The hottest is Poland	225
France is unanimous on the subject . . .	225
Demands of England	225
Russia refuses to execute the Treaty of 1815 . .	225
Poland destroyed her rights by her rebellion in 1830	226
France refuses to join in the demands of England . .	226
They sent a concurrent note with Austria .	227
Resistance of Poland for ninety years	227
She is a rallying point for revolutionists . . .	227
The independence of Poland the only remedy . .	228
Her population is too scattered	228
The kingdom of Poland could maintain itself . .	229
Would their neighbours let them alone? . . .	230
The insurgents have shown great courage and fidelity to their cause	230
A congress of little practical use	231
Disunion among the insurgents	231

Wednesday, April 15th.
CONVERSATION WITH MADAME CORNU.

The Emperor cannot attract the old aristocracy . .	232
The aristocracy he has created is rich . . .	232
Dance at the Hôtel des Affaires Etrangères . . .	232
Party at Madame de Montalembert's . . .	233
Reception at Madame d'Haussonville's . . .	233

CONVERSATION WITM MADAME D'HAUSSONVILLE.

Rank in France and in England	233
The grandson of a duke a commoner . . .	233

Thursday, April 16*th.*
DINNER AT DUCHÂTEL'S.
CONVERSATION WITH DUMON AND M. AND MADAME DUCHÂTEL
French are becoming less insane on the Polish Question . 234
Difficulties of the expedition 234
A war with Russia would be unpopular . . . 235
The Emperor does not wish for one . . . 235
Challenge of young Wielopolski 235
The Prince should once for all decline such challenges . 236
Public opinion in France would not support him . 237
Madame Castiglione in a *tableau vivant* 238
Duchâtel fears a war with America . . . 238
Appointment of Admiral Wilkes 238
Madness of North America 238
To be always pacific does not ensure peace . . . 239
The *Trent* outrage a case in point . . 240

Friday, April 17*th.*
CONVERSATION WITH CIESKOWSKI.
Possibility of an independent Polish kingdom . . 240
Claims of Poland 240
On that ground England may claim the South of France 241
Populations of Polish territories 241
The sympathy of the people the chief ground . 241
The peasants have not joined in the insurrection . 242
They care for forms though not for doctrines . 242
Only the nobles wish for independence 243

CONVERSATION WITH URISKI AND MICHEL CHEVALIER.
There are not sixteen millions of Poles 243
Poland would not be strong enough to remain independent 243
It would be the slave of Russia 243
The Poles have no capacity for self-government . . 244
The best thing would be to become united to Prussia . 244
Folly of the idolatry of nationality 244

xxvi   CONTENTS.

	PAGE
As shown in the Ionian Islands	244
The Crédit Mobilier	245
Expense of living in Paris	245
Dinners from *restaurateurs*	245
Democracy the bane of refinement	246

April 18th.
DINNER AT THE EMBASSY.

News from Rome	247
Madame Duchâtel at the Embassy	247
Orleanists do not go there	247

Sunday, April 19th.
CONVERSATION WITH THIERS.

No remedy for the Poles	247
Unless they try to make their government work well	247
French assistance impossible	247
Sweden is burning to recover Finland	248
Duty of interfering with a friendly sovereign	248
Sweden expects France to help her	248
All Europe would rise up against her	249
Russia will not grant Polish independence	249
Motive of the Federals for insulting England	249

Monday, April 20th.
CONVERSATION WITH MADAME CORNU AND MAURY.

Interview with the Emperor	250
Cause of his high spirits	250
Pressure on him to take up the Polish cause	250
Nonsense talked about Poland	251
A war for Poland would be popular	251
Louis Napoleon may find it difficult to resist	251
Emperor's candidature for the Academy	252
His *Cæsar* very good	252
English writers seldom improve after fifty	253
The case is different in France	253

CONTENTS.   xxvii

	PAGE
Voltaire improved till he died	253
Adoration of style	253

Tuesday, April 21st.
CONVERSATION WITH AUGUSTE CHEVALIER.

He is editing the *Constitutionnel* and the *Pays*	254
Temptations of newspaper editors	254
The former editor put in by Mirès	255
Nothing to be done with Rome	255
Relations between Prince Napoleon and the Emperor	255
Nothing to be done about Poland	256
Sedative administered to the Pope	256
The Emperor intensely Southern	257
No one can prophesy about the French	257

CONVERSATION WITH BUFFET.

The Catholic Church is infallible	257
Mr. Gorham's a parallel case	257
A Catholic may inquire	258
The Church affirms the damnation only of Judas	258
The Athanasian Creed intolerant	258
It is necessary to believe in the Immaculate Conception	259

April 22nd.
CONVERSATION WITH CIRCOURT.

Chance of Russia attacking Sweden	259
Finland is well governed and loyal to Russia	259
The Fins are Lutherans, Poles are Catholics	259
Outrages at Minsk a fabrication	260
Polish peasantry better than the nobles	260
The insurrection is subsiding	260
The peasants have not joined in it	261
Russia is anxious to conciliate Poland	261
The conscription not the cause of the insurrection	261
The mine was prepared by the Anarchists	261
Russian institutions rapidly improving	262

	PAGE
Success of the emancipation of the serfs . . .	262
State of the Polish *petite noblesse* hopeless . . .	262
Incurable folly of the Polish nobility . . .	263

April 23rd.
CONVERSATION WITH DUC DE BROGLIE.

The Emperor is trying to envenom the relations between England and America	263
He wants a *coup de théâtre*	263
Difficulty of a war with Poland	263
Wishes to join England against North America . .	263
Incomprehensible conduct of the North . . .	264
England sympathised with the North at first . .	264

April 24th.
CONVERSATION WITH CIRCOURT.

Future map of America	265
The Federals seem bent on suicide . . .	266
They will not drive England into war . . .	266
England should join France in Mexico . . .	267
And recognise the Confederates	267
Note on M. de Circourt . . .	268

April 27th.
CONVERSATION WITH GUIZOT AND CHANGARNIER.

Four great bodies in France	269
The Military the only good one	269
Subserviency of the other three	269
The army only is free	270
It is the friend of order	271
Emperor is not popular in it	271
Blunders of the Austrians	271
Emperor was surprised at Montebello, Magentâ, and Solferino	272
Cigars consumed by him at Magenta and Solferino .	272

CONTENTS.

	PAGE
Absorbing effect of responsibility	273
Louis Napoleon is popular with the 'Garde'.	273
Difference between the 'Garde' of the First and the 'Garde' of the Second Napoleon	273
Enmity between Louis Napoleon's 'Garde' and the 'Ligne'	274
The 'Ligne' would join the 'Émeutiers' and destroy the Empire	275

CONVERSATION WITH GUTIERREZ DE ESTRADA.

Sketch of his history	275
Terrible change for the worse in Mexico in 1840	275
Wishes the Mexicans to return to Monarchy	276
Commission from Santa Anna in 1854	277
Disturbances in Mexico between 1855 and 1860	277
Misgovernment of Juarez in 1861	279
Proclamation of the Allies	279
United States would not allow Mexico to become a Monarchy	280
Estrada visits the Archduke Maximilian	280

April 30th.
CONVERSATION WITH DROUYN DE LHUYS.

He is puzzled by the conduct of England	281
Her interest is to establish good government in Mexico	281
Letters from Sir C. Wyke to Lord John Russell describing the miserable state of Mexico	282–288
English jealousy	288
Lord John's letter to the English Admiral	288
Our object only to protect British interests	288
Can be done only by establishing good government there	288
Ultimatum of the French Admiral	289
The Spanish and English refused to adopt the ultimatum	289
Each party has fulfilled its threats	289
The Archduke would have been established if England had joined	290

England would be glad to see Mexico an Algeria	290
It would be a mistake for France	290
Mexico may still be made a Constitutional Monarchy	291
Otherwise it will become a great slave-holding Republic	291
French troops no longer popular there	292
Evil of England keeping aloof	292
Unpopularity in France of the war	292
The opposition will be much stronger in the new Chamber	293
The English distrust universal suffrage	293
Do not believe that the Mexicans wish for Maximilian	293
England should interfere frankly	294
The word 'non-interference' has a magic power	294
Madame Viardot's 'Orfeo'	294
Absurdity of the libretto	295

May 1st.
CONVERSATION WITH RENAN.

His view on inspiration	296
The Gospels compiled in the first century	296
Gospel of St. John	297
Prediction of the end of the world	297
And the end of the Temple	298
Scanty memoranda of Christ's teaching	299
Time when the Gospels were successively written	300
Impression of melancholy erroneous	300
The Pagan and Jewish Golden Ages	301
Beauty of Palestine	301
Charm of Nazareth	302
Beauty of Nazarene women	302
Our Saviour's delight in Galilee	303
Eastern lower classes unlike ours	303
Every previous religion was ascetic	304
Cheerfulness of Christ's teaching	304
He sympathised with all testimonies of affection	305
Harmony of the band of disciples	305
Expectation of the kingdom of Heaven	305

Joyousness of these pilgrimages proclaiming the 'Good News' 305
The kingdom foretold was a spiritual kingdom . . 306
Immense superiority of Christian countries . . . 306

April 26th.
CONVERSATION WITH MR. DAYTON.
Conduct of America to England 306
Opinions of Frenchmen 307
Influence of the *Times* 307
Appointment of Captain Wilkes 307
Mr. Cassius Clay's despatches 308
Conduct of England in the *Alabama* 308
The Confederates conceal their dislike of England . . 309
No interference could stop the war 309
The South will be starved out 310
The English should have stopped the *Alabama* . . 310
She should stop the Ironsides 310
Conduct of the United States in the Crimean war . . 310
They stopped the building of ships for Russia . . 310
The English should amend their laws 310
If not, the American people will become ungovernable . 311

CONVERSATIONS.

1862.

[AFTER the death of Cavour (June 6, 1861), Italy for a time ceased to advance.

Cavour was succeeded by Ricasoli, a man of unbending integrity, but unpopular with the majority. He succumbed to a party intrigue in March 1862, and Rattazzi became Prime Minister in his stead. The French troops still remained in Rome, and Venice continued in the hands of the Austrians.

The chief object of interest at this time was the American war. England was greatly excited by the capture, while on board a British steamer—the *Trent*—of Messrs. Slidell and Mason, and two other commissioners from the Southern States, on November 8, 1861. In consequence of the earnest representations of the British Government, they were set free in the following month.

Affairs had for some time been going on in a very unsatisfactory manner in Mexico. The situation of foreigners had become so intolerable, that, after much vain negotiation, the English, French, and Spanish Governments signed a convention, engaging to combine hostile opèrations against Mexico. On the 8th of December, 1861, the Spanish troops landed at Vera Cruz. It surrendered on the 17th, and on the 7th and 8th of January the British naval and French military expeditions arrived, and issued a proclamation to the Mexican Government. A conference with commissioners chosen by Juarez was appointed, in which the French commissioner, M. de Saligny, refused to take part.

Perceiving that the real object of the French was to overturn the whole government of Mexico, and to set up a sovereign of their own nomination (the Archduke Maximilian), the English and Spanish Governments resolved to take no further part in the expedition, and withdrew their troops, leaving France to carry on the war alone.

The increased freedom of debate granted by the Emperor of the French in 1861 was productive of more harm than good to his government. In consequence of the success obtained by General Montauban in Cochin China, the Emperor wished to confer on him the title of Count de Palikao, and to create him a Senator, with a dotation or *majorat* in perpetuity of 2000*l.* a-year, by means of a bill to be passed in the Chamber. It met with so much opposition in the Corps Législatif, that General Montauban wrote to the Emperor asking that it might be withdrawn. To this Louis Napoleon, however, would not consent, and in his reply to the General he wrote that '*degenerate nations* alone dole out public gratitude.' This expression gave much offence, and the Emperor was forced to yield, and to withdraw the bill.—ED.]

Paris, Hôtel Bedford, Rue de l'Arcade, Saturday, March 8.—We reached Paris yesterday evening, but before I begin a Paris journal I must record a conversation which I had in London the day before yesterday with Mr. Hotze, a South American, sent to England by President Davis, with a commission to act as consul as soon as the Confederacy shall be recognised. He is of Mobile, in Alabama, where he has long edited the principal newspaper. He was a strong opponent to secession ; but when it had taken place he joined the Confederate army, and served for six months.

I asked his theory as to the origin of the rupture.

Hotze.—It was not the tariff. The South itself is protectionist wherever, as in the cases of sugar and tobacco, it thinks that it can gain by protection. It was not slavery. The Abolitionists are, at least were, a small and unpopular party. We all knew Lincoln to be as convinced of the fitness of slavery in countries where whites cannot labour as we are ourselves. · It was, in the language of the Divorce Court, incompatibility of temper. No two European nations, not the Dutch and the Spaniards, are so different as the Northern and Southern Americans. The Yankee does not loathe the Negro more than we loathe the Yankee. We despise his selfishness, his avarice, and his vanity; we are disgusted by his vulgarity; we fear and detest his fraud. While we could keep him down, while indeed he was only our equal, we tolerated the Union. At first there was no difficulty. We were the superiors in numbers and in wealth. But the climate and the ports of the North, and its concentrated, exclusive, unscrupulous devotion to gain and to accumulation, turned the balance in its favour. It required the greatest skill and unremitting vigilance on the part of the South, to hold its position.

Senior.—The South was not very scrupulous.

Hotze.—It was not. The purchase of Louisiana, the breach of the Missouri compromise, the annexation of Texas, the invasion of Mexico, and the Fugitive Slave Law, were all acts of aggression. We could defend ourselves only by sallying out. But the time came when we saw that further resistance was impossible. The election of Lincoln showed that the North had obtained a decided preponderance, a preponderance which every year would increase. An American President, as you know, is far more powerful than an European sovereign, for he appoints almost every federal official. If we had not seceded, or if we were now to re-enter the Union, we should be a degraded caste, such as the impure castes are in India, such as the Irish Catholics were during the Protestant ascendancy. I myself vehemently opposed secession. I doubted its success, and dreaded its miseries. But I now think that it was wise.

Senior.—Do you doubt its success now?

Hotze.—Not in the least. We are now, notwithstanding these new Northern victories, in a position far better than we ever expected to be. We expected the North to overrun us. We expected them to occupy our ports and our cities, and that we should weary them out by bush-fighting and hardship. We never hoped that we should have, as we now have, 400,000 men in arms. We never hoped that we should keep them at bay for a year, and blockade the Potomac.

Senior.—What is your estimate of the comparative efficiency of the two armies?

Hotze.—I believe that the Federals exceed us in number by about one-third. I believe, too, that they are better drilled, that is, in marching and in manual exercise. But they are not, as our men are, masters of their weapons: they are not seasoned to hardship and danger. You have heard of our poor whites. You probably suppose them to resemble your paupers, the refuse of your cities. They much more resemble savages than paupers. They are men who hate city life and city employments, and dwell in our thinly inhabited woods, living chiefly on the half-wild cattle and the produce of the chase. They form a large portion of our army, and a most formidable one ; for every Southerner can ride and every Southerner can shoot. Another portion, or rather *the* other portion, consists of our planters and merchants, and their sons. In my company all were gentlemen, clothed and fed by themselves.

Senior.—But how do the families of the poor whites live, when their husbands and sons are with the army?

Hotze.—Their women can and do work as well and as hard as the men. The sun does for them more than half of what labour and capital do for a Northerner. It supplies the place of fuel, and, to a great degree, of shelter and clothing. The fertility of the soil, and the abundance of half-wild cattle, make life in the back settlements and in the woods easy and cheap. But our great superiority is in our officers. Almost all the regular army has taken part with us, and our volunteer officers are very different from the clerks, shoemakers, and lawyers whom the North is forced to employ. They are the sons of planters, accustomed to live for months in shooting parties in the desert; accustomed to rely on themselves, where there are no roads or houses to find their way by the compass, to sleep under trees, and, above all, accustomed to act together—to obey and to command.

Senior.—What was the health of your army while you served in it?

Hotze.—Admirable ; far better than that of the

Federals, as might be expected from the superior military training of the men.

Senior.—What are your pecuniary resources? You have no customs, and you cannot impose direct taxes to any considerable amount.

Hotze.—Our great resources have been the zeal and confidence of the people. The Government has issued about sixty millions of dollars in Government paper, to be converted into stock as soon as we have organized our public debt, and there are about forty millions issued by the banks, and secured by the deposits of specie.

Senior.—Does the specie itself circulate?

Hotze.—No; there is none in circulation. The banks are forbidden to pay in specie. Probably there are about 100,000,000 of paper current, which is about fifty per cent more than was current before the war. As yet there are no symptoms of depreciation. The Government notes indeed, being current throughout the Confederacy, are preferred to local notes. Prices have not risen, except as to things affected by the blockade; and as we have scarcely any commerce, the test of foreign exchanges is wanting. We had at the beginning of the war about 20,000,000*l.* sterling in Europe. This has been lent to the Government, and we have paid out of it for the arms and saltpetre which we have imported.

Senior.—The North relies on an Unionist party among you.

Hotze.—It does; but it is an illusion. In

one or two scattered districts votes were given to Lincoln, and in those districts there are Unionists. But they are a contemptible minority even there, and totally absent everywhere else. I do not believe that history relates an instance in which there has been such unanimity among eight millions of people.

Senior.—And the slaves?

Hotze.—The slaves know well the bitter hostility of the North towards their colour. They know that emancipation would be another name for death by misery and cold. There is no fear of them. Their ill-treatment is a very rare exception.

Senior.—Under these circumstances, what are your expectations? I do not ask for your hopes, but for your sober expectations.

Hotze.—My sober expectations are, either that Europe will interfere, or that the war will last for fifty years. Each party is equally determined. We certainly shall not give in, and I see no symptoms of yielding on the part of the North. But I believe that Europe will intervene. It will begin by recognising us.

Senior.—What good will that do to you? It will not give you a man or a ship.

Hotze.—It will discourage the North. They will no longer be able to call us rebels. Their finances, depending on the interests of the capitalists, not on their zeal, will dry up when they see that all Europe believes that the South will conquer its independence. They will force an accommodation.

Senior.—And what accommodation will that be?

Hotze.—The absolute independence of the States south of Virginia. We shall lose Maryland, Western Virginia, Kentucky, and Northern Tennessee, and keep the rest.

Senior.—Including New Orleans?

Hotze.—Yes.

Senior.—I think that the North might allow New Orleans to be a free city—not to be a member of your Confederacy.

Hotze.—We might submit to that, if New York were made a free city, not otherwise.

Senior.—What do you suppose to be the motive which has induced the North to make such sacrifices in order to bring you back?

Hotze.—Mortified vanity and ambition. They could not bear to see their vision of enormous, almost unlimited, empire and domination fade away.

Senior.—But this motive ought to have influenced the South as much as the North. By breaking off from the North you sacrifice empire as much as the North does.

Hotze.—Much more so; for the North, with its twenty millions of whites, which in twenty-five years will become forty millions, must soon regain its preponderance in the civilised world.

Senior.—If it hold together.

Hotze.—That is a danger common to both of us—perhaps still more likely to befall the South. Our confederacy will be founded on the right of secession. Perhaps what is most to be wished is, that the North, the South, and the West, should all separate, and form independent republics, not one of which would be strong enough to domineer over the others. But my answer to your question, Why *we* can bear the loss of empire, and the North cannot? is, that we have much less political ambition than the North. The North is an upstart, composed of immigrants from all Europe, without a history, and seeks food for its vanity in the idea of the power and wealth of the United States—of what it calls the Great Republic. We cling to our English descent, we are proud of the great part which the English nation has played and is playing in the world. We desire no future glories which we are to share with the North.

I went this morning to the 'Institut,' and found the room unusually full.

A member of the Academy of Moral and Political Science was to be appointed. There were only two candidates who had any chance :—M. Husson, who has published statistical works ; and M. Vuitry,* President of the Financial Section of the Conseil d'État.

When I entered, Passy was pleading in favour of Husson,—or, rather, against Vuitry.

'There is one subject,' he said, 'and one only,

---

* For a conversation with Vuitry, see vol. i. p. 220.—ED.

which, from its constitution, the "Institut" cannot examine, and that is, practical politics. We may study the sciences from which the art of government draws its principles, we may inquire into those principles, but we cannot inquire into their application.

'Now the only claims of M. Vuitry to the distinction for which he asks, indeed for any distinction whatever, are his labours as a practical politician. I do not affirm that they are not great. I do not affirm that he has not written excellent reports; or that he has not honestly and intelligently presided over his Section of the Conseil d'État; but I say that these are matters out of our jurisdiction,—out even of our cognizance,—on which we cannot exercise our judgment without descending from the region of theory into that of practice, without becoming politicians instead of Academicians.'

He was followed by a member whose name I do not know, who objected to Vuitry on the same grounds, adding that he had not undergone the test which the Academy required,—that of having written a book.

Guizot answered them. He said, 'that it was true that Vuitry had not published what is technically called " a book," but that he had written reports of high excellence ; and that, of the two, a good report was often a greater work than a good book.'

'How few books,' he said, 'are equal to the Duc de Broglie's Report on Slavery, or to Talleyrand's on Public Instruction ! What has Tocqueville written better than his Report on the Revision of the Constitution?

'A report,' he continued, 'ought to have all the merits of a book,—knowledge of the subject, logic, arrangement, style—and others, which do not belong to a book,—such as the selection of the best ends, the recommendation of the best means, the power of distinguishing between what is practicable and what is merely desirable; the power of brushing away sophistry, of conciliating those who are hostile, of allaying the fears of the timid, and clearing the doubts of the scrupulous. A hundred men can write a book for one who can write a report.

'As for politics being out of our jurisdiction, where does M. Passy find that laid down? It is a field into which we ought to enter cautiously; but how can we avoid it, if, as M. Passy admits, it is our duty to examine into the principles of the art of government? Are we forbidden to inquire what are the proper limits to the freedom of trade, or to the freedom of the press? Is not *that* descending from theory to practice?'

The result was that in an assembly of thirty-five voters, Vuitry had eighteen, Husson sixteen, and one voting paper was blank; so that Vuitry, having an absolute majority, was elected.

Though in the service of the Emperor, he was supported by most of the Orleanists. He had protested against the confiscation of the property of the House of Orleans. This was alluded to by several of the speakers, under the general terms of his independence of character.

Tuesday, March 11th.—I spent the morning with D. E. F.

We talked of apartments in Paris.

D. E. F.—This house contains five floors, besides the ground-floor and the garrets. It is about 100 feet long and 50 broad. On each floor are two apartments, consisting each of a kitchen, four very small sitting-rooms and three bedrooms. Each apartment on the first floor lets for eleven thousand francs (440*l.*) a-year. In the two stories of garrets are the bedrooms of the servants of all the twelve families; allowing three servants to a family, which is the minimum, there must be thirty-six servants—probably there are forty,—to whom must be added the girls attending the four shops on the ground-floor; so that about fifty persons inhabit the garrets. Each has a room, but so small that it may be called a coffin. The room of my wife's maid holds only a small bed, a table, chair, and washing-stand. It is so low that she cannot stand in any part of it. I doubt whether she can sit in her bed.

You may conceive what schools of vice these garrets are, into which fifty persons, mostly young, are crowded. It is almost impossible to get or to keep a decent female servant in Paris.

Senior.—How do you communicate with them?

D. E. F.—Generally through caoutchouc tubes from each apartment to the garrets of its servants.

There are many inconveniences in your system of separate houses. It increases the number of your servants, trebles your distances, and prevents the intimacies which depend on neighbourhood; but those inconveniences are nothing to the evils arising from our close congregation.

He asked whether, in our Swiss tour, we had come across General Charras.

Senior.—No; my illness detained us at Ouchy.

D. E. F.—Next time that you go to Switzerland, I must give you a letter for him at Basle. You will find him honest and intelligent. He is now writing a history of Napoleon's French campaign in 1814, which will be as remarkable as his history of that of 1815 was.

Senior.—I had to examine the campaign in order to write notes to my daughter's translation of Napoleon's letters, and I came to the conclusion that the merits of the first part of that campaign, from the 10th of February to the 18th February, were at least equalled by the blunders and irresolutions of the second part, from the 27th of February to the 31st of March.

D. E. F.—Such is the opinion of Charras. It is not, however, so much about French affairs that you ought to talk to Charras as about Italian ones. When Lamoricière, in 1860, took the command of the Pope's army, the Italian republicans asked for the services of Charras. He met Bertani, Mazzini, and Garibaldi.

Senior.—Tell me something about Bertani.

D. E. F.—Bertani is a physician at Genoa, but he prescribes much more for the State than for his patients. He is the creator of the Provvedimento Society, which excited and carried on the late revolutions in Italy, and will excite others. He organized Garibaldi's expedition; he drove the Grand Duke from Tuscany; he is a republican, but his grand object is Italian Unity; and while Victor Emmanuel will serve that cause, he will maintain his sovereignty. In this he differs from Mazzini, who is more Republican than Unitarian. Nothing will reconcile Mazzini to a king. He scarcely tolerates Victor Emmanuel as an instrument, with an obstinate determination to break him as soon as he can do without him.

As for Garibaldi, he is a royalist, not so much on principle,—for he has scarcely any political principles, except hatred of foreign domination, or even influence,—as from admiration for the King's courage, and perhaps sympathy with his ignorant, unscrupulous rashness. Charras told me that as long as the three were together they let Mazzini take the lead, and apparently agreed in his republicanism; but that each separately disavowed the two others. Bertani, as soon as they were alone, said,—

'Now you must come to the King.'

'The King!' said Charras; 'why, I thought that we were acting independently of him. I thought he was friendly to the Pope.'

'On the contrary,' said Bertani; 'it was by his order that I sent for you. I could not tell that to such fools as Mazzini and Garibaldi, Mazzini would have become your enemy, and Garibaldi would have blurted it out. Come to the King, who is eagerly expecting you.'

Charras, however, refused to see the King. The want of real concert among the republicans disgusted him, and he did not trust the sort of troops that were offered to him.

Senior.—Lamoricière's were not much better.

D. E. F.—Still they *were* better; and though Charras is a good officer, he is not vain enough to think himself equal to Lamoricière. He wisely, therefore, declined the command of unacknowledged, ill-disciplined bands, and forced the King to declare himself, and to invade the dominions of his friend the Pope with a regular army.

Senior.—What are the means, and what are the objects, of the Provvedimento Society?

D. E. F.—The objects are those of Bertani—unity, with or without the King. The means are great, for half Italy belongs to it, and amongst those means is assassination.

Senior.—Assassination rarely succeeds.

D. E. F.—Because the assassin generally wishes

to escape; but a fanatic, who surrenders his own life, has a fair chance of taking another's.

Senior.—I can conceive such fanaticism in a religious enthusiast, who believes that death in the cause of the Church will take him to Paradise. But the assassins of whom the Provvedimento disposes disbelieve in a future state. They must be ready to die, without even knowing the result of their attempt.

D. E. F.—They will be found, however, and in numbers sufficient to render ultimate success certain. This Louis Napoleon knows. This was the fear that drove him into the campaign of 1859. This is the fear that will force him to give up Rome. He would do so immediately, if he were not afraid of the clergy. What he will do is this, he will permit the Piedmontese to draw nearer and nearer every month, till the Pope is confined to Rome. Then he will allow revolutionary mobs to terrify the Pope, until he believes that he is not safe. The French garrison will then escort him to Civita Vecchia, and the French fleet will take him to Marseilles. The Piedmontese will enter Rome as Goyon leaves it, will protect the Cardinals and the Papal officials, and the Provvedimento will grant to Louis Napoleon, if not perfect pardon, at least a reprieve.

Senior.—And will this farce deceive the clerical party?

D. E. F.—Perhaps not, but that party, though strong—most mischievously strong in the provinces

—is weak in the army, and in Paris. Opposed as the liberals are to a military tyranny, they fear still more an ecclesiastical one. This is the force of the Bonapartists, and of the Orleanists. They have common enemies in the priests and the Legitimists.

Senior.—What do you know of Rattazzi?

D. E. F.—Rattazzi is clever. So far—and so far only—he resembles Ricasoli. Ricasoli is a man of birth and fortune—proud, frank, honest, and absolute. He scarcely conceals his contempt of the ignorance and of the tastes for his Piedmontese King, and used him merely as an instrument for the consolidation of Italy.

Rattazzi is an adventurer. His own aggrandisement, and then that of Piedmont, are his objects. He cares as little about Italy as Ricasoli cared about Victor Emmanuel. Like all his countrymen, he distrusts and hates Louis Napoleon, but will truckle to him as long as he thinks that he can get anything by doing so.

It was by means of the Countess Rosine—the King's mistress *en chef*—that Ricasoli was turned out; and I expect every day to hear that the King has married her.

Senior.—Who was this Countess?

D. E. F.—The daughter of the King's coachman—Countess by royal creation.

Senior.—Do you believe in Italian unity?

D. E. F.—North of the Neapolitan dominions I do. Lombardy, Parma, Modena, and Tuscany, are unitarian. But Naples—though it joined the kingdom of Italy in a moment of excitement, and to escape from its terrible government—hates its northern fellow-countrymen and its northern King.

Senior.—I am surprised to find here, in a very high position, C——, one whom I always heard of as a Republican.

D. E. F.—You may be surprised at C——'s acceptance of office; but when you know the state of his fortunes, you will not be surprised at Louis Napoleon's having offered it to him. He belongs to the class from which tools are selected—the poor rich men. He has a large nominal income, but so encumbered that he has more than once been forced to ask the Emperor for money.

Wednesday, March 12*th.*—I went this morning with Lord Cowley's ticket to the diplomatic tribune of the Corps Législatif, to hear the best of the Government speakers—Billault.

The galleries were all full. They are so high above the speakers, and the Hall is so ill built for hearing, that I lost much of his speech. His tone and manner were those of a lawyer, not of a statesman. He speaks, in fact, avowedly as a mere advocate, as a minister *sans porte-feuille*—in our language, without a department; he does not pretend to utter sentiments of his own. He was listened to, however, attentively, and the interruptions—the constant proof that a French speaker is efficient—were numerous.

Two or three others spoke, but not with much force. The French have much to do before they regain—if ever they do regain—the parliamentary eloquence which was silenced in 1848.

I had some difficulty in getting away, the avenue to the tribune being filled by a crowd pressing to get in.

The Senate is inaccessible.

The Constitution says, 'The deliberations of the Senate are secret.' They are reported, however, at full length in the *Moniteur*, and every member has a right to complain, and exercises it, if a word of his speech be omitted. But by a curious inconsistency, though every one may read them, no stranger can hear them.

Thursday, March 13*th.*—I dined with Prince Napoleon. The ladies were Madame de ——, the Princess, and her two ladies-in-waiting. Among the men the only ones that I knew were General Kalergi, the man who, after having in 1843 headed the Greek revolution, and pointed his cannon against King Otho's palace, now represents him in Paris; Pietri; M. Petinet—formerly Prefect of Upper Savoy, now Director of the Imperial Printing Office; Colonel Claremont, the English military *attaché*, and several others whose names I could not ascertain, whom therefore I must designate by letters.

When we retired into the *fumoir*, the Prince became the centre of an animated political discussion. As is generally the case in Paris, it turned more on general propositions than on particular facts. The Prince gave us a sort of essay on the French nation.

Prince Napoleon.—The great fault of the French is, *qu'ils n'ont pas de caractère.* This shows itself in their dread of being in a minority. On every question the instinct of a Frenchman is to ascertain on which side is the majority, and to join it. It shows itself also in their want of elasticity; they have no backbone. A blow from the Government strikes them down, and they lie flat and torpid. It was the same 300 years ago. There was at that time a strong Protestant feeling in France; but it could not stand persecution.

Next to this, their great fault is their hatred of superiors. The peasant, lying at the bottom of society, hates every one who wears a coat, and still more every one who wears a cassock.

Pietri.—And yet he would rise if you were to pull down his *clocher*.

Prince Napoleon.—In some departments, perhaps in twenty out of the eighty-six, he likes his *clocher*, but in every department he hates his *curé*.

Pietri.—The *bas clergé*, however, are the best.

Prince Napoleon.—The least bad. The other day a storm was raised in the Senate because I was supposed to have said that Napoleon re-entered France in

1815 with the cry, '*à bas les prêtres.*'* If I had said so it would have been the truth. The only country in Europe in which the priest is popular is England; and he is popular there because he is a gentleman, a man of the world, a *père de famille*, and above all, because he is rich and is charitable. Our priests are poor; they eke out their incomes by exactions from the people, they are turned out of their seminaries ignorant of everything except a scholastic divinity which, even if it be comprehensible, no one understands; they spring from the same class as the peasants, over whom they claim absolute authority, they interfere with the *ménage*, they set the wife and the daughter against the husband and the father. Every government and every party that relies on their support is doomed.

Senior.—Does the peasant hate the Prefect?

Prince Napoleon.—No. In the first place, he never sees him. To him the Prefect is an abstract idea, or at most, an impersonation of the government; and the peasant clings to the government as the enemy of his enemy—the bourgeois. What the *ouvrier* hates most is his *patron*. When I had to select a couple of hundred *ouvriers* to send them to London for the Exhibition, I offered them 40,000 francs towards the expense. They accepted it from *me*, but they all said that they would not take a sou from their masters.

---

* What he really said was '*À bas les traîtres.*'—ED.

Next to his *patron*, the *ouvrier* hates the *bourgeois*. Louis Philippe and his bourgeois Chamber of Deputies were abominations to him. So was the Provisional Government and the Constituent Assembly. All the *ouvriers* were behind the barricades against Louis Philippe in February 1848, and against Cavaignac in the following June. He hates constitutional government, with its checks and counter-checks, and hierarchy of power. His affection is given only to what he supposes to be revolutionary principles, the absence of an aristocracy, that is to say, of any intermediate between the government and the mass of the people.

As for the bourgeois, he hates everybody, because he fears everybody. He hates and fears the people, he hates and fears what aristocracy we have left to us, he hates and fears the government.

Senior.—Why the government?

Prince Napoleon.—Because it taxes him, because it imposes free trade on him, because it makes war, subjects him to the conscription, and interferes with trade.

X.—Because it emasculates his newspaper, *internes* him, or sends him to Cayenne if he talks too loud, and because it interferes with the course of justice if he is defrauded by one of its favourites.

Senior.—And the aristocracy?

Prince Napoleon.—There is no aristocracy except the aristocracy of office, which gives influence but no respect, and the small aristocracy of military and civil talent. Our officials, and generals, and orators, and littérateurs, are something while their office or their talent continues, but their influence is transient.

Y.—A great speaker is always a considerable man in France.

Prince Napoleon.—He was nothing from 1852 to 1861, and who knows how soon he may be reduced again to nothing?

W.—A great proprietor, such for instance as Falloux, has influence in the provinces.

Prince Napoleon.—Certainly; but how many of them are there? And how many of those have qualities which make them capable, or even desirous, of exercising influence? As for titles, they are worth nothing, and birth—which has some little value in a few circles—is seldom authentic. Not one family in a hundred in the Faubourg has any right to the name which it bears.

The consequence of all this is that there is no desire for liberty, or, indeed, possibility of it. For liberty cannot exist without intermediate bodies—centres of resistance—between the throne and the people, breakwaters for the throne and bulwarks for the people.

I bitterly deplore it, but I am in a small minority. France is not liberal in government, in commerce—in any thing, in short, except religion, and its religious tolerance arises from its disbelief. Even the schoolmaster does not affect to have any faith in the doctrines which he is obliged to pretend to teach.

Pietri.—We must trust to the gradual operation of the press.

Prince Napoleon.—I, too, trust to the press. Though it has done positively but little, it has done comparatively much during the last ten years. It has enabled the Emperor to give us an instalment of free trade, and of free discussion.

Illiberal as France still is, she is much less so than she was in 1852; much less so than she would have been if Louis Philippe had continued. But we shall not see fully the useful influence of the press till it is free. I say *useful* influence, for the positive influence, the influence for evil, is probably greatest under a system of compression. In America, where there is perfect freedom, no one newspaper has much influence. In England, where the enormous expense of founding and keeping up a newspaper gives a monopoly to a few great capitalists, a few newspapers have considerable power; but not half the power which they have in France. The fiscal burthens, the *cautionnement*, the liability to suppression, the stamp, keep the number of papers lower even than it is in England, and the notoriety of the fact, that they all publish, and indeed exist, only on the sufferance of the government, gives importance to their censures. Everything that they say in opposition to the government is taken as an admission. What I wish for is not so much the liberty of the press as its anarchy.

Senior.—By its anarchy do you mean that there shall be no such thing as a *délit de la presse ?*

Prince Napoleon.—I mean that there shall be no stamp, no *cautionnement,* no forced signature, no *avertissement.* At present, the press is under the *régime* not of *l'arbitraire,* which is bad enough; but of *le caprice,* which is intolerable. I wish a journal with only two hundred *abonnés* to be able to live. I wish to have a hundred, or five hundred such journals; their errors and their falsehoods would neutralise one another. But while every opposition journal calls in question the principle of the government and of the dynasty, we must have some *délits de la presse.*

In England *you* have practically abandoned political prosecutions, because these questions are never raised. No newspaper in England writes against Christianity, or royalty, or property.

Still the system of *avertissement,* if it were not managed by a fool or a madman, has many advantages.

Petinet.—I detest it. To be tried, warned, and suppressed, without being heard, is intolerable.

Prince Napoleon.—Still it is better to be suppressed than to be imprisoned. You would not find the tribunals much more liberal than M. de Persigny.

Senior.—But a jury might be so.

Prince Napoleon.—The jury would consist of bourgeois. A jury, when it is frightened, is worse than even a judge, for it is not responsible even to public opinion. *Et les bourgeois sont en permanence de peur.*

Petinet.—I have had some experience, for I have appeared before the tribunals seventeen times.

The conversation passed to the dissolution or expiration of the Corps Législatif.

R.—In the next Chamber there will be at least thirty opposition members. We see the influence of only six.

Prince Napoleon.—Among them I hope to see Thiers. He could certainly be returned for Rouen; and with little difficulty for Lille.

Pietri.—He will give trouble!

Prince Napoleon.—Unless he is bought,—not with money; Thiers is above that,—but by flattery. Never did the Emperor spend a compliment better than when he called Thiers '*un historien illustre et national.*' Thiers has not forgotten it.

Pietri.—Nor does he let anyone else forget it.

Prince Napoleon.—Paris will return ten Rouges. If I were to go to the Faubourg St. Antoine, I should be elected by the *ouvriers* unanimously; especially if the *patrons* opposed me. But the opposition, though it may give trouble, will do little good. The Corps Législatif has no influence. 'The deputies,' say the people, 'are named by the Prefects, *we* named the Emperor.'

One thing, however, the next Chamber will do,—if it be not done before,—it will force the evacuation of Rome. We cannot remain the supporters of that odious tyranny, and the obstacles to Italian unity. Every motive requires us to escape from such a situation.

Pietri.—Billault says that it will take centuries to consolidate Italy.

Prince Napoleon.—An additional motive for losing no more time.

At about half-past nine, we returned to the drawing-room, where we found the Princess, her two ladies, and Madame de ——.

I talked to Madame de —— about Rome.

Madame de ——.—I never would have created the temporal power of the Pope. It injures his spiritual influence, just as his spiritual functions interfere with his political ones. But he has it, and I dread the immediate consequences of his losing it. I would keep the *status quo* if I could. And such are the opinions of almost all whom I see.

Senior.—Not *here*.

Madame de ——.—Not on one side of the Palace, but very strongly on the other.

The conversation passed to Savoy. M. Petinet

maintained that the annexation was popular among all excepting the priests.

Prince Napoleon.—The people never, from 1815 to 1859, gave up the hope of returning to France. Thousands of families kept little tricolors as sacred deposits. They loved, indeed, the house of Savoy, but they hated Piedmont, and felt degraded by the prospect of being swallowed up in the great kingdom of Italy.

Senior.—They are swallowed up now, in a still greater empire.

Prince Napoleon.—Yes; but in an empire with glorious recollections, with a glorious present, and with a glorious future. The kingdom of Italy is glorious only in its hopes.

The Princess sat at first near the fire, with her ladies, but she afterwards came into the middle of the room, sat on an ottoman, with a circle round her, and joined easily in a general unconstrained conversation.

We spent a dissipated evening, going to Madame de Circourt's and Madame Duchatel's and Madame A. B. C.'s. We talked at Madame de Circourt's of Madame Mohl's book on Madame Récamier.

Madame de Circourt.—One of my friends is going to translate it in the *Revue des deux Mondes*, and begs me to write a preface. Now I am too French and too foreign.

Too French to criticise impartially Madame Mohl's

comparison of French and English society, and too foreign to write safely in French. My only qualification is my delight in the book. Besides, I never knew Madame Récamier. She took for her *salon* the day which I had taken for mine, and it was full of idolaters. Now, I hate idolatry, and, with all the merits of Chateaubriand, I could not worship so selfish and capricious a deity. I liked to see him and to hear him in his wife's *salon*, where he was only a mortal.

Senior.—Tell me a little about Madame de Chateaubriand.

Madame de Circourt.—She was a *petite bossue*, full of talent, vivacity, and *caractère*. When she was ambassadress at Rome, she found that the old etiquette requiring the first visits to be paid to the French ambassadress had become obsolete. She resolved to restore it: the Roman ladies would not consent. So for four months she was in a sort of quarantine.

Chateaubriand was not satisfied with the diplomatic and English society; he wanted to shine before a larger audience, and kept remonstrating, but she persisted, till at length they yielded and came to her.

Augustin Thierry was one of my subjects, and one of Madame Récamier's slaves.

He was blind and paralytic, and yet she scarcely exceeded him as a *teneur de salon*. He knew by the voice who every one was, and where every one was. By the rustle of the gown he knew how every one was dressed. I came to him one evening with natural flowers in my hair: 'Ah!' he said, 'you have taste enough to wear real flowers;' he distinguished them by the smell.

Madame Récamier kept him at Madame de Chateaubriand's as a spy in the enemy's camp. He was in fact a treble spy, for he told to each of us what happened in the *salons* of the other two.

After Chateaubriand had begun to read his memoirs at Madame Récamier's, he wished them to be heard by some who did not visit there. He went to Thierry's to settle who they should be. A list of auditors was, after much discussion and much revision, finally settled. At the top were Monsieur de Circourt and myself. Chateaubriand took it away, as he said, to think it over, but in fact to show it to Madame Récamier. She struck us out.

At Madame Duchatel's we found all the Orleanist aristocracy. Duchatel inhabits one of the great hotels of the *ancien régime*. Its fine rooms were filled, and I heard scarcely an untitled name announced.

I became Monsieur Le Marquis de Seigneur.

I talked much to Lavergne, who tells me that there is great uneasiness respecting the Mexican expedition. It seems that *we* have sent no land troops, that the Spanish force is insufficient and provokes fierce opposition, and that a considerable addition to the French army is required. There is much sickness, and the want of roads and of means of transport is embarrassing.

Senior.—The Mexicans of Montezuma were more numerous, richer, and more civilised than the modern Mexicans, yet Cortez conquered them with 800 men.

Lavergne.—With the assistance of the people of Tlascala. We shall find no allies. We are getting tired of these distant, fruitless wars. I live in fear of hearing a general cry that, if we are to be constantly at war, it ought to be for something worth having, and that means the Rhine.

At Madame A. B. C.'s, I walked with A. B. C. up and down his ante-chamber, and asked him if he shared Lavergne's fears.

A. B. C.—My alarm probably exceeds his. I fear that Louis Napoleon has embarked us in a long and disastrous enterprise.

Your force is merely naval; and, as the Mexicans have no navy, it might almost as well be absent. You are there only for form's sake. The Spaniards have not money or men to march 250 miles over a mountainous country, thinly inhabited, and by men who have been fighting for years. We shall be forced to bear the burden ourselves, and that in a cause in which we are scarcely interested. More troops have been sent for, and many more will have to follow.

Then the base of our operations is a country at all times eminently unhealthy, and, in the hot months that are coming, mortal. But we must go on,—the honour of our flag is engaged, and so is the vanity of our master. He cannot recall his troops and so acknowledge himself beaten.

Senior.—What was his motive for making this war?

A. B. C.—There was a plausible motive in the misconduct of the Mexican government. It had cheated us, broken faith with us, and allowed our fellow-citizens to be murdered with impunity. But the real cause was Louis Napoleon's restless eagerness to do something. He is not satisfied with European greatness. He wishes to be not only Russicus, and Italicus, and Sericus, and Africanus, but also Americanus. That quarter of the globe is unoccupied. If he could have induced you to join him in breaking the blockade, he might have earned that title at the expense of the Washington government. Failing in that, he is looking for laurels from Mexico.

But his peculiar mode of action subjects him to great difficulties. He makes war and peace *en conspirateur*. He wishes to dazzle by unexpected *coups de théâtre*.

To be unexpected, his acts must be ill prepared. If I dress in my own room I know what I am about. I know where all my things are. But if I dress behind a sheet in the dark, I am sure to make mistakes. In 1859, he sent his army across the Alps and the Apennines, ill clad and ill armed. He had not studied the country; he had not prepared the means of transport. He improvised his Villa Franca peace, knowing himself little of the real state of Italy, and asking no one for advice or for information. He has put his head, or rather our heads, in the same blind way into this Mexican wasps' nest.

Senior.—Does he hope to conciliate Austria by giving a throne to the Archduke Maximilian?

A. B. C.—He may hope to do so, but he is mistaken. Austria has told him plainly that, though she would not refuse her consent, she does not desire such an event. It would make Anglo-America furious; and some months hence Anglo-America may again be formidable. Nor would *you* like to see a new Transatlantic monarchy?

Senior.—There you are mistaken. The only decent Transatlantic governments, Brazil and Canada, are monarchical. We shall be satisfied with any government that will trade with us, pay its debts, and keep the roads and the towns safe.

A thin, dark, intelligent-looking man came in.

A. B. C.—That is Gutierrez de Estrada, who has held high office in Mexico. I will introduce him to you. He will give you good information.

I asked Estrada if he agreed with A. B. C. in thinking that the French had engaged in a difficult enterprise.

Estrada.—The only difficulty is occasioned by the presence of the Spaniards. If the French and English, or either of them alone, had entered Mexico, not a hand would have been raised against them. They might have marched to the capital in triumph. The Mexicans are so thoroughly sick of the anarchy of the last four or five years, of the robbery and murder which threaten to reduce the country to a wilderness, that any foreigners but Spaniards or Anglo-Americans would have been received with transport. But the horrible cruelty of the Spaniards in our war of independence, and the treachery, rapacity, and barbarity with which the United States treated us in the war in which they robbed us of more than half our territories and hanged our citizens because they refused to acknowledge that a proclamation of an American general had turned them into subjects of the United States, would induce us to prefer even our present calamities to any remedy proposed to us by such *soi-disant* friends.

Senior.—Would you accept a monarch?

Estrada.—We would accept from you, or from the French, any thing, or any body.

Senior.—Then you justify our interference?

Estrada.—I think it not merely justifiable, but absolutely necessary. Absolutely demanded, not merely by your interests, but by common humanity. We cannot raise ourselves from the misery, degradation, and anarchy to which the war with the United States and the intrigues of the Americans before and after that war reduced us. A foreign prince, unconnected with our factions, possessing European habits and knowledge, might save us. I pray every day for Maximilian.

Baron Gros, just returned from China, joined us.

He congratulated me on the news that we are at last going to interfere and protect some portion of the civilised Chinese from the Taepings.

Gros.—The toleration of their barbarities is a scandal to civilisation. A small French or English force would destroy them far more easily than we destroyed the Chinese whom we encountered before Pekin. But you seem to have a strange affection for rebels in the East as well as in the West.

Senior.—I hope that you will urge us to interfere. You are now an Asiatic power; for I suppose your recent conquests in Cochin China are considerable.

Gros.—The territory is almost as large as France, but it is a delta, very unhealthy and very fertile.

Senior.—I delight in your occupation of it, and I hope you will add to it Madagascar, which I find you claim as a province of France.

Far be it from us to oppose you there, unless indeed we do so for the mere purpose of exciting you to conquer and to retain it. The possession of distant dependencies is the strongest motive to keep the peace. *We* should not be so pacific if we were not spread over the whole globe, and vulnerable everywhere.

March 15*th.*—I called on Madame Cornu, and asked after her friend, Louis Napoleon.

Madame Cornu.—He is in vigorous health, and thinking of nothing but his *History of Cæsar.* The first volume will soon appear, and he is in all the anxieties of authorship.

Senior.—He ought to be hardened against criticism, for he is a veteran author.

Madame Cornu.—Yes; but he had much less to dread from criticism when he was Monsieur Bonaparte. Now he addresses the whole world.

Senior.—Do you think that Prince Napoleon has any views on Naples?

Madame Cornu.—Not in the least. His father-in-law offered Naples to him in the beginning of 1860, and he refused.

Senior.—Would the Emperor have sanctioned it?

Madame Cornu.—Not openly; but he would have permitted it, probably have liked it. It would have been the best arrangement for France. The kingdoms of Northern Italy and Southern Italy, neither strong enough to stand alone, would have been our dependents. But the Prince cannot bear to quit Paris. All his friends, good and bad, all his pleasures, good and bad, are here. He enjoys his success as a *causeur*, and still more as an orator. Among over thirty-seven millions of Frenchmen, he is the only one absolutely free. He says what he likes, and from a tribune whose echoes fill the world. He is delighted to call himself a republican, and at the same time to feel himself connected with the oldest families in Europe. There is only one crown for which he would exchange this existence.

I asked if M. Cornu was still painting.

Madame Cornu.—Not at present. He is preparing the exhibition of the Campana collection. The Emperor wishes it to open on the 1st of May, or indeed sooner. He thinks that Paris will then be full of persons on their way to London.

Senior.—Campana ruined himself to make that collection.

Madame Cornu.—Campana was ruined in consequence of having made that collection, but not by his own extravagance or want of judgment. The collection was worth much more than it cost him. But the cunning of his enemies and the weakness of the Pope made it the occasion of his ruin. He was a lawyer, and a favourite of the Pope, who ennobled him, and put him at the head of the Mont de Piété. He was an enthusiastic collector. He had large balances in his hands, and he could employ them advantageously in purchases and excavations. He asked the Pope's permission to do this, stating that the Mont de Piété could not suffer, as his collection, which he then valued at six millions, would be a security. The Pope assented, and Campana bought and excavated boldly, but judiciously and successfully. Antonelli hated him. They were rivals for the Pope's favour. He suspected what was going on, and one day without warning examined the treasury of the Mont de Piété. It was deficient by six millions and a half. Campana was arrested, his collection was sequestered, and he was prosecuted for breach of trust. He said that his collection was worth more than eight millions, that it was pledged to the Mont de Piété, that the Pope had been cognisant of the whole transaction, and that he was blameless. Pio Nono, afraid of Antonelli, and afraid of public opinion, was weak enough to say that he did not remember Campana's conversation with him; and there was nothing in writing. The collection was valued by the Pope's officers at three millions, at which price the Pope proposed to take it. Campana was condemned to the galleys for twenty years.

But the annexations began. The Pope's treasury was exhausted, and the collection was put on sale. The Russians were allowed to select articles to the amount of 800,000 francs. Your consul, Mr. Newton, also obtained permission to select to the same amount. The Emperor heard of it, and sent my husband to Rome to buy. He found that he should be the last, after the Russians and Newton had taken the best things, and knowing well that he should be supported by the Emperor, offered to buy the whole. Newton was less bold, but he immediately set out for England in order to obtain permission to bid against my husband, and urged Antonelli to do nothing till he heard from him. The instant he was gone, my husband went to Antonelli, offered him 5,200,000 francs for the whole, but requested an answer in twenty-four hours. If his offer was not accepted in that time, he should return to France. Some Roman bankers, however, offered 6,000,000 francs, and it seemed likely that the price would rise extravagantly. But in that case the Mont de Piété would have been more than reimbursed, and Campana must have been pardoned. This did not suit his enemies. So the Pope was made to answer that he would sell only to a sovereign, and the French offer, being the best royal offer, was taken; so that Campana was still considered as having robbed the Mont de Piété of 500,000 francs.

Senior.—What became of Campana?

Madame Cornu.—The Pope was, I believe, thoroughly ashamed of his part in the transaction. He used to talk of the *Povero Campana*, and at last got his imprisonment changed into banishment. He is living, I believe, in Naples with his wife, an Englishwoman, in great poverty.

Have you been to Madame A.'s exhibition?

Senior.—No. Who is she?

Madame Cornu.—She was a very successful trader on her own personal merits, and having ruined more men than it usually falls to the lot of such ladies to be able to do, she has retired from business, and is to marry an *avocat*. But he has his scruples. He insists that before the marriage she shall part with all the presents which a series of victims have heaped on her. So they are to be sold. There are pearl necklaces worth thousands, and diamonds without end. You know that there is a strange, morbid curiosity among Parisian ladies about these women. Novels are written on them; their habits are described, and their *bon mots* are repeated. It has been thought that an exhibition of the genuine stock-in-trade and spoils of one of them might be attractive. The entrance costs ten francs, and I hear that the rooms are crowded.

I spent the evening at Mrs. Digby's, and found there a large party. Among them were the Pope's nuncio, Monsignor Chigi, the Montalemberts, and a little, dark, round-shouldered man, who was introduced to me as M. Gérard.

The nuncio is an agreeable, gentlemanlike man. M. Gérard turned out to be the great lion-killer. He told me he was collecting a party, with whom he intended to cross Africa from north to south.

Gérard.—What has prevented or has impaired the success of African travellers has been that they have gone alone, or with few companions. We intend to be at least thirty, besides our servants. We shall take dromedaries, be well armed, and obtain the respect and the gratitude of the natives by killing their most formidable enemies, the beasts of prey. A single lion in Algeria destroys every year live stock worth 6000 francs, and perhaps half-a-dozen human beings. Wherever I killed a lion I became a sort of hero among the Arabs.

I asked his opinion of Chaillu, and was surprised to find that he had not read his book.

March 16*th*.—I went to Notre Dame to hear the sermon. Only the aisles were open, but long before the sermon began they were filled. It took me a quarter of an hour with the aid of the Suisse to push my way to my reserved seat, I lost therefore the preacher's introduction.

The three insurrections of *la raison contre la foi* formed the subject of his sermon.

'The first,' he said, 'was in the fifteenth century, the least dangerous, because, though it dethroned the Church, it retained the New Testament; though it deprived the Protestant of the intercession of the saints and of the Holy Virgin, it left to him the sacrifice and the teaching of the Saviour; though it deprived him of a living and infallible interpreter, it left to him a divine revelation in the gospels, and inspired commentators in the epistles. It was the most illogical because, while it held the contemporaries of Our Saviour to be inspired, it denied that claim to their successors, and drew a line, perfectly unauthorised, between St. Luke, St. Mark, and St. Paul and the saints who have followed them.

'The next insurrection was that of the eighteenth century. That was an insurrection against the supernatural. "In early times," it said, "everything was attributed to the direct interference of a supernatural being—called a god. Jupiter caused rain, or fair weather. If a ship reached its port, it was by the favour of Neptune; if it perished, it was because he raised a storm. If the Hebrews crossed the Red Sea, they were led by Jehovah. If the Egyptians were caught by the returning tide, it was Jehovah that overwhelmed them.

' " With every advance of knowledge," it said, " the frontier of the supernatural has receded. Astrology has been given up; ghosts no longer appear, miracles are no longer believed. The affairs of the world appear to go on according to unaltered, and apparently unalterable, rules. If there be the supernatural being called 'a God,' he does not interfere. To be believed, his existence ought to be manifested."

' This insurrection was soon put down. It was opposed to all the instincts of humanity. Denying a Creator, it in vain attempted to account for a creation.

' The infidelity of the nineteenth century is more modest. It denies nothing; but it affirms nothing. " A God," it says, " is an incomprehensible idea, because that word is a mere negation of attributes. It supposes a being who has had no beginning; who will have no end; who fills no space; who has no passions. Such a being," it says, " may exist; but, as he cannot be conceived, he cannot be the object of reverence, or of love, or even of fear. There may be a God," it says, " though he does not show himself to us. There may have been miracles, there may now be miracles, though we never saw one, or even saw a person who had seen one. There may have been revelations, though we hear of them only in obscure, barbarous corners of Syria or Arabia."

'This insurrection will fail, as that of the eighteenth century failed. Religion is natural to man. One of the greatest philosophers of the century ranked doubt as the worst of calamities. The Head of our Church in heaven—Christ; the head on earth—the Holy Father; the ministers of both our secular and our regular clergy, offer to everyone, to the lowest as well as to the highest, certainty instead of doubt, revelation instead of ignorance, hope instead of despair, and every year, nay, every day, these blessings are accepted by a larger and larger majority.'

To be heard by three or four thousand persons, in a lofty, narrow building, he was forced to scream, so that his voice was unmodulated, and often indistinct.

He seemed to me to use the word '*Foi*' in different senses. Sometimes as expressing the Roman Catholic faith, sometimes as expressing religion, sometimes as expressing belief, and to suppose that in every one of those senses it may be opposed to reason. Now a man's reason may be opposed to the Roman Catholic faith, it may be opposed to any religion whatever, but his reason cannot be opposed to his belief. We are so constituted that we cannot believe except by means of our reason. The grounds of our belief may be absurd, but some grounds there must be.

If you ask a Roman Catholic why he believes in the intercession of the Holy Virgin, he necessarily answers, because it is affirmed by the Church. If you ask him why he believes in the Church, he probably answers, because his priest tells him that his Church is infallible. If you ask, why he believes the priest, he answers—or at least he ought to answer—because he is a learned man and has inquired into the matter.

From Notre Dame, I went to A. B. C.'s, and found with him M. de Corcelle.

We talked of the late debates.

A. B. C.—They have been mischievous to Louis Napoleon, and will be still more so. A policy like his, if policy it can be called, cannot bear discussion. When, after having carefully studied the motives on every side, a man has decided on his course of action, he can defend it. He has merely to repeat what has already passed through his own mind. But when a man has obeyed the impulse of the moment, some sudden caprice of vanity or of fear, he cannot explain to others what perhaps he can scarcely explain to himself.

Read Billault's speeches. He is obviously an advocate who knows that his cause is indefensible. He begins by admitting that all the Emperor's promises have been broken, that all his wishes have been disregarded, that all his expectations have been falsified. 'Therefore, Messieurs,' he says, 'trust to the wisdom, the fidelity, and to the good fortune of the Emperor, and all will come right.'

After Palikao's pension had been refused, the

deputies came to me as proud as peacocks. '*Vous êtes un tas d'imbéciles,*' I said. 'If you wished to oppose the Government, it should not have been when a very moderate recompense was given to a man who has performed well a difficult service. You say that you are opposed to *majorats,*—no one will believe that a set of *hobereaux,* chosen by the prefects for their retrograde opinions, care about *majorats.* There is not one of you with any money who would not wish to entail it for the next ten thousand years. You thought that Montauban, an adventurer mixed in the Strasburg affair, a personal friend of our master, and therefore unpopular, was a safe subject for your opposition. You have disgusted the Army and done good to the Emperor by showing how unfit you are to govern. And what is the consequence? The Emperor has submitted. He does not press the law for giving to M. de Montauban, with the assent of the Chambers, 50,000 francs a-year; but he substitutes for it a law, by which he is to give away a million or two millions a-year to any one whom he likes, and without consulting anybody.

'And this is the compromise for which you deputies fell into one another's arms and wept tears of joy.'

Ought I to try my chance at the next elections?

Senior.—Certainly. The Corps Législatif has in its hands instruments with which it can govern the country. What it wants are men like you, who can excite it and teach it to use those instruments.

A. B. C.—It seems to me that this state of things cannot continue. An Assembly elected by the people, discussing freely all the acts of the Government, and itself not allowed to govern, or to choose who shall govern, must degenerate into an opposition, and will carry with it the people.

Senior.—But this Assembly was not elected by the people. It was nominated by the prefects.

A. B. C.—Some nine or ten of its members were really elected by the people. And some of the Government's nominees, such as Keller, have turned against it.

It is always dangerous to prophesy, and in no country so dangerous as in France. Your journals must be full of unfulfilled prophecies—many of them mine. But if the whole state of affairs be not soon altered by some great military success of *Celui-ci,* or by some great military reverse, I predict that in a couple of years he will be forced either to resign his arbitrary power, or to keep it by a *coup d'état.* He will be forced either to admit the Corps Législatif to dictate his policy, which will be an abdication ; or to suppress its discussions, which will be a *coup d'état.*

Senior.—Some of my friends believe his views have been changed by the birth of his son,—that they are altogether dynastical, that he sees that it is only in constitutional states that the succession is regular, and that therefore in the interest of his son he intends to make the Empire constitutional.

A. B. C.—I utterly disbelieve this theory. His desire of power—of uncontrolled power, or unshared power; of power, not merely unshared, but unsuspected of being shared—is insatiable. You offend him if you compliment him on his good choice of ministers—even of generals. All that is done, must be done *auspiciis Cæsaris.* You would annoy him if you were to praise his cook. All must be supposed to be done by his will, without the intervention of inferior agents. ' Let there be a dinner, and there was a dinner.' Hence his hatred of the clergy, of the bishops, and of the Pope. They do not depend on him.

A schism which should create a Gallican Patriarchate, with him for its Patriarch, is his dream. The steps of his progress are to be Cæsar, Pontifex maximus, Divus. Necessity only, a necessity affecting himself, will force him to change it.

Senior.—You agree with Keller.

A. B. C.—Necessarily; for when Keller said, '*Lorsque le pouvoir temporel du Pape n'existait pas, César était tout, César était Souverain Pontif, César était Dieu,*' he stole that sentence from me.

You are an observant traveller. Tell me what you hear about us.

Senior.—I dined the other day with one of your great men, and he gave us a lecture on the character of the French, beginning by saying that in the French sense of the word they have no character.

Corcelle.—That is quite true. The first idea of a

Frenchman, as soon as he finds that he has the misfortune to be in a minority, is to join the majority.

Senior.—Next, he told us that everybody hated everybody. That the peasant hated everyone who wore a coat, and still more everyone who wore a cassock.

Corcelle.—That is not true. Your great man can never have lived in the country. The curé is generally the son and the brother of a peasant. He knows the peasant's wants, he sympathises with him, he advises him, and, having no adverse interests, his advice is sincere.

A. B. C.—The peasants and the bourgeoisie are the religious portion of the French. The former from routine,—irreligion has never been preached to them ; the latter from interest and from habit. Under the Empire and under the Restoration, the bourgeoisie was irreligious. The Church was then allied to the Government, and shared its unpopularity. But 1830 frightened the bourgeoisie. What it worships above all beings, and above all ideas—property—was for an instant threatened. It saw the value of the religious sanction. The fathers conformed without much belief. The sons have been educated as Roman Catholics, and they are the young men who fill the churches. Their belief, it is true, is not founded on inquiry, but perhaps it is the more undoubting.

Visitors came in and I went away.

Monday, March 17*th*.—Yesterday, at Notre Dame, or somewhere else, I caught the prevalent disorder in Paris, *grippe*, or, as we call it, influenza. I am, therefore, confined to the house, and see only those who call on us.

To-day we had, among others, Monsieur and Madame Jules de Lasteyrie. We talked of the passion for *égalité*, attributed to the French.

Lasteyrie.—It is political, not social *égalité*, that we seek, or, at least, that we enjoy. There is far less social *égalité* in France than in England. There birth seems to have little value. In France it is all-important.

Senior.—Birth in England, if it be notorious, if it be marked, for instance, by a title, or by a well-known descent from some great family, is valuable, particularly in the country.

Lasteyrie.—In the country, especially in the hunting-field, I have seen all classes together, and they seemed to meet on a footing of perfect equality.

Senior.—Sport, like politics, levels all distinctions. The gamekeeper talks to his master in a tone which no other servant assumes, and the master loses his reserve when he talks to the gamekeeper.

Lasteyrie.—But in London society the power of interesting or of amusing seemed to me to be the passport to social distinction. The people to whom my hosts were proud to introduce me were not lords and ladies, but political or literary men, or artists, or men of science.

Senior.—I find them in Parisian circles.

Lasteyrie.—Yes, but not their wives. It is in marriage, above all things, that the difference in ranks is shown. Sometimes a noble marries a *roturière*, but it is a marriage of interest. Never does a *roturier* marry a noble. I never meet a physician or an advocate in Parisian society, and very rarely a clergyman.

Senior.—You meet Odillon Barrot and Berryer.

Lasteyrie.—Yes, as politicians, but not as advocates. You say truly that politics level all distinctions; and though there is much political equality, a man of birth, while elections were free, had a great advantage.

Senior.—Tocqueville treated his birth as an obstacle, and ascribed to it the loss of his first election. He was met everywhere, he said, by the proverb, ' *Les chats prennent les souris.*'

Lasteyrie.—That occurred under Louis Philippe, when the bourgeoisie formed the *Pays Légal*. My observation refers to the time of universal suffrage. There were eighteen of my family in the Constituent Assembly.

Tocqueville in 1837 was little known, and was suspected of illiberal opinions. His father was a Legitimist, and so were his brothers. He himself refused to serve Louis Philippe, or even to accept assistance from the Government in his candidature.

The Lasteyries were followed by Circourt.*

I repeated to Circourt Lasteyrie's opinions, and asked if he agreed with them.

Circourt.—Perfectly. The society of Paris is the most aristocratic in Europe.

Senior.—You must except Vienna.

Circourt.—That is true, but it is the only exception that I can make. There are about three thousand families in Paris, noble, or received as noble, and they are almost omnipotent in society.

Senior.—How do you arrive at that number?

Circourt.—We know that in 1789 there were about 220,000 persons in France *censés* to be noble. At least nine-tenths of these families perished in the revolution, or became extinct, or sank into poverty so abject as to be now unknown. In my country, Lorraine, there were then about 250 families of recognised nobility. In 1815 only eleven were left; now there are only six.

The creations by Napoleon, by the Restoration, by Louis Philippe, and by *Celui-ci*, have not been enough to affect much the number. If there are now in France 22,000 nobles, it is the maximum; at three to a family, they form 7333 families, of whom about one-third, or 2444, inhabit Paris.

Lasteyrie is right in saying that the distinction

---

* Nov. 21st, 1879. M. de Circourt has just died of a sudden attack of apoplexy.—ED.

shows itself most in marriage. A young man of rank, though poor and insignificant, finds easily a rich, well-educated wife in the bourgeoisie.

Not long ago, a M. E——, a banker of some eminence, told me that he wished his daughter to marry in the Faubourg St. Germain. The person on whom he had fixed—not from knowing him, but from his reputation as a well-disposed young man— was a Baron de la Bouillerie.

'I give to my daughter,' he said, ' immediately 500,000 francs, and 100,000 more on the birth of each child; but I fear that is not enough to compensate the difference of birth.'

'I admit,' I said to him, 'that there is a difference in birth, but I think that the advantage is all on your side.

' M. de la Bouillerie's barony was created by Louis Seize. Your ancestors filled for centuries high municipal offices in Bordeaux. Your wife was a Hope of Amsterdam. Your daughter's ancestors were considerable people when the la Bouilleries were nothing. But I will enter on the negotiation for you.'

Young Bouillerie received the proposal coldly. He was not sure that he should like the young lady, or the family. I told him that the girl was charming, and the family thoroughly honourable and respectable. So he agreed to meet them at my house. Both parties were pleased, the marriage took place in a few weeks, and has turned out well.

My wife arranged just such another marriage a few months ago.

Senior.—I find excellent society, and of the highest rank, at Madame Anisson's, yet the Anissons must be bourgeois.

Anisson's father was a partner with Réveillon, the paper-maker, the destruction of whose property was the signal for the revolution in 1789.

Circourt.—It is true that there is no society in Paris better than that of the Anisson's, and scarcely any so good. They, and two or three other families, hold an exceptional position. Their character, their wealth, their intermarriages, and the political importance of Anisson, the father, have placed them in the aristocracy.

Senior.—What position do the Chevreux hold?

Circourt.—A very high one, but a different one. They are at the top of the bourgeoisie; their daughter refused the Duc de St. Aignan, and I can scarcely tell how many great aristocrats. She said that she was resolved to marry in her own sphere, and did so.

Senior.— She was the friend for whose loss Ampère is inconsolable.

Circourt.*—Yes; he has devoted the last years of his life to her, and since her death to her parents.

---

* In his latter years, M. de Circourt had the same sort of romantic friendship for Madame d'Affre and her daughter, the Duchess Colonna. The Duchess was a woman of great beauty and talent. She excelled in sculpture, and some of her works were in the Exhibition of 1862. She died at an early age of consumption.—ED.

His own tastes carry him to Rome, but theirs take him to Pau.

The noble young ladies dislike this state of things; they complain that the rich bourgeois girls spoil their market.

Senior.—They refuse to marry the bourgeois young men.

Circourt.—Utterly. A friend of mine, of good family, but small fortune, is now becoming an old maid. 'If I were a man,' she says, 'I should have married long ago, whether a noble or a *roturière* would not have signified; but I cannot marry a bourgeois, and I have no chance against the rich bourgeoises.'

Friday, March 21*st.*—I have nothing to record of the last four days, having spent them neither agreeably nor profitably, in influenza and headache.

To-day Cornelis De Witt called on us. We asked him whether he thought the position of the Emperor altered since we met this time last year.

De Witt.—Sensibly deteriorated. He has been sinking ever since the *attentat* of 1858. The shock impaired the obstinacy, the self-confidence, and the intrepidity, which were among the causes of his early successes.

Senior.—And yet his Italian campaign—the only great thing that he has done—was done after 1858.

De Witt.—Do you call that a great thing?

Senior.—Certainly. For a man of fifty, who never saw a gun fired, to take the command of 250,000 men, opposed to a still greater force of some of the best troops in Europe, and in two months gain two victories, and dictate a peace, is one of the greatest things recorded in history. I do not recollect anything that resembles it.

De Witt.—That is the outside, but when you look into it, you find that the Austrian army, though good, was wretchedly commanded; that neither Magenta nor Solferino was decisive; that he himself took no part in either; that the peace was not such a one as he wished, or had promised to France and to Italy; that he was not able to enforce its stipulations; that the result has been to give us on our very frontier a neighbour twenty-two millions strong, instead of a dependent ally. And that this has been done in defiance of his wishes, of his entreaties, of his remonstrances, and almost of his commands—that the Pope has refused even to listen to him, that Cavour behaved to him contemptuously, and Garibaldi insolently. The only sovereign who has treated him with deference is Mr. Lincoln.

Then there is no doubt that there is considerable distress. His friends attribute it to the American civil war, his enemies to the enormous unproductive expenditure of the government, and, influenced by the government, and imitating it, of the higher classes. The public at large, to the commercial treaty. I believe that all these three causes have contributed to it, and that the third cause is the least efficient. But the operatives and capitalists put it foremost, and cannot perceive that it must be temporary, and that, as all commerce is barter, there cannot be a permanent increase of imports, without at least an equal increase of exports. Simple as this proposition is, the French cannot understand it, and if you read the debates, you will see that Pouyer Quertier and others do nothing but exaggerate our imports, and that Auguste Chevalier and Baroche waste all their time in showing that they are smaller than they appear to be, and that they will diminish.

Senior.—You believe that there is great distress?

De Witt.—I do.

Senior.—And in Paris?

De Witt.—In Paris, perhaps more than anywhere else. A friend of mine—a very charitable man—told me that in visiting his poor people, *il avait flairé la détresse.* He had found in many of their rooms a smell of spirits. For the workman, when he cannot get sufficient food, often keeps up his courage, and obtains temporary strength, by the use of alcohol.

I attribute much of the distress to a fourth cause, a sense of political insecurity. When the Emperor's letter to Montauban, calling the French a degenerate people, was published, an acquaintance of mine, a great manufacturer, dismissed seven hundred of his workmen.

The general result is, that there is deep and wide discontent. I do not think a 24th of February impossible. A conspiracy to effect one was discovered a couple of months ago. It is said that

Persigny wished to allow it to break out, but that all the ministers advised its being stifled, by the arrest of the leaders. We are told that two hundred are in prison. It is difficult to know how to deal with them. To try them will be dangerous; it will put evil thoughts into people's heads. It is dangerous to let them loose, and there are among them men, such as S——, a great manufacturer, who cannot be secretly disposed of.

Senior.—But while he has the army, need he fear an *émeute?*

De Witt.—The army sympathises with the nation. An attempt has been made to render it prætorian, by encouraging men to enlist for long terms, but it has not had much success. The service is not popular. The conscript submits to it from necessity, and from a feeling that he is bound to pay his six years of service to his country; but he counts the days till he can return to his cottage and his field, and despises the *remplaçant* as a mercenary. The army cannot be depended on against a really popular *émeute.*

Senior.—The officers, however, who have adopted the army as a profession—seldom men of any property, whose only home is the garrison or the camp—sympathise little with the civilians.

De Witt.—That applies principally to the inferior officers. Those in the higher commands have wider views, and are citizens and politicians as well as soldiers. They have a well-founded contempt for

Louis Napoleon's military talents, and from them that contempt has spread through the whole army. These distant expeditions, too, to unhealthy climates, for unintelligible purposes, are unpopular. Trochu refused to command the Chinese expedition, not, indeed, directly, but by imposing impossible conditions. He said that he must command the fleet as well as the land forces.

Fould's exposure of the state of our finances has done Louis Napoleon immense harm. It convicts him not only of waste, but of deception. Year after year he maintained, through his ministers, that the receipts fully equalled the expenditure, and now a deficit of forty millions sterling is shown. Soon after Fould's letter was published, I went to Val Richer. My friends at Lisieux and Pont l'Evêque could talk of nothing else. 'You told us all this,' they said, 'last year and the year before, but we could not believe you. Now it is the minister himself who tells it to us.' If there were a general election, I could come in by acclamation, merely because I should be an opposition candidate.

The deficit requires fresh taxation, unless we are to borrow to pay the principal of our debts, and to borrow more, in order to pay the interest of the new loan.

When the new tariff was imposed on us, in the form of a treaty, because no Chamber could have been nominated servile enough to pass it as a law, the country was bribed by the promise of a remission of taxation. If some of us were to suffer as producers, all were to gain as consumers. Eighty millions of taxes were remitted.

Immediately afterwards the taxes on tobacco and alcohol were augmented by fifty-two millions, and now M. Fould asks for one hundred and twelve millions more of new taxes, to be imposed chiefly on the necessaries of life—on sugar and on salt—so that instead of a remission of eighty millions, there will be an increase of eighty millions. And it is in the face of all this that the Chambers are opened to the public, and that the policy of the Government, and of the head of the Government, is canvassed with a boldness which would scarcely be used in your Parliament.

Senior.—I am struck by this passage in a speech made yesterday by the Marquis de Pierre, in the Corps Législatif :—

'*Si j'en puis croire quelques signes fâcheux au plus lointain de l'horizon, le Gouvernement aura peut-être un jour plus besoin d'amis courageux que d'admirateurs obséquieux. Le suffrage universel est un puissant élément: mais on n'y peut naviguer qu'à condition d'une popularité sans bornes. On n'y comprend pas beaucoup les raisons métaphysiques de la liberté, mais on s'y laisse vivement impressionner par les questions d'argent. Que le gouvernement qui croyait cette mer sans fond ne néglige plus d'y jetter souvent la sonde. Il pourrait toucher à des écueils qu'il ne prévoyait pas.*'

De Witt.—It was a solemn warning, and a premeditated one, for the speech was written.

When I consider the mobility and impetuosity of the French character, and our tendency to join what appears to us to be a majority, I feel that a mere suspicion that the Government is shaking may make every one rush to overturn it.

Senior.—Not only does M. de Pierre intimate this suspicion, he tells us that a Government based on universal suffrage cannot subsist, unless it enjoy universal popularity, which certainly is not the case with yours.

De Witt.—Then there are dissensions at headquarters. What the relations between the Emperor and his cousin may be no one knows. But we see that the Prince is in opposition, that he condemns the Emperor's Italian policy—or rather want of policy.

Senior.—Some of my friends think that, however we dislike and fear Louis Napoleon, we ought not to wish his Government to become seriously unpopular, because, when pushed to extremity, he will take the most effectual mode of withdrawing the attention of the French from their own affairs, a war with England.

De Witt.—That is possible, but I do not think that it is probable. It is so dangerous an expedient that he will defer and defer it, and the blow that is to strike him down—if it is to come—will probably come unexpectedly.

Saturday, March 22nd.—Jules de Lasteyrie called on us. We talked of M. de Pierre's speech on Thursday.

Senior.— What is the Marquis de Pierre? He calls himself a friend of the Government.

Lasteyrie.—He is an Absolutist.

Senior.—A Legitimist?

Lasteyrie.—Not sentimentally so. He is for any government that will protect property, enforce the game-laws, and protect agriculture. He is a Tory country gentleman, and such are the majority of our provincial deputies. They are Bonapartists only so far as they are anti-Republicans.

I am told that the deputies are overwhelmed by letters from their constituents, urging them to vote against the proposed taxes. To impose new taxes is always difficult, indeed dangerous, in France, and never was a time for doing so worse chosen.

Every interest is suffering; you know what is the state of our commerce and of our manufactures; and our agriculture is perhaps in a still worse state.

In the first place, it is affected by the general *malaise*. The cultivator is no longer a *prolétaire*, who sows and plants principally for his own consumption. In my department, *Seine et Marne*, almost a third of many farms is in *betteraves*,* and the farmer pays his rent by sugar and alcohol. With

---

* Beetroot.

the general distress the demand for these things falls off.

And, secondly, last year's harvest was deplorable. You have heard that instead of exporting, as we generally do, we have this year imported four hundred millions worth of grain. This is sixteen millions sterling taken from our agriculturists. I am inclined to think that the proposal of new taxes must be withdrawn. The result must be still to increase our debt, and to render necessary a still heavier taxation, or a still larger loan next year. And the Emperor's imprudence, and Fould's vanity, have made all this notorious. All confidence in the Emperor as an administrator is gone. It is clear that he knew nothing of the state of his finances, and now that he does know it, he proposes no real retrenchment. I believe, however, that he will be forced to withdraw the law enabling him to pension his military favourites. The Palikao business did him great harm. Neither the time nor the man was well chosen.

Another of his mistakes is his quarrel with the Society of St. Vincent de Paul. It disposed of a large revenue very usefully, and it was a wanton quarrel. The Society is not political, and would not have opposed him if he had left it quiet.

Senior.—You told us the other day that you never met a clergyman in society. I am invited to meet on Monday the Cardinal Archbishop.

Lasteyrie.—I do not envy you; he will be dull,

and the cause of dulness. It is thought correct when a mere bishop is present to be formal. What must it be in the presence of a Cardinal? Many subjects must be avoided; vices must be treated as sins, and errors lamented, not ridiculed. What remains to be laughed at?

Senior.—In Rome the Cardinals are good company.

Lasteyrie.—Yes, for there the Church is at home, and therefore at her ease. Here in Paris she feels herself a stranger. During the fifty years that preceded the Restoration, when infidelity was aggressive, an ecclesiastic was always in danger of hearing things which he could not tolerate without some loss of dignity, or reprove without making a scene. The clergy, therefore—even those whose birth, and education, and fortune, would have enabled them to mix in society—gradually withdrew from it.

That danger no longer exists; no clergyman in good company would hear anything that could offend him. But the habit has remained, though the cause has ceased.

In some country places, where there is a great proprietor—a squire—the curé dines with him on Sunday; but this is rare. In fact, the clergy are seldom fit to be our companions. The ignorance, even of the higher ecclesiastics, and even on their own subjects—theology and Biblical history—is astounding. They never read, they never talk to educated men. Their doctrinal sermons are therefore pitiable. They do not know what are the objections which require refutation, or what are the difficulties that require explanation. The Benedictines for many years before the Revolution had been engaged in the great work called 'Gallia Sacra.' After the restoration they resumed it, but made so little progress that it was taken from them, and given to a layman, who, in about ten years, has done more than the whole Benedictine Order did from 1815 to 1848.

The monks, however, having nothing else to think about, are good administrators of their estates, and the clergy in general learn something of human nature, especially of female weaknesses, in the confessional.

Lasteyrie was followed by Circourt.

Senior.—M. De Lasteyrie has been talking to us of the ignorance of the French clergy.

Circourt.—It is wonderful. Père Lacordaire was perhaps the most ignorant man that ever entered the Academy. His history and theology were full of originality. Indeed they were absolutely original, for he invented them as he went on. This gave to his sermons the charm of perpetual novelty. They never resembled one another.

Sunday, March 23rd.—Still confined, and therefore forced to give up the Père Félix to-day.

The Léon Says called on us.

He asked me whether I found Louis Napoleon stronger than he was last year.

Senior.—The general opinion seems to be that he is weaker.

Say.—That is my impression. 'Wolf,' however, has been so frequently cried, that I am *blasé*. Still it must be borne in mind that in this country a power suspected of being weak is thereby weak. It will be difficult to impose these new taxes, and dangerous to withdraw them. He has suffered the veil to be lifted and the rottenness of our finance to be nakedly exposed. The blindest Imperialist must see that to continue in times of peace the system of deficits and loans is the road to bankruptcy. And bankruptcy with a debt so enormous, and so spread among the lower classes as ours is, would be revolution.

His strength consists in our dread of revolution. But where will it be when we perceive that his conduct is bringing on a revolution?

Senior.—In the event of his being overthrown there are five possible successors to his power,— Henri V., the Comte de Paris, the Imperial Prince, Prince Napoleon, and the mob—which has the best chance?

Say.—You ought not to include Henry V. or the little Imperial Prince. I do not think either of them possible—at least, now.

It would lie, I think, between the Comte de Paris and Prince Napoleon.

But all this is barren speculation. This Government will fall, as all its predecessors have fallen; and it will fall as they fell—by some unforeseen blow, and in some unforeseen way. And its successor will probably owe its power to some cause equally unforeseen.

March 24*th.*—Captain Hore, the naval *attaché*, and his wife, Kergorlay, and Circourt, breakfasted with us.

I asked Hore if the French naval preparations were active.

Hore.—Not active. They are going steadily on to complete the scheme laid down ten years ago. Their existing fleet is so large in proportion to their sailors that they have been forced to oblige men who had already served to serve again. Their invention of iron-plated ships was a brilliant one: it gave them for a year or two the advantage over us. The English Admiralty was warned, but pooh-poohed the idea, and would not even try experiments, until the success of the *Gloire* opened their eyes.

Senior.—Is she as fine a vessel as the *Warrior?*

Hore.—Not so good a sailor, but less vulnerable, for she is completely armed. She is a very formidable Channel ship.

Senior.—Shall we ever come to ships of war of solid iron?

Hore.—It seems that iron requires the support of wood. A solid iron target of great thickness was knocked to pieces at Shoeburyness the other day without difficulty.

The Hores live in the Champs Elysées. I congratulated Mrs. Hore on inhabiting a quarter where no barricades could be raised; since the breadth of the Champs Elysées and the slope towards Paris would give irresistible advantages to the attack.

Mrs. Hore.—You do not mean that such considerations influence the choice of a residence in Paris?

Senior.—I do not know whether they do so; but I am sure that they ought to do so.

Let us ask Circourt whether he thinks that Paris is ever safe from an *émeute?*

Circourt.—It has not been so during my remembrance. It is not now. One seemed to be imminent two months ago. A dynasty cannot be opposed by Pretenders more dangerous than the Orleans family. Their mere number renders them formidable. A single childless competitor—a Henri V.—may die. Nothing but an Eastern massacre, like that which Jehu executed on the royal family of Ahab, could extirpate the descendants of Louis Philippe.

Then there is not one of them who is not distinguished by the qualities which the French most esteem and admire.

Senior.—Were the French Princes right in taking service in the American contest?

Circourt.—No one can deny that as a general rule

foreigners ought not to take part in a civil war. But I think that this was an exception. The cause of the Federals is a just one. The secession of the South was not justifiable on the only grounds on which a rebellion can be justified—illegal government or intolerable oppression. It is tainted by slavery. The Princes have a right to consider themselves as fighting in defence of the principle of lawful authority and national coherence. And, probably, though with less right, they think that they are fighting against slavery.

Then a French Prince ought to be a soldier; the opportunities of an exile are rare. I think that the Princes are right in seizing all that offer. MacClellan's school may not be a first-rate one, but war is to be seen there on a gigantic scale. Half a century has passed since such enormous armies have had to be moved over such enormous distances. I hear that the young Princes are among the best officers in the Federal army; and that the advice and the influence of the Prince de Joinville are great, and have been very useful. It seems that Lincoln had obstinately determined not to surrender the Commissioners, and that, having resisted the majority of his own cabinet, he yielded to the remonstrances of the Prince de Joinville.

Senior.—Many of the friends of the Princes regret their conduct.

Circourt.—Of course they do. The friends of Princes always disapprove of everything that they do.

To please them a Prince must imitate Henri V.,—

> ' Who never did a silly thing,
> Nor ever did a wise one.'

The conversation turned on language.

Senior.—How many words go to the vocabulary of a peasant?

Circourt.—Of words that he understands more or less vaguely—perhaps four hundred.

Senior.—And how many to that of a lady of the Faubourg?

Circourt.—Not many, except proper names. But of these, perhaps five hundred. They form the stock of the conversation. ' Where were you, madame, last night? Whom did you meet there? How did So-and-So look? How was So-and-So dressed?' The terror of a Frenchwoman is to be supposed to be guilty of originality, to be supposed to express any opinion that is not universally received; and she escapes by expressing none.

I have stayed out visitor after visitor at a lady's morning reception, and never heard anything but the same questions and the same answers about the same people.

Senior.—I was walking in Cairo with a Turk, and we saw two Turks meet. They talked together with great volubility for about five minutes. I asked my companion what they were talking about. ' They are repeating,' he answered, ' the same questions over and over again, and the same answers. " How do you do? "

"How do you do?" "Very well." "Oh, very well." "God be thanked!" God be thanked!" And so on.

Circourt.—Well, the conversation of the Faubourg is much the same.

I went out for the first time since last Monday and called on D. E. F. He asked me what appeared to me to be the prevalent political opinion in Paris.

Senior.—An opinion that the Imperial throne is shaking. But I have heard that opinion so often that I almost cease to attend to it.

D. E. F.—You never heard it from me.

Senior.—Yes: in the beginning of 1854.

D. E. F.—That is true. I thought him in danger then; and he was so, and was saved by the Crimean War. A war with England, or a war on the Rhine, if successful, might save him again. But I tell you *now* that I believe that his throne *is* shaking. The power that—when it chooses to do so—governs France, is the bourgeoisie. Its fear of the Rouges, and consequent inaction, enabled him to make the *coup d'état*. By coquetting with the Rouges he has lost its confidence, and he has not obtained that of those whom he is now courting. His position is one which it appears to me that a sovereign, unsupported by powerful bodies between the throne and the people, cannot maintain—that of being the object of universal distrust.

Senior.—Does the army trust him?

D. E. F.—The army trusts him so far, that it

believes him to be its friend, or rather its servant; that it believes him to be anxious to give it promotion, and pay, and privileges. But it does not respect him : it hates his military policy, his distant expeditions, and his choice of generals. The army is substantially an army of citizens, and sympathises with the classes from which it was taken and to which it is eager to return.

I was the other day in an *atelier*, where a year ago he was popular, where every one tried to find excuses for his faults. Now they are finding fault with his attempts to serve them.

'You must,' I said, ' be grateful for his having relieved the *maître sans compagnon* from the *droit de patente.*'

'Not in the least,' they answered. 'The consequence will be that thousands of *compagnons* will be discharged. And what do you think,' they added, ' of the new tax on salt, and of the new tax on sugar; or of his sacrificing the French workmen to his English alliance; or of his sacrificing French soldiers and French money to keep up the Pope?'

His tortuous, insincere conduct disgusts even those whom it is intended to please. The clerical party hates him as much as it could do if he had pulled down the Pope; the bourgeois and the *ouvriers* as much as if he cordially supported the Pope.

Senior.—I am told that the bourgeoisie form the religious portion of the French.

D. E. F.—You heard that from Corcelle, or from Montalembert, or from Lasteyrie. Do not believe it. The bourgeois has no more belief than the *ouvrier*.

Senior.—Who, then, are those who fill the churches ? The 2000 men whom I saw at Notre Dame listening to Père Félix seemed to me to be bourgeois.

D. E. F.—So were the 1000 persons whom I saw last Sunday at the Oratoire listening to Père Gratry. But they went, as I went, to hear a piece of rhetoric. The hatred of the bourgeois for the clerical party overthrew the Restoration, and mainly contributed to the fall of Louis Philippe.

Senior.—Louis Philippe, who chose Protestants to be his daughter-in-law and his minister, could not be accused of favouring ultra-Catholicism.

D. E. F.—What he, or rather his Government, was accused of, was of favouring hypocrisy. No one sinned in that way more than Cousin. His advice to all his pupils was, 'Talk as if you were believers.' And such was the tone of the Château. Such, too, is the tone of the present Government. A professor of history at the Lycée Bonaparte, named Weiss, is a Protestant. A year or two ago he had to talk of Luther, and treated him with respect. He was warned by the Minister of Public Instruction that it would not do : that if Luther were mentioned it must be as an apostate monk. Well, these young men, who were not to hear Luther treated seriously, were among the students who wanted to give Renan an ovation for calling Jesus Christ a man. Nothing irritates the French so much as hypocrisy. And as hypocrisy in religion, in morals, in foreign politics, in domestic politics, in the management of the press, in the management of the elections, and, above all, in the Constitution itself, is the very essence of this Government, you must not be surprised if I think it tottering. Père Gratry asked St. Marc Girardin and me to hear him read a portion of his *Conférences du Carême.* He wished to insert in it nothing that could expose him to prosecution. The subject was our social duties, and, among them, our duties towards the Government. 'That you may understand them,' he said, 'I must first explain to you the nature of our existing Government. Our Government, my brethren, is a despotism; and a despotism may be defined as the power of one individual *écrasant tous les autres.*'

We stopped him short. 'You wish,' we said, 'to avoid prosecution, and you propose to print such a sentence as that?'

'Why not?' he answered. 'It is a mere definition. Is not our Government a despotism, and what other definition of a despotism can I give?'

Senior.—Did he persist?'

D. E. F.—No; he gave up the publication, for this was only one of other mere definitions. But he was unconvinced, and I believe still thinks that we made him suppress an inoffensive book.

The conversation passed to foreign literature.

D. E. F.—I share the general incapacity of the French to speak foreign languages. This narrows much my power of enjoying the most delightful species of literature—poetry. I cannot perceive the rhythm of English, or of German, or of Italian verse. I am confined to Greek, Latin, and French poetry, or rather to Greek and Latin; for the monotony, the artificiality, and the pedantry of what the French call poetry, weary me to death.

We dined with Kergorlay, and met Mr. Dayton, the American Minister.

Dayton.—The question whether the Union will or will not be restored depends on a fact as to which we have no certain information—the existence or non-existence of a Union party in the Gulf States. We have ascertained that there is such a party in the Border States. In Maryland, Kentucky, and Tennessee, they appear to form the majority, though their voices were at first drowned by a more active and more vociferous minority. It is very strange if there be not in every state such a party, though it may not be large. It is very strange if, among five millions of whites, who have for eighty years under the Union enjoyed a prosperity, and made a progress, of which the world does not afford another example, there are not scattered everywhere some persons who deplore the sacrifice of that progress and prosperity to the vanity and ambition of a few politicians. In three months we shall have penetrated into the South sufficiently to enable this party to show itself. If it does not do so, if we have reason to think that the Gulf States are unanimously hostile to us, we must leave them to their folly, keeping to ourselves, however, New Orleans and the command of the Mississippi.

March 25th.—I called on Mr. Slidell, the Southern Commissioner. He is a gentlemanlike, intelligent man, about sixty or sixty-five. He asked me what appeared to me to be the state of opinion in Paris on American affairs.

Senior.—Sympathy with the North.

Slidell.—That is not my experience, except among the Orleanists, and they sided with us, until the Princes entered the Federal service; then they turned sharply round.

And what are their expectations?

Senior.—They believe that the issue depends on the existence or non-existence of a Unionist party in the South.

Slidell.—They are right; and as there is no such party, I have no doubt of the result. I do not believe that there ever before was so near an approach to unanimity in so numerous a people.

Senior.—And what are your own expectations?

Slidell.—I have told you what are my expectations as to the final result. The Union will never be restored. But whether this war is to terminate in three months, or six months, or in six years, depends on Europe. We supposed that long before this time you would have recognised us. It was clearly your interest to do so.

Senior.—But what good would our recognition have done to you? It would not have given you a man or a gun.

Slidell.—It would have relieved us from the blockade. Seward would have declared war against you. He told you so plainly. I wonder that a threat did not lead such proud nations as you and France to recognise us immediately.

Senior.—Seward was silly enough to write and to publish the threat, but I do not believe he would have been mad enough to execute it; and I do not think the time is even yet come at which the practice of nations authorises us to recognise you. Our object from the beginning has been to follow strictly the rules of international law.

Slidell.—Those rules seldom influence the conduct of nations.

Senior.—Not of despotisms, whether the despot be one or many. But a constitutional government, in which there is a strong opposition, cannot safely do anything which it cannot defend on legal principles.

Slidell.—Lord Palmerston might safely have recognised us, for Lord Derby would have done so, and would do so to-morrow, if he were in power.

Senior.—That is possible; but yet, if Lord Russell had recognised you, I have no doubt that Lord Derby would have attacked him; and, as I said before, you would not have been any nearer to the raising the blockade.

Slidell.—I hear that the distress among your work-people is great, and increasing. Will not that force you to raise it?

Senior.—We are getting cotton from India, we are adapting our machinery to it, we are looking forward anxiously to the time when we shall no longer be dependent on you. I do not believe that the war will be ended by an European intervention.

Slidell.—Then, it may last for years. The two parties are equally obstinate. I have spoken of the unanimity of the South; I believe the North also to be unanimous. *We* are ready to sacrifice everything to our independence. The *North* is ready to sacrifice everything to its ambition.

Senior.—Will not some more success, by satisfying the vanity of the North, induce it to offer terms which you can accept?

Slidell.—I have no such hope; success will only inflame them. They will try to use it, not for the purpose of conciliating, but of subjugating us, of trampling us down, of extirpating us. This they cannot do. If, therefore, you are right in thinking that Europe will not interfere, there is no prospect but of war for an indefinite number of years.

Senior.—There is an opinion among the friends of the South that when you have achieved your independence you will gradually abolish slavery.

Slidell.—We shall abolish the odious laws by which the intrigues of the Abolitionists forced some of the States to protect themselves, such as forbidding the slave to be taught to read; or to be allowed to possess property; or to be master of his own time, paying a rent to his master; or to be emancipated. But slavery, as an institution, must continue in our Southern States. The white man cannot cultivate the land; exposure to the sun kills him. All domestic services may be performed by whites, so may all factory work.

Indeed, for factory work, which is unhealthy to all races, and for that sort of field-work which even the negro cannot stand, we prefer whites.

To dig a drain up to the knees in water, under a nearly tropical sun, is a work to which no planter would set his own negroes. He contracts with an Irishman, who puts a hundred of his countrymen in it, fills them with whisky, loses ten per cent of them, and makes a handsome profit.

Senior.—But is it necessary that your coloured agriculturists should be slaves? Will not you gradually emancipate them?

Slidell.—We are convinced that a superior and an inferior race cannot inhabit the same country on terms of equality.

Senior.—Your proposition seems to me to be too

general. In our islands the two races live together on such terms.

Slidell.—In a few of your small islands, where the density of population enables the owners of land to exercise over the blacks a pressure equal to that of slavery, that is true.

But in the islands containing uncultivated land, on which the negro can squat, you are forced to do your field-work by imported Coolies. The negro is essentially idle, improvident, and without self-command. We firmly believe that he was intended by Providence to be the submissive instrument of the superior race. He is a sort of domestic animal, meant to be governed and directed by the white man. He feels this himself. It is a mistake to suppose that he frets against slavery. He accepts it as his natural state. He knows that he is not fit to take care of himself. He frets, of course, against a bad master, but bad masters are as rare as bad husbands and bad fathers.

The separation of families, of which Northern writers talk so much, is rarer still. The selling of children is a myth.

As the population on a Virginian estate becomes too large, the excess is sold; but it is sold in families.

In my State—Louisiana—emancipation is constantly going on, but it is the emancipation of the elderly, faithful servants, the *élite*, and in fact produces little change in their situation. This emancipation will continue, probably increase; but it will never amount to the annual excess of births. The slave population, therefore, will increase, perhaps at nearly the same rate that it does now.

Senior.—In that case you may have eight millions of slaves twenty-five years hence, and sixteen millions in fifty years.

Slidell.—I do not see why that should not be the case. Freed from the interference, the emissaries, and the firebrands of the North, our negroes will be happier and more contented than they are now; and even now they are the happiest and most contented peasantry in the world.

Lavergne called on us.

Lavergne.—Louis Napoleon may try to console himself for his failures here by his success with you. He has not been so well treated by your newspapers since 1858.

Senior.—He has behaved to us admirably in the *Trent* affair; and we believe him to be more pacifically disposed than he has been since 1858.

Lavergne.—I believe that you are right. Ever since the opening of the Session he has been playing the part of a constitutional king.

Senior.—Except in the Palikao letter.

Lavergne.—That was an ebullition of ill temper. It seems that his private wishes were irritated.

But could Queen Victoria have recognised more frankly the rights of the Corps Législatif?

He had proposed an enormous budget, to be provided for by new taxes.

The Corps Législatif tells him that it regrets that new taxes should be thought necessary. It tells him that it will carefully study the question, taking into consideration both the demands of the Exchequer and the power which the country has to meet them. '*Il serait à desirer,*' they add, '*qu'on pût trouver dans la réduction des dépenses improductives le moyen d'équilibrer le budget, et de poursuivre l'exécution des travaux publics.*'

I doubt whether any Queen's speech ever received such an answer. It would have turned out the strongest ministry.

He replies:

'*Ces questions vont être examinées d'un commun accord, et je ne doute pas qu'avec un esprit de conciliation la commission du Budget et le Conseil d'état ne s'entendent pour amener une solution conforme aux vœux de la Chambre et à l'intérêt général.*'

The sum is, he asks a large budget and new taxes. They answer that they regret that new taxes should be demanded, and suggest that it would be better to supply the deficit by the reduction of the unproductive expenses. He replies that he has no doubt that they shall come to an agreement; and ends by disclaiming any intention to dissolve them. This is very different from his tone when he claimed to be appointed by Providence to act and think for France.

Senior.—Will this new humility do him any good?

Lavergne.—Not in the least. We have no wish for constitutional government. In some states of mind we wish for excitement and glory; in others for quiet and prosperity; but never for self-government.

Senior.—And will he obey the orders of the Chamber and consent to reductions?

Lavergne.—I think so. If Fould had not spoken out, he might have gone on with loans, and concealed the deficit by fraudulent budgets. But the secret has been betrayed. All France is watching his finance. He must reduce his expenditure. He is not supported by any great party, or by any great principle. There are Legitimists, Orleanists, and Republicans in France, but no Bonapartists.

Senior.—He inscribes on his flag the principles of the Revolution of 1789.

Lavergne.—He might as well inscribe on it the principle that the earth goes round the sun. All the objects of the Revolution of 1789 had been gained in 1793. Four years sufficed to deprive France of her aristocracy, and to rivet on her the chains of centralisation. We are as likely to return to the Ptolemaic system as to the *ancien régime.*

Senior.—I thought that Napoleon was a sort of St. Denis, the guardian saint, the local god of the French, and that the worshippers of that name formed the Bonapartist party.

Lavergne.—There are no such worshippers; the first Napoleon is almost forgotten.

Senior. — How then do you account for this man's six millions of votes?

Lavergne.—It was fourteen years ago. The forty-five centimes had made Cavaignac unpopular. The Republic was hated, and *Celui-ci* was elected to destroy it. He has done his work, and we are tired of him.

The only Bonapartists are those who hope to get from him money or office (and they are comparatively few); those who look to him as their bulwark against the Rouges (and they are losing their confidence in him); and those whose sole desire is—at any price, and by any sacrifice—to avert another Revolution, who prefer the evils of despotism to those of change.

Alphonse Jobez,* a great proprietor in the Jura, a deputy under the Republic, came in while we were talking.

Jobez.—I perfectly agree with Lavergne. There are no Bonapartists except the three classes whom he has mentioned, only the third of which is considerable; and that class consists of Quakers. They will not fight against a revolution, since to avoid fighting is their principle.

Senior. — Do you agree with Lavergne, that Napoleon is forgotten?

---

* M. Jobez is a politician and a writer. His *History of the Reign of Louis XV.* has not long been completed. He is brother-in-law to M. Buffet.—ED.

Jobez.—By the masses, and as an historical personage? Yes. It is wonderful that a man who died only forty-one years ago, who, if he were now living, would not be older than some of my friends, should have passed into a sort of legend. The people have a vague idea that he put an end to the Revolution, and that he gained great victories. But over whom, or when, they never inquire and cannot tell.

Louis Napoleon's six million votes were owing partly to a considerable expenditure of money, partly to the unpopularity of his opponent, and, above all, to his name being known. In that respect Strasburg and Boulogne, silly as they were, did him good.

In the provinces, under universal suffrage, all depends on notoriety. The peasant does not know the names of a dozen public men; he has the vaguest ideas as to the characters of the few whom he does know. The probability is that he will vote for the name that is most familiar to him. This is the cause of the almost omnipotence of the Government in elections. It allows only its own candidate to publish addresses, to distribute voting papers, in fact to announce himself as a candidate, in every way except by personal canvas.

An opposition candidate started in my department. The Prefect sent a circular to the printers, warning them that if they allowed the opposition candidate to make any use of their presses, their *brevets d'imprimeur* would be withdrawn.

They were succeeded by St. Hilaire.

Senior.—Do you join in an opinion which I have just heard, that there is no Bonapartist party?

St. Hilaire.—Certainly. There are individuals, such as Fould, Walewski, and Persigny, who have sold themselves to Louis Napoleon, who have wealth and power while he can reign, and will be nothing when he falls; but they are not numerous enough to be called a party. Never since the *coup d'état* have I thought so ill as I do now of the prospects of this dynasty. It survived the destruction of liberty, the fettering the press, the increased conscription, the deportations of 1858, the scandals of its corruption; but it cannot survive a bankruptcy, or the visible approach of a bankruptcy.

Senior.—Do you give it ten years?

St. Hilaire.—Not five; and when it falls, it will not leave, as Louis Philippe did, and as the Restoration did, a strong vivacious party anxious to restore it. Not a spar, not a plank of the great vessel, will remain floating.

Senior. — Do you think that he himself is alarmed?

St. Hilaire.—No; he is a fatalist, he is *insouciant*, he is indolent, he is absorbed by petty vanities and sensual pleasures. He lets things take their course. Every one feels that there is no one at the helm. That neither abroad nor at home is there any settled policy; that the most important measures are taken up capriciously, and executed precipitately. I hear now that we are to send 30,000 men to Mexico. A few weeks ago he wanted to borrow in London four millions sterling, in order to facilitate the conversion of the four per cents, by buying up the threes which might be thrown on the market. He had contracted for the loan at six per cent.

A question was asked in your House of Commons, and this Government denied the negotiation, on which your capitalists broke it off, and he has borrowed the money from Rothschild at ten per cent. All the important measures of the last two years—the treaty of commerce, the Chinese and Mexican expeditions, the liberty of debate; and, above all, the revelation of the true state of our finances, have been undertaken inconsiderately and blindly. The worst of them, probably, is the Mexican expedition. It will complete the ruin of our finances, and, as I said before, that ruin will ruin the dynasty.

I dined with Masson, and met Changarnier, Duvergier, Corcelle, Lanjuinais, and Buffet.* · We talked of the debate on the address.

---

* M. Buffet practised as an advocate before the Revolution of 1848, when, being returned as a representative of the people by the department of the Vosges, he voted as a rule with the old dynastic Left, which became the Right of the Constituent Assembly, and distinguished himself by his zealous opposition to Socialism. He accepted the Republican constitution, and declared that General Cavaignac had deserved well of his country. After the election of December 10, he gave in his adhesion to the govern-

Masson.—It was amusing to find all the nominees of the Emperor, who were selected as the representatives of his opinions, the fiercest opponents of his policy.

Duvergier.—Yes; but though they spoke against the address, they voted for it.

'How could I do otherwise,' said B. to me, 'I was the Emperor's candidate?'

Lanjuinais.—This was what Louis Napoleon

---

ment of Louis Napoleon, who intrusted him with the portfolio of Commerce and Agriculture after the dismissal of M. Bixio. Both as minister and as representative, he supported the party of order, but he refused to follow completely the policy of the Elysée, and accordingly he quitted the ministry with Odillon Barrot, December 31, 1849. Re-elected by his department—at the head of the poll—he exercised great influence in the Legislative Assembly. After the crisis which followed the dismissal of General Changarnier, he returned to office with M. Léon Faucher, 1851. He resigned with his colleagues, 1851, when the President declared in favour of the withdrawal of the law of May 31. A few days later he was nominated a Chevalier of the Legion of Honour.

After the *coup d'état* of December 2, 1851, M. Buffet declined to accept any public appointment for several years, except that of Member of the Council-General for the Canton of Thillot. In 1863, however, he came forward as an Opposition candidate in the first circonscription of the Vosges, and was elected. M. Buffet quickly became one of the most prominent members of the Corps Législatif, where he was one of the leaders of a 'Tiers Parti,' which endeavoured to reconcile Liberal reforms with loyalty to the dynasty. He was re-elected for his department in May, 1869; and in the short session which commenced in the following month, alluded to when he said that the vote had restored the confidence which the debate had disturbed.

Morny said to a friend of mine, 'I am angry, I am indignant at the Emperor's policy. At last I could stand it no longer, I was forced to give vent to my feelings, by writing to him a letter of remonstrance, "*Je lui ai bien lavé la tête.*"'

'And how did he take it?' said my friend.

'Why, in fact,' said Morny, 'the letter was so

---

he greatly contributed to the victory of the Liberal centre, and was one of the promoters of the famous demand of interpellation, signed by 116 deputies, which elicited the message and the project of the *Senatus consulti*, containing the promise of a return to parliamentary government. After the prolonged negotiations in connexion with which his name was so constantly mentioned, respecting the formation of the first parliamentary ministry, M. Buffet became a member, as Finance Minister, of the cabinet formed by M. Emile Ollivier, on January 2, 1870. His financial policy gave general satisfaction; but when M. Ollivier consented to the *plébiscite*, M. Buffet deemed it his duty to resign at the same time as his colleague, M. Durer, April 10.

After the disaster of Sedan, and the Revolution of September 4, he retired for a short time into private life. However, at the elections of February 8, 1871, he was returned by his department —again at the head of the poll—to the National Assembly. M. Thiers offered him the portfolio of Finance, but he declined it, for fear of the susceptibilities which might be wounded on account of his having held office under the Empire. M. Buffet took his seat in the Right Centre. On April 4, 1873, he was elected President of the National Assembly in the place of M. Grévy, and he was re-elected to that office, May 13, 1874. In 1875 M. Buffet became Prime Minister : he resigned in 1876, and was succeeded by M. Dufaure.—Ed.

VOL. II.

strong, so uncompromising, it contained so many bold truths, *que, ma foi, je l'ai mise dans le feu.*'

Masson.—A deputy, after declaiming against the new taxes, the treaty, the treatment of the Pope, and the imperial government in general, ended by saying to me, 'But for *one* reason sixty of us would have voted against the address.'

'What reason?' I asked.

'Because we must have voted with Jules Favre.'

Duvergier.—You may estimate the importance of the opposition by the sacrifice which Louis Napoleon made to conciliate the Chamber. He has promised not to dissolve it.

Senior.—This is not a good moment for a dissolution.

Duvergier.—No, but next year the Chamber expires. By giving up the power of dissolution he has given up the power of choosing a favourable occasion for a general election. Things are bad now, but they may be much worse in the autumn of 1863.

Have you seen Persigny's declaration in the *Constitutionnel?* He says that he does not intend to resign until he has been able to show his devotion to the Emperor at the next elections, by his fearless patronage of the friends of the Government, and by his fierce opposition to his enemies. It is an instructive comment on the freedom of election.

Corcelle.—The Emperor has tried his hand at making a new constitutional machine. It contains elements never tried before, and, I suspect, unfit to work together. Till last year its action was concealed. No eye penetrated into its mysteries. Now it works in the face of day, and all its doings are recorded by the merciless stenographer. The system of ministers *à porte-feuille* and ministers *sans porte-feuille*—the first to plan and to carry out their measures, but not allowed to explain or support them ; the second not consulted as to those measures, but brought into the Chamber merely to defend them, is one never tried before. No one was absurd enough even to think of it. The consequence is, that the defence does as much harm as the measures themselves.

Billault's* speech is called eloquent. He begins by speaking contemptuously of Rattazzi's ministry— a ministry supposed to have been brought in by the Emperor. He then tells us that the Piedmontese army has been ruined, by being swamped by the Tuscan, Roman, and Neapolitan *canaille*. He tells Europe that the Papal government is detestable, and that the Pope is an obstinate old man, who is walking with bandaged eyes towards a precipice. He deplores any attack on Venice, but adds, that if the Italians are unwise enough to make one, France must support them.

Thus he insults all our friends, and ends by admitting that, if they act in opposition to our wishes,

---

* Billault died suddenly in the autumn of 1863.—Ed.

our interests, and our advice, we shall, notwithstanding, support them.

'Pray come to terms with Victor Emmanuel,' he says to the Pope; 'but if you *will* not do so, we shall still protect you.'

'Pray do not attack Venice,' he says to Victor Emmanuel; 'but if you *will* do so, we shall help you.'

Corcelle. — Louis Napoleon insults the Pope, because he does not fear him; but the Pope has arms which he may use if pushed to extremity. The average age of our bishops is a little under seventy. Vacancies, therefore, occur every year. They are filled by servile Bonapartists. As yet the Pope approves them; but he might refuse. Diocese after diocese would be left vacant. This would be not merely an inconvenience, but a scandal. It would be instantly notorious that the Church was opposed to the Emperor. His best friends are among the agricultural population, who in most districts are religious. His party—if he has a party—is now very weak. He cannot afford to weaken it still more.

March 26*th.*—We went to Madame Duchatel's instrumental concert, carried on by seven of the best players from the Conservatoire. The reception-rooms, large as they are, were full. There must have been six or seven hundred people. The concert-room, and the two rooms next to it, were occupied by ladies. The men were principally in the dining-room, and in two rooms between the dining-room and the drawing-rooms. We were so far off that we could talk without annoying the players.

I talked principally to Dumon and Corcelle. Dumon's views of Napoleon's position agree with those of St. Hilaire.

Dumon.—I, too, am *blasé* as to the prophecies of the fall of Louis Napoleon; but I cannot resist the proofs of his great and growing unpopularity. I ought, perhaps, to use a stronger word. He is what is much worse than unpopular—despised. A *laisser aller* government cannot live in France, and since the peace of Villa Franca this government has been almost passive.

Senior.—It has made the commercial treaty.

Dumon.—Which, for its immediate interest, it had better have let alone. Justice will be done to the treaty hereafter. Long after this Second Empire has ceased to exist, the introduction of free trade will be recollected as its principal glory. But coinciding with a bad harvest, a ruined exchequer, and senseless foreign wars, it threatens his destruction. All that I hear in Paris, and all my letters from the country, are in the same sense. All the distress—and there is much—is attributed to his folly and to his obstinacy.

Senior.—He seems inclined to yield to the Corps Législatif, and to withdraw the new taxes.

Dumon.—It seems impossible for him to do so, and at the same time to continue his enormous expenditure, except by a loan—indeed by a system of constantly increasing loans—and he has allowed Fould to disclaim loans in time of peace. I suspect that he will press the new taxes, except perhaps the salt tax. It now produces thirty millions, about eighty-one centimes per head on the population; and as the poor, who live much on a vegetable diet, consume as much per head as the rich, it is a poll-tax. At four to a family, it is a tax of three francs four sous a family. If doubled—as is the proposal—it will be a tax of six francs eight sous a family—about two days' wages of an *ouvrier*, and three days' wages of a peasant— a tax which, coming at a moment of distress, will be heavily felt.

Corcelle.—I have just heard a characteristic story of the Emperor. He drove himself the other day, with only Fleury, his *aide-de-camp*, to the Gare of the Strasburg railway to meet the Duchess of Hamilton. He was received in the waiting-room set apart for great personages.

The train was late, he got tired, and went out, and walked up and down the platform. It was a cold, draughty day, and M——, the *chef* of the Gare, warned him that he was in a dangerous atmosphere. He went back to the waiting-room, got tired again, and returned to the platform.

M—— went up to him, and repeated his advice.

'None of us,' he said, 'venture to walk here in such weather unless well wrapped up.'

The Emperor, however, continued his walk.

Fleury came to M——, and said, '*Vous avez abordé Sa Majesté deux fois. Vous aviez donc quelque chose de bien pressé à lui dire?*'

'*Ma foi!*' said M——, '*je lui ai dit qu'il s'enrhumerait.*'

'*Mais,*' said Fleury, '*savez-vous que vous avez fait une chose bien grâve? On ne parle pas à l'Empereur sans avoir une audience concédée par Sa Majesté.*

'*Par exemple, aujourd'hui Sa Majesté est allée vers la Gare du Nord au lieu de la Gare de Strasbourg. Mais je n'ai pas parlé jusqu'à ce que Sa Majeste m'ait dit, "Fleury, je crois que nous nous trompons de chemin." Alors, étant interpellé j'ai osé répondre, "Oui, Sire, nous nous trompons de chemin."*'

March 30*th.*—We dined with the Mohls, and met M. J——. The story of Fleury and the Emperor was told.

Senior.—Is Fleury a sample of his *entourage?*

J——.—A fair one. About as servile as the others. Do you know the story of De Dreux?

Senior.—No.

J——.—De Dreux was a celebrated horse-painter. The Emperor ordered from him a portrait, large as life, of a favourite charger. He was so pleased with it that he proposed to De Dreux to paint another.

De Dreux did not receive the commission with the gratitude that sovereigns expect. 'Such a picture,' he said, 'takes much time.'

'But,' said the Emperor, 'it is well paid for. Fleury gave you from me 30,000 francs.'

'I received,' said De Dreux, 'only 6000.'

An altercation followed, Fleury affirming that he had paid 30,000 francs, and De Dreux that he had received only 6000; and then a duel, in which De Dreux was killed on the spot.

All this must come to an end, and not a very distant one. All that is wanting to a successful *émeute* are twenty or thirty men ready to sacrifice their lives.

There were many such in 1832 and in 1833; there were some such in June 1848. I was behind the barricades in 1832. When I saw that success was impossible, I said to those around me, 'We have nothing more to do. We are not soldiers, acting under orders, and bound by our engagements; we are citizens, obeying our own impulses, and engaged only to ourselves. Let us disperse and save ourselves for another opportunity.'

Many did so; some refused. 'Whether we live or die,' they said, '*c'est égal*. When we took up the good cause, we knew that our chances of life were almost desperate. We shall remain here.'

And so they did.

There were no such men in 1851, or the result of the *coup d'état* would have been different. They are now reappearing. They are the natural offspring of distress and discontent under an absolute government, which meddles with everything, and therefore is held responsible for everything.

Celui-ci trusts to the army; it will fail him. The men sympathise with the people, the regimental officers with the Bourgeoisie, and the higher officers are Orleanists.

Everybody knows that the end is approaching, but few know how near it is.

April 1st.—I called on Auguste Chevalier.

A. Chevalier.—You have been three weeks in Paris, what are your impressions?

Senior.—The thing that strikes me most is the apparent weakness of the dynasty. Last year it seemed to be firmly established, now, no one believes in its permanence.

A. Chevalier.—To you who have not watched the progress of our opinions, the change must be marvellous. To me, who have seen its gradual growth, it seems natural.

In 1852 Louis Napoleon had two courses open to him. One was to carry out the representative constitution which he had invented, or rather copied. To let the elections be honest, the discussions unrestrained, and the press free, and gradually to make the Chambers a part of the Government. The other was to nominate, through his prefects, the Corps Législatif, to render the press servile, to suppress all record of the discussions in the Senate, to mutilate or suppress those of the Corps Législatif, to confine both Chambers to the mere voting or rejecting laws, and to govern absolutely under the screen of representative bodies. The latter was the course which he selected. It had succeeded with his uncle, and he is essentially an imitator. He had been following it for nine years, when you were in Paris last year. He had enormous advantages at the beginning. The selfishness, faction, jobbing, and want of public spirit of Louis Philippe's Chambers, and the ignorance, unstatesmanlikeness, indecision, and vulgarity of the Republican assemblies, had disgusted everybody. We were sick of parliamentary government.

For some time things went on pretty well. The press was paralysed, the Chambers were submissive and generally silent. If any damaging discussions occurred they were unreported. Success made him confident. He was told that the glories of the second empire eclipsed those of the first. He wished for flattery which should appear to be independent, which should be uttered by a full chorus, and should re-echo over all Europe. He resolved to unmuzzle the Chambers, to allow them to consider, not merely *projets de loi*, but the whole character and conduct of his policy, to open every session by a debate on the state of the nation. As his ministers were not chosen for their rhetorical talents, indeed for any talents at all, except those of a court, he invented ministers *sans porte-feuille*, mere talkers, whose duty it should be to explain and defend measures on which they had not been consulted, the measures of other men, their rivals perhaps, or their enemies.

The time chosen by Louis Napoleon for this revolution was when he had quarrelled with the Church, had quarrelled with the press, had allowed the affairs of Turkey to take a course injurious to our power, to our honour, and to our vanity, had sacrificed the immediate interests of our manufacturers to the English Alliance, had incurred a deficit of forty millions sterling: and in the face of an unavoidable distress occasioned by a bad harvest and the American war.

These were the auspices under which the parliamentary campaign began.

What was to be expected but defeat and discredit? *Il est sur une pente, où il ne peut pas se cramponner.* He must sink into the valley of parliamentary government, or climb back to the *plateau* of absolutism. If he allows things to go on, his ministers *sans porte-feuille* will be inferior in every debate, for they will be opposed by men who have studied far better than they can do the subject in question.

Baroche, though he was on the right side, did not know how to use his advantages, he mistook kilogrammes for francs, left out a line in his figures, and was beaten by Brame and Pouyer Quertier, as Billault was by Jules Favre and Keller.

The opposition can always choose its points of

attack, and the follies of this government lay it open on every side. The real ministers must be taken from the Chamber, they must be taken from among the men in whom the Chamber has confidence, and that is what I have called descending into the valley of parliamentary government. This he will not tolerate. It is opposed to all his prejudices and to all his tastes. It was to avoid it that he made the *coup d'état*.

He will take the other course. He will, as Morny threatened, abolish the debate on the address, and allow only such parts as he thinks innocent of the other debates to be published. This will be a movement in retreat. Like all such movements it will be an avowal of defeat: it will be a small *coup d'état*.

Senior.— But it will be a *coup d'état* which will not excite the Bourgeoisie or the people. They do not care for the debates.

A. Chevalier.—When a government is falling everything is important. As I said before, it will be an acknowledgment of weakness, an acknowledgment that his policy cannot bear discussion. Never was a government more a government of opinion than this is, for it has no root in the affections of its subjects. Such a government is like a bank : as soon as its solvency is suspected there is a run on it. As soon as a few of the leaders have declared against it, there will be a general *sauve qui peut*.

Senior.—To what leaders do you allude? France seems to be without leaders. In 1848 you had men each of whom had his followers. There was Guizot, there was Odillon Barrot, there was the Duc de Broglie, there were in every province men who were looked up to. They were divided, but the common danger united them, and returned the great Constituent Assembly which broke to pieces the socialists and gave you a government which, if you had not chosen a Pretender for your President, might have lived respectable and respected till now.

A. Chevalier.—It is true that ten years of despotism have destroyed all organization among the Bourgeoisie and the aristocracy. It is true that among them there are now no leaders. But there are still three organized bodies—the army, the Church, and the Secret Societies : none of them are his friends. The army despises his affectation of military ability, the secret societies hate and dread him. It is on them, and especially on their chiefs, that his massacres and his deportations have fallen. And I need not tell you what are the feelings of the Church. At this instant the most popular man in the army, perhaps in France, is MacMahon. He is honest, sensible, modest, an excellent officer, of long experience in every sort of war—the partizan warfare of Algeria, and the *Grande Guerre* of Europe—and a liberal in politics. He is one of the few eminent men who ventured to oppose the *loi de sureté générale*, and he is an Orleanist.

Senior.—Do not Randon's position and character give him influence?

A. Chevalier.—Randon is an excellent administrator, a man of sense and of probity, a good general of division, but not a general in the high sense of that word. His name inspires respect, but not the unlimited confidence which is required for a leader in a crisis. He will follow MacMahon.

Senior.—What will Changarnier do?

A. Chevalier.—I will not guess; but he will not exercise great influence. Ten years ago his talents, his courage, his reputation, and his boundless ambition, made him dangerous. But military reputation passes quickly in France. There are too many competitors, and the army changes too rapidly. A few *remplaçants* are the only soldiers that recollect Changarnier.

Senior.—You do not expect the initiative to be taken by the army? It seems to me that that must be done by the people.

A. Chevalier.—And, therefore, the leaders of the secret societies are so important. No leaders are so blindly obeyed, partly from love, but still more from fear. You have heard of the Reign of Terror. That has passed. *Au lieu du Règne de la Terreur, nous avons le Règne de la Peur.* What will be the folly or the blunder that will occasion the explosion I cannot guess. All that I know is that follies and blunders will not be wanting.

Senior.—I rather expect that when I am here next year I shall find him in a better situation than he is now. There will probably be a fair harvest, the American war will be over, the temporary evils of the commercial treaty will have almost passed away;

there will be a revival of trade, and with good wages and cheap food the discontent will abate.

A. Chevalier.—Supposing all these contingencies to turn in his favour, there are other sources of discontent which will probably be aggravated. Our foreign relations, under his management, must go from bad to worse.

Senior.—He has not always mismanaged them. In 1851 he found France weak and discredited, with no ally but England, and threatened by a coalition headed by Russia. In 1855 she had humbled Russia, had added Austria and Piedmont to her allies, and was feared throughout the Continent.

A. Chevalier.—Very true; but his foreign policy from the end of 1851 up to the middle of 1855 was managed, not by him, but by Drouyn de Lhuys. And what has been its progress since Drouyn de Lhuys left him? Austria has become his bitter enemy. Piedmont, raised by him to a first-rate power, distrusts and hates him. So do all Germany, Holland, and Belgium. So does Spain, which he proposed a couple of years ago to partition. *You* are avowedly arming against him. It is true that he is feared. By doubling in ten years our national debt he has created an army so great that it cannot be kept up, and a fleet too large to be manned. I feel convinced that our foreign relations will be worse next year than they are now. So will our finances be. What will be the cost of this Mexican war? I expect no really important reductions, and I expect little from the new taxes. The civil list is said to owe fifty millions. The Church is becoming more hostile to him every day, and all the monarchical parties belong to it. The enemies of the Church are also his enemies, for they are republicans. His mind is formed out of three dissimilar elements—Creole, Corsican, and Dutch. As a Creole, he is indolent, prodigal, vain, and self-indulgent; as a Corsican, he is false and cunning; as a Dutchman, he is phlegmatic, reserved, silent, and intrepid. It is to his Dutch qualities that he owes his success. I have watched him narrowly in circumstances of great difficulty. His courage never flinches, his self-command never deserts him—*il ne s'étonne jamais.*

Military men of ordinary, or less than ordinary, talents have often beaten in the field of battle men far superior to them intellectually. In a battle there is everything that can confuse and disturb the mind. Suppose five men to be engaged, whose respective intellects are represented by 100, by 75, by 50, by 25, and by 15. If the man of 25 preserves all his powers of mind, while those about him sink down to 15, he beats them. Just as a general commanding 100,000 men may be beaten by one commanding only 50,000, if the whole 50,000 can be brought into action against only 40,000 out of the 100,000.

Now Louis Napoleon brings all his wits into action. Louis Philippe in quiet times had far more talents, but they deserted him on the approach of danger. So it was with Guizot; so it was with Thiers.

Senior.—Such a frame of mind seems to fit him peculiarly to resist what is his greatest danger—an émeute.

A. Chevalier.—No courage, or skill, or presence of mind, will avail if the mob attack him and the army does not support him. Those are the events which I expect, but whether next year, or four or five years hence, I cannot guess.

Senior.—What is the history of Lavalette's return from Rome ?

A. Chevalier.—He comes to ask that Goyon's instructions and his may be assimilated. At present they are opposed. He is ordered to encourage Victor Emmanuel, Goyon to encourage the Pope and the ex-King of Naples. But he will fail. Louis Napoleon will persevere in his double policy, and perhaps he is right. To desert Victor Emmanuel would exasperate the Carbonari; to desert the Pope would exasperate the Clergy, and having a double policy he must have double instruments.

Wednesday, April 2nd.—I went with Jules Simon to visit a M. Rencontre, a working shoemaker, living in a by-street leading out of the Rue de Sèvres.

He received us in his little room on the second floor, divided into two by a partition.

I asked him what were the political opinions of the men of his own class.

Rencontre.— We, the *ouvriers*, are all of us republicans.

Senior.—La République sociale et démocratique ?

Rencontre.—No ; la République libre. Socialism if it were possible would be the worst of tyrannies.

Senior.—We are told that the republicans care more for equality than for liberty.

Rencontre.—Unhappily there is much truth in that. Though we all desire liberty we do not all understand it. But *Celui-ci* is giving to us a political education. He is showing to us that there may be an equality of weakness, of intolerance, in fact of slavery. He is showing to us that such equality is destructive, not only of our dignity as men, but of our *bien être* as animals. He is showing us that there can be no good government under a despotism, and no prosperity without good government.

Senior.—What do you say as to his quarrel with the Pope ?

Rencontre.—Oh, with that we are delighted. But we wish that he would manage it more honestly. We see with indignation French troops mounting guard over the Roman liberals and supporting the Neapolitan brigands. We are all Italians.

Senior.—Unitarians ?

Rencontre.—Unitarians. We trust that the time is at hand when France and Italy free and allied will lead the liberal party in Europe.

Senior.—What will your clergy say ?

Rencontre.—They will say whatever they may be paid to say. We shall not know much about it. We never speak to them, or listen to them.

Senior.—You talk of the incompatibility of despotism and prosperity. Has there not been much prosperity under the Empire?

Rencontre.—Only in a few trades, such as the builders and the makers of military stores. Ever since 1851 the prices of the necessaries of life have been steadily rising, some, such as lodgings, have almost doubled. Ten years ago these rooms let for 200 francs a-year. I now pay 350 for them; and I should have to pay taxes besides if the *concierge,* who is *bonne fille,* did not return them as letting for only 250 francs a-year, and therefore exempt.

Senior.—But you get more for your shoes?

Rencontre.—Very little more, not nearly in proportion to my increased expenses.

Senior.—And to what do you attribute these increased expenses?

Rencontre.—As to lodgings the cause is obvious. A fifth part of Paris, and the most populous part, has been pulled down, and the new houses are such as we cannot inhabit. As to other things, we suppose that if 700,000 strong hearty young men are kept walking and standing about as soldiers, and as many more in building fine houses, and making fine furniture and fine clothes for the Court and courtiers, there must be fewer employed in raising the food and making the things we *ouvriers* have to consume.

Senior.—Baroche tells us that wages have risen as much as prices.

Rencontre.—Baroche lies; wages have risen very

little. The wages of printers, for instance, are what they were thirty years ago. The printers have demanded an increase of 20 per cent ; the masters have offered 10. Several men have been arrested, some for advising their fellow-workmen to refuse the masters' offer, others for having refused to work.

Senior.—Is that an offence ?

Rencontre.—An offence severely punished. The Crown and the Bourgeoisie make our laws. Of course they prohibit everything which might render the workman independent of his master.

A pleasing young man of about twenty-one came in, the shoemaker's son. He is doing very well, he told us, as a carpenter.

After we left the house, I heard the young man's story.

Simon.—About this time last year he completed his twentieth year, and had to stand the ballot for the conscription ; 300,000 young men are subjected to it every year, half of them are unfit for service, and out of the remaining 150,000, 100,000 are taken. So that the chances are two to one against escape.

The father came to me in terror. ' To think,' he said, ' of a son of mine serving Bonaparte ; and yet all that I can hope to raise by selling all my furniture, even the bed from under me and my wife, is 500 francs, and to insure for a substitute costs 1500.'

I went about to beg for them. D'Haussonville

gave me 500 francs, and in a few days I collected the whole 1500.

I went with it to the garret. 'Shake hands with me, Rencontre,' I said.

'Ah,' said the wife, '*Je vois qu'il a la vie de notre fils dans la main.*'

Senior.—What would you have had to pay if you had waited till he was actually drawn?

Simon.—2500 francs, twice as much as was paid under Louis Philippe. The conscription is an engine not only of oppression, but of extortion. The Government demands 2500 francs, and procures a *remplaçant* for half the money. It squeezes in this way about a million and a half sterling a-year, by the most unequal of all taxes—a poll-tax.

Saturday, April 5th.—We dined at Madame Anisson's and afterwards went to Thiers.

At Madame Anisson's we met M. de Barante, Lanjuinais, Viel Castel, Circourt, and the younger Anissons.

The remark which I have been hearing for four weeks—the *décadence* of Louis Napoleon—was repeated by every one, and by none more strongly than Viel Castel.

Madame Anisson talked about English habits.

Madame Anisson.—There is one institution which governs your whole lives, which I could never tolerate—the luncheon. Luncheon and breakfast destroy the whole morning. Your breakfast is so early, that nothing can be done before it. It lasts till about eleven. Then, in winter, you must go out, for there is no going out after luncheon. At two comes luncheon, it is over by three, and by four it is dark. The drawing-room is deserted, you sit in your own room till half-past seven, and then you are expected to dine, though you in fact dined only four hours and a half before. Our plan of breakfasting at half-past eleven gives us two or three hours before breakfast, and the whole day from half-past twelve to half-past six free.

Senior.—I am quite ready to surrender luncheon, if you will give up a French institution—a lady's having a day for morning receptions.

Madame Anisson.—I abominate it, and never submit to it. I pay a morning visit in order to talk to a friend. What conversation can there be in a room of twenty people, when somebody is coming in and somebody is going out every ten minutes?

Roger Anisson.—The institution which I envy you most is that of downs and commons. We have *biens communaux*, but they are generally in wood, or let by the commune to individuals. The village green, round which cottages with their little gardens, and sometimes the houses of the smaller aristocrats of the village—the doctor, the clergyman, and the retired tradesman are scattered—is almost unknown to us. So is the great open down, on which I have ridden in England for ten miles.

Senior. — The land of England has been for

centuries possessed by the rich, and has been used as much for pleasure as for profit.

Roger Anisson.—With us it is merely a source of profit. Commons and downs produce little even to their owners, and scarcely anything to the Government. They give no stamp duties, as they are not sold or mortgaged, and little *impôt foncier*. The Government always tries to force the communes to sell their lands, and to invest the price in the funds. And as the funds give five per cent, and the land not two and a half, this process goes on so rapidly that in a short time we shall have no *biens communaux* left.

At Thiers' I found St. Hilaire, Duvergier, Masson, and three or four others.

I asked Thiers if he shared the general opinion that Louis Napoleon's prestige was diminishing.

Thiers.—It is gone; his reign as an absolute monarch is over. I told you six years ago that the amount of liberty which he left in the Constitution, like a young tree that has rooted itself in an old wall, would grow and extend, until it burst the obstacles by which he thought he had confined it. His wars, one just, the other, though absurd, successful, diverted public attention, but now it is fixed on him. We have long seen the folly and weakness of his foreign policy. Now he has himself told us that his domestic policy has been as mischievous, that he has wantonly ruined our manufactures, and, with a revenue twice as great as that of his uncle, has incurred a debt which will weigh us down until we shake it off by a bankruptcy. All this he has proclaimed to Europe from the tribunes of the Senate and of the Corps Législatif.

Senior.—Will he silence these tribunes ?

Thiers.—If he does he must give us something in their place—*le droit d'interpellation* for instance.

Senior.—That seems to me to be the last thing he will give. For a man who generally has no plan, and when he has one, conceals it, and plays the statesman *en conspirateur*, nothing could be more offensive than to be required to state precisely what it is that he intends to do.

Thiers.—Some such concession, however, he must make. The country will not bear to return to the Constitution of 1852, under which the Chambers were to ignore politics. The next step will be to take his ministers from the Chambers, and that is parliamentary government.

Senior.—And do you think that he will submit to that ?

Thiers.—I think that if he sees in time the necessity he will do so. His great merit is, *qu'il sait reculer*. He is obstinate in his ends, but not in his means. But he may discover the real nature of his position too late. He may fall, as Louis Philippe did, unexpectedly. His great strength is the conviction of the Bourgeoisie that the government which follows him must give liberty of the press, and that a free press will produce revolution after revolution until a new despot again fetters it.

We talked of the Mexican expedition.

Thiers.—I believe that nothing but European intervention can save civilisation in Mexico. I should be glad to see Europe interfere, as it did in Greece and in Belgium, for a joint purpose and at a joint expense. But that France, on her road to bankruptcy, meeting with no real assistance from England and only obstacles from Spain, should send an army and a fleet for the purpose of raising an Austrian Archduke to a Mexican throne, is a madness which has no parallel since Don Quixote undertook the cause of the Princess Autonomasia.

Senior.—What put it into his head?

Thiers.—I believe that it was the Empress. Mexico has behaved outrageously to Spain, as she has to every country with which she has had any relations. Spain has long been threatening her with little effect, as she was not supposed to be able to execute her threats. The Moorish campaign raised her spirits and her reputation. She has recovered St. Domingo, and is forming more extensive plans. The Empress is a true Spaniard, with all the pride and ignorance of her race. I believed that she hoped to send a Spanish prince to Mexico. But the Emperor refused to countenance a Bourbon.

Senior.—I have reason to believe that he expressed his willingness to see the Duc d'Aumale king or emperor of Mexico.

Thiers.—If he said so it must have been on Talleyrand's principle that the use of language is to conceal thoughts. The proposal of Maximilian came from the Mexicans. Some of them took on themselves to offer the crown to him. He caught at it eagerly, and wrote *la plus basse des lettres* to Louis Napoleon asking his consent and assistance. Both were given, and I suppose that we shall have to add the Emperor Maximilian to Queen Pomare, and King Ramadan, and the Pope, and the other sovereigns whom, to our great honour and glory, but little to our profit, we protect.

April 7th.—I called on Madame Cornu. We talked of Louis Napoleon.

Madame Cornu.—A single day changed his character. Until the death of his elder brother he was mild, unambitious, impressionable, affectionate, delighting in country pursuits, in nature, in art, and in literature. He frequently said to me—not when he was a child, but at the age of nineteen and twenty, ' What a blessing that I have two before me in the succession — the Duc de Reichstadt and my brother, so that I can be happy in my own way, instead of being, as the head of our house must be, the slave of a mission.' From the day of his brother's death he was a different man. I can compare his feelings as to his mission only to those which urged the first apostles and martyrs.

Senior.—What is the sense in which he understands his mission?

Madame Cornu.—It is a devotion first to the

Napoleonic dynasty, and then to France. It is not personal ambition. He has always said, and I believe sincerely, that if there were any better hands to which he could transmit that duty, he would do so with delight. His duty to his dynasty is to perpetuate it. His duty to France is to give her influence abroad and prosperity at home.

Senior.—And also extension of territory?

Madame Cornu.—Not now. I will not say what may have been his wishes before the birth of his son, but what I have called devotion to his dynasty is rather worship of his son. One of his besetting fears is the revival of an European coalition, not so much against France as against the Bonapartes, and the renewal of the proscription of the family.

Senior.—I have been told that he leans towards constitutionalism as more favourable to hereditary succession than despotism.

Madame Cornu.—I believe that to be true, and that it is the explanation of his recent liberalism. He hates, without doubt, opposition; he hates restraint; but if he thinks, submitting to opposition, or even to restraint, will promote his great object—the perpetuation of his dynasty—he will do so. He would sacrifice to that object Europe, France, his dearest friends, and even himself. One of his qualities—and it is a valuable one—is his willingness to adjourn, to change, or even to give up, his means, however dear they may be to him, if any better or safer occur to him. Another is the readiness with which he confesses his mistake.

Senior.—His last confession was, perhaps, too full and too frank.

Madame Cornu.—So I think; but by making it he enjoyed another pleasure, that of astonishing. He delights in *l'imprévu*, in making Europe, and France, and, above all, his own ministers stare. When it is necessary to act, he does not consult his friends, still less his ministers; and perhaps he is right, for they would give him only bad advice; he does not conscientiously think the matter over, weigh the opposing means, strike the balance, and act. He takes his cigar, gives loose to his ideas, lets them follow one another without exercising over them his will, till at last something pleases his imagination; he seizes it, and thinks himself inspired. Sometimes the inspiration is good, as it was when he released Abd-el-Kader. Sometimes it is very bad, as it was when he chose the same time for opening the discussion of the address, and revealing the state of our finances.

Senior.—Auguste Chevalier treats his phlegm as his greatest quality—*qu'il ne s'étonne de rien.*

Madame Cornu.—Did Auguste Chevalier ever describe to you his fits of passion?

Senior.—No.

Madame Cornu.—Probably he never perceived them. His powers of self-command are really marvellous. I have known him after a conversation, in which he betrayed no anger, break his own furniture in his rage. The first sign of emotion in him is a swelling of his nostrils, like those of an excited horse. Then his eyes become bright, and his lips quiver. His long moustache is intended to conceal his mouth, and he has disciplined his eyes. When I first saw him in 1848, I asked him what was the matter with his eyes. 'Nothing,' he said. A day or two after I saw him again. They had still an odd appearance. At last I found out that he had been accustoming himself to keep his eyelids half closed, and to throw into his eyes a vacant, dreamy expression. I cannot better describe the change that came over him after his brother's death than by saying that he tore his heart out of his bosom, and surrendered himself to his head.

One day I found him reading *Hernani*. ' How wonderfully fine it is! ' he said.

'I know,' I said, 'what you admire in it. It is the picture of a man driven on by an irresistible destiny. You are thinking of the Hernani *qui n'est pas un homme comme les autres.*'

' Ah,' he answered, ' *que vous m'avez bien deviné.*'

Senior.—Pray show me the passage to which you referred.

She took down the ' Théâtre de Victor Hugo,' and read to me the following verses from the scene of the third act of *Hernani* :—

> ' Tu me crois peut-être
> Un homme comme sont tous les autres, un être
> Intelligent, qui court droit au but qu'il rêva,
> Détrompe toi. Je suis une force qui va.

> Ou vais-je ? Je ne sais, mais je me sens poussé
> D'un souffle impétueux, d'un destin insensé,
> J'avance et j'avance, si jamais je m'arrête,
> Si par fois, hâletant j'ose tourner la tête
> Une voix me dit, Marche !'

Now when, as he thinks, his mission is fulfilled, his former nature is returning. He is becoming mild and affectionate; many parts of his disposition are feminine. He adores his child, with the affection rather of a mother than of a father. He puts me in mind of the pictures in which the Virgin is looking on the infant Jesus with an expression half-love and half-worship. The boy is intelligent and serious—no common child.

Senior.— What are his relations with Prince Napoleon?

Madame Cornu.—The affection is chiefly on the Emperor's side. Prince Napoleon is much the younger. The Emperor educated him. For three years they slept in the same room. He feels to him as towards a younger brother. Prince Napoleon has great talents, and is not without affection, but he is devoured by ambition and vanity. Men are easily deceived as to their own popularity, and princes especially. He believes himself to be popular, which is a great mistake. If the Emperor and his son were to die now, it would not be Prince Napoleon that would succeed. On the whole, the best of the Bonapartes is the Emperor, and, as I said before, power is improving him, notwithstanding his detestable *entourage*. He is a bad judge of men, he is shy, he hates new faces, he hates to refuse anything to anybody; and he keeps about him men unable, and if they were able, unwilling, to give him advice, whose only object is to plunder him and the public purse.

Senior.—Do you agree in the general opinion that he is sinking in public estimation?

Madame Cornu.—I do, and I suspect that he feels it himself, and, as I said before, that he is trying to recover himself, by promoting public prosperity, and by an approach to constitutional government.

Senior.—I expect when I am here next year to find that you have renewed your old relations with him.

Madame Cornu.—I do not know. When people once intimate have been separated for ten years, there is a shyness on both sides. In the meantime he is constantly writing to me. On the *jour de l'an*, though he had been receiving people and addresses all day, he found time to send me a note to say that he could not let the day pass without expressing his good wishes. He knows, too, how much I detest his *Idées Napoléoniennes*. If we talk, it must be on the neutral ground of his *Life of Cæsar*. There we shall sympathise, for it will be very good. From time to time he is absolutely engrossed by it; and he has all the help that money and power can procure.

I called on Montalembert. I found him furious

against Italian unity, and against England for having promoted it.

Montalembert.—The next thing will be German unity. The Continent will be divided among a few great sovereigns, some of them already absolute, and the others ready to become so, who will combine to render escape from their despotism impossible. And you, who call yourselves Liberals, encourage all this for the mere temporary object of preserving the balance of power.

Simon came in, and the conversation turned to French affairs.

Montalembert.—I had to see our master yesterday, to announce to him M. Feuillet's election by the Academy. I found him rather fatter than when we met last, but apparently in great health and strength. Our conversation, if so it can be called, was a monologue. He said that he was enchanted to see me; I bowed. That it was very long since we had met; I bowed. That we had made an excellent choice, as M. Feuillet was a very great writer; I bowed. That he was very sorry that circumstances had separated us, that common pursuits and common studies ought to unite all literary men, and that he trusted that the separation would not continue; as I had no such trust, I could only bow again and be silent. As I looked at the titled *valetaille* round him, I thought of the senators of Tiberius. I doubt, however, whether even he so thoroughly despised those whom he called *homines nati ad servitutem*, as our master does. I doubt whether he would have taken for his Home Minister a man without talents, without education, without even the full use of the little reason which nature gave him.

I was in the Pyrenees a few weeks ago with Maillet. At the gates of Perpignan our passports were asked for. We had none, so I said, '*Sujet anglais*.' The man made me a low bow, and went to Maillet. '*Et lui aussi*,' I said, '*est sujet anglais et ne sait pas le Français*.' Another low bow, and we passed on. Can Persigny, mad as he is, think that such distinctions do not humiliate us?

What has become of young Veuillemont?

Simon.—I have not yet been able to do anything for him. His history may interest *you*, Mr. Senior. He is a clever young man, scarcely twenty-one. He edited a paper, well known in the Quartier Latin, was prosecuted for two articles which offended the Government, and sentenced to two months' imprisonment for one, and one month for the other. He came to me as soon as he had been discharged. For heaven's sake, I said, do not come near *me*, or near any known Liberal; keep at home till you are forgotten. He kept at home for a few days, and then went to call on a friend near the Issy Faubourg. As he passed the Column of the Bastille, a man standing at an open door said to him: 'I believe that I have the honour of addressing M. Veuillemont. Pray step into this room.' In the room he was seized by two gens-d'armes. The only answer to his remonstrances was, that it was a measure intended to prevent his committing some folly. He was kept six weeks in the horrible prison of Mazas, and then turned out without apology or explanation. What gives me hopes is the feeling of the young men. Ten years ago they were apathetic. The follies of the Republic had disgusted them. Ten years of tyranny have opened their eyes. All the men between eighteen and twenty-five are steady anti-Bonapartists.

The conversation turned on the comparative expensiveness of London and Paris.

Montalembert.—You have so much reduced your expenditure on matters of mere ostentation, and we have so much increased ours, that I believe Paris to be a dearer residence than London. Our great economy is in servants. A respectable family not keeping a carriage has seldom more than three. If you have a carriage there must be five. One reason for trying to have as few as possible is, that it is difficult to get good ones. There is little mutual attachment. A servant leaves you as you leave a shop, from the slightest motive. A lady's maid, as soon as she has saved a trifling capital, sets up for herself as '*Couturière, à domicile.*' She will be worse fed, and clothed, and lodged, and warmed, but she will be her own mistress.

Senior.—Not worse lodged?

Montalembert.—Our servants are lodged as well as we are.

Senior.—What do you, Simon, say to that?

Simon.—I say that M. de Montalembert talks *en grand seigneur*.

Montalembert.—I am not a *grand seigneur*, I wish that I was; but I know that in this hotel the servants are well lodged.

Simon.—How many families are there?

Montalembert.—Two.

Simon.—So I thought. In the house that I inhabit there are fourteen. The kennels in which their forty servants sleep, are hot in summer, and cold in winter, and pestilential in all seasons. They are not, however, much worse than the average habitations of the lower orders, for the French are frightfully indifferent to stifling rooms and bad smells. They care nothing for ventilation or drainage.

We talked of Lacordaire.

Montalembert.—He was my oldest and my most intimate friend.

Senior.—Did you know him before his conversion?

Montalembert.—No; but he has often told me the story. His mother was a religious woman, and educated him as a Christian; but he lost his faith at school, and was remarkable both at the *école de droit de Dijon*, and during the years that he practised as barrister for the violence of his anti-Catholicism. It was not by reading, or by conversation, or by meditation, that he was converted. A sudden inspiration, what he called *un coup de la grâce*, made him in one day a Christian. The very next day he resolved to take orders, and in 1824, at the age of twenty-two, he entered the seminary of St. Sulpice, and was ordained in 1827. Such conversions are not uncommon in our Church. What unhappily is uncommon, is that he remained as liberal when a priest as he had been when a barrister.

Senior.—Was his success as a preacher rapid?

Montalembert.—Very slow. I went with Corcelle and Ampère to hear his first sermon. It was at St. Roch, in the spring of 1833. His failure was complete. He felt it to be so. 'I may be useful,' he said, ' as a teacher; but I have not the voice, or the rapidity of conception, or the versatility, or the knowledge of the world, which a preacher requires.' Even as a teacher he was at first unsuccessful. His Conferences at the College of Stanilas in 1834 were too bold for the then state of the Church. He was accused of republicanism, and almost of impiety, and interdicted by Monseigneur de Quélan, the Archbishop.

Senior.—I have been reading your account of his *Conférences de Notre Dame*, addressed to the members of the ' Société de St. Vincent de Paul.' I am accustomed to your boldness, and yet I could not read without a mixture of fear your lamentation that the greatest work of Christian democracy had been destroyed *par une de ces mains étourdiment cruelles auxquelles Dieu livre la puissance humaine quand il veut montrer aux hommes le peu de cas qu'il en fait.*

Simon.— Ce *monsieur* has tried two falls with M. de Montalembert and was worsted each time. I do not think that he will venture a third.

Senior.—A century hence this passage will be quoted as a proof that the press was substantially free under Louis Napoleon, as we quote *Præter atrocem animum Catonis,* and *secretosque pios, his dantem jura Catonem,* as proofs that there was liberty of writing under Augustus.

Montalembert.—As respects books, the press is substantially free, for books cannot be attacked without incurring the risk of a trial. It is against journals which cannot defend themselves, which may be extinguished by a mere *avertissement,* that M. de Persigny shows his courage.

Senior.—Had Père Lacordaire much learning?

Montalembert.—He must have had some knowledge of law, as he studied it for five years. He had a schoolboy's acquaintance with the best known classics, and with as much of ancient history as he could get from Justin and Cornelius Nepos. He had picked up the history of his own times from newspapers and conversation. This was about all the history that he knew. Like his master, Lamennais, he was profoundly ignorant of mediæval history. In theology he was a Thomist, in discipline he was an Ultramontane.

Senior.—Of course he was an Ultramontane. Having become a Christian, not from inquiry and reasoning, but from a sudden impression, to use his own words, by a *coup de la grâce*, he must have relied solely and implicitly on authority, and, as the highest authority, on that of the Pope. He could not have been a Gallican.

Montalembert.—Certainly not; he denounced Gallicanism as a disguised schism. His great intellectual qualities were his imagination, his rapidity of conception, and his force and facility of expression.

Senior.—That he should have been deficient at first in the qualities for which he afterwards was most distinguished, is a strong proof that *orator fit*.

Montalembert.—I should not say that these were the qualities for which he was *most* distinguished; for high as were his intellectual excellencies, his moral excellencies were still higher; and it was to them that his wonderful power as an orator was chiefly due. His impressive and exciting delivery, his clear, and brilliant, and unpremeditated language, were merely the forms in which his boundless love of God and of man, of liberty and of piety, was embodied. Never, I believe, did God create a mere human being more approaching to faultlessness. He had no vanity, though continually breathing the incense which most intoxicates, that which is burned before an orator; no love of power, though he reigned over the opinions and the consciences of thousands; no wish for money, or for rank, or even for fame.

The possession which he most valued was *un cœur détaché de tout*, a heart in which there should be no selfish desires or selfish fears. Perhaps the greatest sacrifice that he made was when he became a Dominican. His passion was freedom. As soon as he took the frock he surrendered his free will. He invested his superiors,—men, as he must have known, far below him intellectually and morally,—with absolute power over all his actions, all his habits, almost over all his thoughts. They might have silenced the voice which re-echoed through the whole Catholic world; they might have sent him, at an hour's notice, to China or to Abyssinia; they might have wasted his wonderful talents in the most trivial employments. But he knew how useful the religious orders had once been to his country. He believed that he could reopen France to them. And for such a purpose he was ready to make, and did make, the total and the irrevocable sacrifice of his freedom.

Senior.—I am told that he sacrificed to it his life, that the austerities of his profession brought on the disease which carried him off at an age at which he might have expected many years of usefulness?

Montalembert.—It is possible, nay, probable, that that may be true. If so, he added to his other qualities that of martyrdom.

April 8th.—I went with Simon to call on M. Corbon.

His history is remarkable. His father was an *ouvrier*, and he began life as a printer, and afterwards took to carving in wood. He was one of the founders in 1839, of the *Atelier*, a paper conducted by working men on revolutionary principles. He fought behind the barricades of 1848 and became a member and vice-president of the Constituent Assembly. He was not re-elected to the Legislative Assembly, gave up public life on the *coup d'état*, and returned to his business as carver. He received us in his simple *atelier*, in which he works with a single journeyman. I asked him as to the strength of the Bonapartist party.

Corbon.—There is no such party.

Senior.—Not in the army?

Corbon.—The army likes '*ce Monsieur*' as the distributor of crosses, pensions, and promotions, but it despises him. It knows that every French government will fawn on the army, that it will get crosses, and pensions, and promotions, whatever be the ruler, and it had rather get them from anyone than from him.

Simon.—The army gets disheartened as soon as it sees that public opinion is against its master. If some fools had not prematurely and unadvisedly raised barricades on the third of December, 1851, and brought on a contest, the army would have turned against the *coup d'état*. It was disheartened by the silence and disapprobation of the people on the second of December. If an Orleans prince could have presented himself, it would have joined him.

Senior.—The means of resisting an *émeute* have been much improved. The cannon in the Caserne Napoléon *enfilades* the Rue de Rivoli.

Corbon.—So have been the means of making an *émeute*. Paris is now undermined. Sewers, gas-pipes, and water-pipes, run under all the great streets. It would be easy to blow up a few houses in every great thoroughfare, and nothing makes a better barricade than the ruins of a house.

The Republicans, a class which comprehends all the working-people, have now their minds turned, perhaps, too much to foreign politics.

Senior.—Do they wish for the Rhine?

Corbon.—Not in the least. The Emperor could not do a more popular thing than if he were to give back Savoy. *Chauvinisme* and ambition are gone. What they wish is to see France surrounded by free countries. They are enthusiastically Italian and anti-Papist.

Senior.—Are they Socialist?

Corbon.—There is much that is good in Socialism, though mixed, as everything human is, with much that is bad. We think that means might be found to free the workman from the extortion of the master—to ensure to every man a fair day's work and a fair day's wages.

When we left him Simon said: 'Corbon is less sensible, though more literary than Rencontre. But

VOL. II. K

absurd as his theory of a minimum of wages is, he is a remarkable specimen of the degree of cultivation which a mere workman, educated at an *école primaire*, and afterwards picking up knowledge from newspapers and lectures, can acquire.'

I talked of Thiers' theory, that one of the great supports of Louis Napoleon was the fear of a free press.

Simon.—I think that a year and a half ago, this was true; but the Imperial *régime* has become so odious, that even the danger of a free press is overlooked. His real support is the uncertainty of his successor. Henry V. is forgotten, and the Orleans family are in danger of being also forgotten.

Hotze and Slidell (the commissioners of the South), Corcelle, Duvergier, and Lanjuinais breakfasted with us.

Lanjuinais asked Slidell whether he had any hope that the negroes would be emancipated within any definite time.

Slidell.—Not only have I no such hope, but I have no such fear. Nothing but the complete subjugation of the South and the destruction of our whole military population could produce such a result.

Lanjuinais.—Then if the South remains independent, slavery is perpetual.

Slidell.—Certainly. The negro was not intended

by his Creator for freedom. If he had been so intended, he would not have been created so indolent that nothing but force will make him work, so improvident that he is incapable of making provision against the wants of to-morrow, so docile that he sometimes seems to have no will but his master's, so dependent that all his pride and his vanity regard not himself but his master. I do not deny that there have been negroes who have risen high above the general level of their race,—whose natural talents and careful education have raised them almost to the level of an ordinary white man. They are the Shakespeares and Homers of the black race. But the average negro is the link, or rather one of the links, between the Caucasian and the dog. I say one of the links, because the negro is superior to the Hottentot, to the Papuan, and to the savage of New Holland, though very inferior to the Kaffir, the New Zealander, and the Bedouin.

The negro, stupid as he is, does not desire emancipation, and will not accept it. It must be preceded, as I said before, by the destruction of the whites, and that destruction will be followed by the destruction of the blacks.

Supposing that we, the Southerners, were ourselves to emancipate our negroes, the consequence would be that the whole population, white and black, would perish. The white man cannot till the ground in our climates, the freed black would not. It would be the destruction of twelve millions of people.

Senior.—At least you could repeal parts of your atrocious negro codes. You could allow your negroes to be instructed, and to be allowed to possess property and to work for themselves, paying a rent to their masters.

Slidell.—Certainly. Those laws were forced on us by the agitation of the Abolitionists. They are not universal, and indeed are seldom enforced.

Senior.—And you could allow emancipation?

Slidell.—Yes; the emancipating master giving security for the support of the emancipee.

Senior.—And you could set bounds to the severity of punishment?

Hotze.—That is done already. It is as illegal to treat a slave with cruelty as it is with you to beat cruelly an apprentice. Moderate correction is all that the law allows.

Senior.—And, that the law may be enforced, you must allow the black to give evidence against the white.

Hotze.—Never. We could not live with our negroes if they had the power to drag their master before a court of justice and give evidence against him. Negro testimony against a white will never be admitted. We may concede much, but against this we shall make a resolute stand.

Senior.—And what, Mr. Slidell, is your expectation as to the result of the struggle?

Slidell.—We believe, in the first place, that Europe will soon become really neutral,—that it will no longer favour the North by acknowledging this ineffective, and therefore illegal, blockade. We shall then get what we want—military supplies, and be able to sell our produce. We believe that Europe will do, what she ought to have done long ago, acknowledge our independence. And, lastly, we believe that Europe will say, as she did in the struggle between Belgium and Holland, and in that between Turkey and Greece, that this frightful, useless war shall cease, and that she will impose on each party fair terms of separation.

If all these expectations fail us, and the superior numbers, and equipment, and wealth of the North drive our armies out of the field, and enable the Federals to do, what as yet they have not done, to march into those parts of our country which are not accessible by water, we shall retire before them, and weary out and destroy them by guerilla warfare, by long marches, by hunger, by fever, and by bankruptcy, until they acknowledge—which is all that we want—our independence.

Senior.—Do you expect to keep the Border States?

Slidell.—Not at first. They are too much in the power of the North. They will adhere to it at first; but as they are weaker, they will be even more oppressed than we have been. They will eventually join us.

Senior.—If the Border States return to the North, on what terms will it be?

Slidell.—Simply those on which they formed part of the Union two years ago. All that the North wants is political power and protectionist tariffs. It will guarantee slavery and give a stringent Fugitive Slave law. It would do so for us if we would put our necks under its collar.

The Abolitionists of the North are few and feeble, though noisy. The other day, Wendel Phillips, an Abolitionist, was driven out of Cincinnati, and Lincoln is no more an Abolitionist than I am. His proposal to buy up the slaves is a mere clap-trap for Europe. He knows that it is impossible. Where is the money to come from? What is to be done with the emancipated slaves in a country where the presence of a black man is a contamination? The Border States will be politically oppressed, but their slave property is safe.

Senior.—In the event of the Border States, only, returning to you, Anglo-America will be divided into two republics, one based on the freedom of the negro, the other on his slavery.

Slidell.—Not two republics. We shall remain a republic because we have an aristocracy, because we have habits of obedience, because we are not cursed with universal suffrage. The North will sink into anarchy or despotism. Which will come first I cannot guess. It may be despotism. Freedom, self-respect, the power, and almost the wish, to resist the central authority, seem gone. The press is silenced, men suspected of Southern tendencies are arbitrarily imprisoned, martial law—the worst of tyrannies—is proclaimed. All the safeguards of freedom are suspended. They may never be re-established.

Or the ruin of the finances, the impossibility to raise loans, or to collect taxes, and consequently of paying this gigantic army, and even of providing for the expenses of civil government, may produce anarchy. The army, whether they attempt to keep it on foot or to disband it, may take the law into its own hands, and then there would be anarchy followed by military despotism.

These are among my reasons for believing that the Border States will eventually join us. We shall be the only free, and the only prosperous, part of what were formerly the United States.

Senior.—Will you make New Orleans a free port?

Slidell.—All our ports will be free. We think custom-house duties the worst mode of raising a revenue. We shall have none. I must correct myself, however, by adding that this is on the supposition that the war is soon ended. If Europe allows it to last until we have been forced to create manufacturing establishments of our own, we must protect them. We cannot encourage them and afterwards desert them. This consideration alone ought to show to Europe the madness of suffering the war to continue.

We dined with Mr. Dayton,* and met Mr. and Mrs. Adams, Mr. Weed (the American commissioner sent by Lincoln on a private mission to conciliate Europe), Mr. Doremus, the first chemist in America, and Mr. Bigelow, a lawyer.

After dinner, all the men, except Mr. Adams, retired into the smoking-room.

'We trust,' they said, 'that we now see the beginning of the end. In a few weeks our troops will be in possession of Richmond, of New Orleans, and of the other important Southern towns. The Unionist party will be able to show itself. It will hang or drive out the traitors who have deceived the country, and will offer, or accept from us, fair terms of reconciliation.

Senior.—And what will be the terms which you will offer?

Weed.—Very simple ones,—merely the abolition of the law by which a master has a vote in respect to his slaves.

Senior.—And, also, the prohibition of slavery in the territories, or in new States?

Weed.—It will not be necessary. As soon as the political value of slaves is gone, slavery, though it may continue where it exists, will not be introduced into any country not now polluted by it.

---

* The American Minister in Paris in 1862.—Ed.

Senior.—Will you give them a Fugitive Slave law?

Weed.—Certainly, and a better one than they have now. The state which assisted the escape of a fugitive, or has even connived at it, will have to repay to the master his value. We offered this law several years ago, but the Southern agitators rejected it. They chose to keep the sore open, to force the officers of the Union and the inhabitants of the free States to be their slave-catchers.

Senior.—Will you repeal the State laws which keep the negro ignorant, allow the separation of families, and the internal slave-trade, and exclude the testimony of blacks against whites?

Weed.—We cannot do so; we cannot interfere with the municipal laws of the State.

Senior.—But you must have a convention, in order to deprive the master of his vote in respect of his slave; a convention is omnipotent, and might abolish the slave laws of the States, or establish a mild, and so far as a slave law can be just, a just slave law throughout the Union.

Weed.—We shall not do so; we shall do nothing that will increase the difficulty of the reconciliation.

Senior.—What will you do with the Southern debt?

Weed.—Assume it as a part of the debt of the Union.

Bigelow.—The North will have to pay the costs on each side.

Senior.—And if the South refuse your offer?

Weed.—Then we employ our last and worst weapon—we emancipate the slaves.

Senior.—By an act of Congress?

Weed.—No, in virtue of the rights of war. Every general will have the power to declare the slaves of a district in his military possession, free. Fremont did this, but it was thought premature.

Senior.—But what is to become of four millions of negroes—ignorant and helpless—suddenly set adrift?

Weed.—That is a question which we choose not to examine.

Senior.—And what is to become of the millions of whites, whose property will be valueless when their slaves are set free?

Weed.—That, again, is a question which we refuse to examine. They have been guilty of the most wicked rebellion that history records. If they refuse not merely fair, but generous terms of reconciliation, their ruin, even their blood, be on their own heads.

Senior.—But you *must* examine these questions. You cannot do acts implying enormous consequences, without inquiring what these consequences will be. If you do, the ruin and the bloodshed will be on *your* heads. Do you look calmly on the prospect of a St. Domingo? Of spreading devastation over a country as large as Europe?

Bigelow.—With respect to the slaves, the North,

by emancipating them, will obtain a right, and will incur a responsibility. It must provide for them, and must require them to do all that they can to lighten that heavy burden. The best mode will, perhaps, be to transplant them to some country where the soil and the climate will allow them to subsist with little labour. I am told that you want people in Jamaica.

Senior.— Yes; but we want thousands, not millions. We do not want men to squat on our waste lands. We want voluntary and hard-working emigrants, not transported slaves.

Bigelow.—Then there is Central America.

Senior.—Yes, but there is no land there without a master; there is no capital to employ them. If 50,000 of your freed negroes were endeavoured to be put ashore on any of the coasts of Central America, I doubt whether they would be allowed to land, and I am sure that they would die of hunger.

Weed.—My belief is that we shall provide for them in a different way. We shall confiscate all the lands and estates of the rebels, and sell or grant them to loyal Northern men; they will be rewards for the army. The slaves on those estates will naturally remain on them. We shall subject them to a kind of apprenticeship, as you did when you emancipated the slaves in your island.

Dayton.—As we did in New Jersey. We did not give to the emancipated slaves perfect or immediate freedom.

Weed.—We shall treat the South as William the Conqueror did England. We shall divide it into territories, make a military man the governor of each territory, give the estates to well-deserving officers and men, and let the slaves, who cultivate them for the rebels, now cultivate them for loyal men. As for the whites, they will not be eight millions; they will not be five millions, for the Border States will return to the Union. Of the five millions in the Gulf States, three-fifths own no slaves, and therefore will be uninjured. The million of slave-owners will be ruined, and they will deserve to be ruined.

Senior.—It will be the destruction of the whole aristocracy of the country.

Weed.—It will, and it deserves to be destroyed.

Senior.—But when you have emancipated the slaves in the Gulf States, what will you do with those in the Border States?

Weed.—Of course they cannot remain slaves, surrounded by free states. We must buy them up. There are about a million of them, worth, at a rough calculation, 400 dollars, or 80*l.* a head. It will cost about eighty millions sterling.

Senior.—And will they be able to provide for themselves?

Weed.—I think so, if they are not too quickly freed from all restraint, and thrown on their own resources. They must probably be subjected to an apprenticeship. But I trust that it will not come to this. I trust that the South will accept our terms, and that in six months' time the Union will be restored.

Senior.—Still you will have to buy up the slaves in the Border States.

Weed.—If those States consent; but it will not be absolutely necessary, for slavery will in that case continue in the Gulf States. In the Border States I hope that it will gradually cease, as it has done in the North, not however so slowly, for the President's message offering the assistance of the whole Union in its eradication is a new element.

Senior.—It appears, then, that slavery can become extinct only in one of three events. If the Gulf States achieve their independence, slavery will continue. If the Gulf States re-enter the Union, slavery will continue. Slavery will be extinguished only in case the Gulf States stubbornly resist, and are conquered, and you believe this to be very improbable.

Weed.—I believe their resistance to be improbable; but if, to use your words, they stubbornly resist, I feel no doubt as to their being eventually conquered. In the meantime we shall exert ourselves to raise a supply of cotton for ourselves, and also for Europe, from the countries in our possession. We cannot but feel that the war would be protracted if Europe were to raise the blockade, and you and the French are becoming impatient. The French nation sympathises with us, but not the Emperor, and the distress is greater here than with you, as it comes on a poorer people. The French, too, are less acquainted with international law, and care less about it. You respect our blockade, because you think that you may yourselves have to use blockades. The French have no such expectation; they probably would not be sorry to see the whole law of blockade abolished. With the slightest encouragement from you, or, to speak more correctly, if not discouraged by you, they would break the blockade, and probably acknowledge the South.

Dayton.—I have often heard of a conversation between Mr. Seward and the Duke of Newcastle, in which Mr. Seward is said to have threatened to insult England, as soon as he should be in office. Can you tell me anything about it?

Senior.—I can repeat it to you as it was told to me by the Duke himself. It was at Governor Morgan's, at the end of one of the enormous dinners of which officials on each side of the Atlantic are guilty. When at last they got into the drawing-room, a little circle was formed in which were the Duke and Mr. Seward.

Seward asked the Duke his impression as to the result of the then approaching Presidential election.

The Duke answered that he had tried to avoid political conversation, but that what he had unavoidably heard led him to expect the election of Mr. Lincoln.

'Well,' said Seward, 'I may be anything that I like in the new government. I have refused to be President. I once thought of going to England, but

I now think that I shall be Secretary. If I am, I know what I shall have to do. I shall have to insult England.'

'So many secretaries,' replied the Duke, 'have insulted us, after professing the most friendly dispositions, that I hope that you will be as inconsistent as they were, and that, having given us the notice, you will spare us the insult.'

'No,' said Seward, 'I shall be forced to insult you. My position will oblige me, but I have not the least intention of war.'

'I fear,' said the Duke, ' that one may bring on the other.'

'Oh, no,' said Seward; 'you cannot go to war with us.'

'I trust,' answered the Duke, ' that you will not act on that supposition, or some fine morning you may find a fleet before New York.'

'There is more English property in New York,' answered Seward, ' than there is American property. You could no more burn New York than you could Liverpool.'

'There are insults,' replied the Duke, 'rather than submit to which we would burn Liverpool as well as New York.'

Such was the conversation.

Dayton.—I do not wonder at Seward's talking all this nonsense. He is fond of ill-timed jocularity. He was at that time elated by the long-deferred, but at length imminent victory of his party; perhaps the length and dullness of the Governor's dinner had tempted him into taking too much wine. But I *do* wonder at the Duke's taking it seriously. There is no man more friendly to England than Seward, but he has lived the little idol of a clique, and does not weigh his words.

Senior.—He does not even weigh the words that he prints, or he would not have printed his letter to you, in which he threatens to declare war against any European nation that should acknowledge the Southern Confederacy—a threat as likely to bring on the recognition as to prevent it.

I begged Dr. Doremus to explain to me his improvement in the manufacture of gunpowder.

Doremus.—It is a simple one. I put a charge of dry powder into a hollow tube of the diameter of the gun for which it is to be a charge, and apply to it, by means of a hydraulic ram, a pressure of about three tons to the square inch. This diminishes it in volume to about one-half. It becomes a compact, smooth mass.

Senior.—Will such a mass explode? I should have expected it to burn like a fusee.

Doremus.—So it would if it were quite compact. Captain Rodman, of your navy, tried the experiment of wetting, and then compressing powder. It became quite compact, and burned instead of exploding. To render it explosive, he was forced to drill holes in it. But if powder be compressed dry, the granular particles do not cohere so closely as to prevent the existence between them of little capillary tubes, which are sufficient to render the mass explosive.

Dayton.—I can show you some specimens.

He produced a couple of cylinders—the one intended for a six-pounder, the other for a four-pounder. They were solid, and shining and grey marks, like those in worm-eaten wood, though much smaller, showed where were the capillary tubes. To one of them the bolt which it was to propel was annexed.

Doremus.—The advantages of the compressed powder are these,—

I. In the first place, it is more efficient than loose powder. The ball has a longer range and greater power of penetration, and its action is more uniform.

II. Secondly, it requires no bag. The bag of a cartridge, of course, takes fire, and the gun must be sponged every time that it is fired, in order to extinguish any remaining burning particles. The compressed powder is its own cartridge.

III. It keeps dry; loose powder attracts moisture, and must be turned at least once a-month—a troublesome and dangerous operation. The compressed powder, if greased, is impervious to water, and even when ungreased, may be left in water for fifteen minutes without injury.

IV. Fourthly, it requires less stowage by one-half.

V. There is less danger of accidental explosion. In the use of loose powder, if a cartridge leaks, a train sometimes is scattered from the guns to the magazine. Many a ship has been thus blown up.

VI. There is less strain on the gun. We ascertained this by experiments with the pendulum-gun. It indicated a considerably less pressure.

Senior.—Do you attribute the increased power of the compressed powder to its more rapid ignition?

Doremus.—No; to its slower ignition. The explosive substances of very rapid ignition, such as fulminating silver, would burst the barrel. The rather slower ignition of compressed powder seems to me to exercise a prolonged influence over the ball.

Senior.—I suppose that you must compress the powder in a hollow cylinder adapted to the bore of every gun in which it is to be used?

Doremus.—Of course, down to a musket.

Senior.—Is the compressed powder as superior to loose powder when used in a mortar as it is when used in a gun?

Doremus.—Much more so. I tried it first in an *eprouvette* mortar, and was astonished by the increase of the range. When used in a gun, though the superiority is great, it is less so.

Senior.—Was your powder used by the *Monitor?*

Doremus.—No; as yet it has been used only by the army. Perrot, who makes guns for the army, as Dahlgren does for the navy, uses it; but when I left America it had not been used by the navy:

as our two greatest manufacturers of powder have taken it up, I have no doubt that it will soon be used in both services.

Senior.—I suppose that you have protected yourself by a patent?

Doremus.—I took out one for America six months ago; and when our difficulty with you ended, I took out patents for England, and for most of the Continental states.

April 9th.—We breakfasted with the Mohls * and

---

* Jules Mohl, of whom a long biographical notice is inserted in page 301, Vol. I. of the *Conversations with Thiers, Guizot, &c.*, was a native of Würtemberg. He came to Paris in 1823, and resided there until his death, in 1876, although the Government of Würtemburg offered him, in the year 1825, the Professorship of Hebrew in the University of Tübingen. He was so distinguished as an Orientalist, that the French Government selected him to translate the *Shah Nameh*, the great Persian poem. The last part was published after his death. He wrote the annual reports on Oriental Research for the French Asiatic Society, he was Inspector of Oriental Topography at the Imprimerie Nationale, and he was an influential member of the Institute.

Besides all these public labours, he was a voluminous letter-writer. His letters to his different correspondents,—among the most frequent were those to the late Queen of Holland, and above all to his wife, whenever he was separated from her, even for a day—are as full of wit and humour as of interest. Among the most curious are those he wrote to Madame Mohl, during the 'Commune,' in 1871. It is to be hoped that some of these letters may be published.—ED.

met M. Renan,* whom Dr. Cureton puts at the head of French Orientalists. I afterwards took two long walks with him. I will throw the three conversations together.

We talked of Cureton's edition of the Gospel of St. Matthew in Syriac.

---

* M. Ernest Renan was in early life intended for the priesthood. He was sent to study at St. Sulpice, and it was at that seminary that his taste for Oriental languages and ecclesiastical studies first showed itself. His turn of mind was far too independent for his intended profession; he therefore left St. Sulpice and devoted himself to private study. In 1848, he obtained the first place in the 'Concours de Philosophie,' and at the same, the 'Volney' prize for an essay on Semitic languages: two years later his essay on the 'Greek Language in the Middle Ages,' was crowned by the Academy. In 1851, he was attached to the Department of MSS. in the Bibliothèque Nationale; and, in 1856 he was elected a member of the Académie des Inscriptions in place of M. Augustin Thierry. At the end of 1860, he was sent on a mission to Syria. In 1862, he was appointed Professor of Hebrew, but did not permanently occupy the chair for fear of a renewal of the manifestations which occurred at his opening lecture in February. In 1863, he published his well-known *Vie de Jésus*, which he wrote after his voyage to Syria, and of which numerous editions have been issued. This work was vehemently attacked by the bishops and clergy, the result being that the author was dismissed from his professorship. M. Duruy, the Minister of Public Instruction, endeavoured to conceal the significance of this dismissal by giving him an office in the Bibliothèque Impériale, which was, however, taken from him in June 11th, 1864. M. Renan was elected a member of the Academy in 1879. He is continuing his series of works bearing on theology.—ED.

Renan.—It is not the oldest copy, for it contains corrections of errors in other copies, but its numerous different readings give to it great value.

Senior.—Do you suppose that the Hebrew which we now read is the Hebrew in which Moses wrote?

Renan.—I have no doubt that it is. I believe, indeed, that Genesis contains fragments older than the time of Moses; such as the more simple and undetailed history of the Creation contained in the fifth chapter, which makes no allusion to the Garden of Eden, or to the fall. All very early books are, to a certain degree, compilations. In Genesis whole poems are sometimes inserted.

Senior.—Can you distinguish in Hebrew writings poetry from prose?

Mohl.—In lyric poetry the iteration, the repeating, in the two members of the sentence, the same thought under different forms, is an obvious mark of poetry.

Renan.—In narrative poetry, of which the story of Joseph and the book of Ruth are beautiful examples, the great mark of poetry is the minuteness of the detail; and I think that I perceive a cadence and a measure different from those of prose.

Senior.—To what age do you attribute the book of Job?

Renan.—To an age in which Hebrew was a spoken language and in its perfection. The style is clear, concise, forcible, and picturesque. This disposes of the opinion that it was written during the Captivity, when Hebrew was becoming a dead language, and those who used it wrote stiffly and pedantically. On the other hand, the peculiar institutions which after the time of Josias completely separated the Hebrews from the surrounding nations either did not exist in the author's time, or were not known to him.

Senior.—Job is mentioned by Ezekiel.

Renan.—Yes, but not this book. Job was probably an historical personage whom the author of the poem selected as an interlocutor. I suspect that if Ezekiel had seen the book, he might háve thought it too bold. I believe that it belongs to the finest period of Hebrew poetry, the age of Hezekiah, in the beginning of the eighth century before Christ.

Senior.—About the time of Homer.

Renan.—It is interesting to compare the two great poems of the Arian and the Semitic races. Both are eminently theistic. The intervention of a God pervades both. But the Homeric Gods are distinguished from men and women only by their power and their irresponsibility. They are shrouded in no mystery. They show themselves to us as they showed themselves to Paris, absolutely naked; and a disgusting exhibition it is.

The God of Job is enthroned in darkness; he speaks out of the whirlwind. His only attributes are wisdom and power. All that takes place, takes place through His direct interference. If He acts according to any fixed rules, those rules are concealed from us. While Homer's gods are merely powerful bad men, or rather bad children, his men are inferior gods. The gods live with them as lovers, as friends, and as enemies. In Job, man is a miserable creature, inferior to many of the brutes in strength, in courage, and in instinct. What are his relations to God it is the great object of the book to discuss. The Christian relation between God and man, mutual love, is not hinted at. There is some worship, but it is a worship of fear. The great problem debated is, 'Is, or is not, God just?'

Job begins by a bitter complaint that he ever was born.

'Wherefore,' he says, 'is light given to him that is in misery, and life unto the bitter in soul?'

His friends answer that it is only to the wicked that life is a misery, and that the good are, on the whole, happy. This Job fiercely denies.

'The earth,' he says, 'is given unto the hand of the wicked. Their houses are safe from fear; they spend their days in wealth, and in a moment go down into the grave.'

He maintains that he is an example of the absence of God's moral government.

'I will say unto God,' he says, 'show me wherefore Thou contendest with me. Is it good unto Thee that Thou shouldst oppress me, and despise the work of Thine own hands? and shine upon the counsel of the wicked? Thou knowest that I am not wicked, and there is none that can deliver out of Thy hand. Thine hands have made me, yet Thou dost destroy me. Thou huntest me as a fierce lion. Wherefore then hast Thou brought me forth out of the womb? Are not my days few? Cease then and let me alone that I may take comfort a little before I go whence I shall not return, even to the land of darkness and of the shadow of death. A land of darkness, where the light is as darkness.'

'Oh, that I knew where I might find Him, I would order my cause before Him, and fill my mouth with arguments. I would know the words which He would answer me, and understand what He would say unto me. Oh, that One would hear me. My desire is that the Almighty would answer me.'

His prayer is granted, and he is answered out of the whirlwind. But the answer is a magnificent description of the power of God and of the weakness and ignorance of man, and of his humble place in creation. The problem is left totally unsolved.

Senior.—The problem really discussed is an insoluble one, the origin of evil. Job assumes that God, as the origin of everything, is the origin of evil, and on that assumption reproaches God with cruelty, first for having created him, and secondly for having unjustly afflicted him. The only attempt at an answer is contained in the last chapter, in which Job is restored to more than his former prosperity, in contradiction to the general spirit of the poem.

Renan.—The contradictions in the poem are innumerable. The Semitic races cannot reason.

Their languages are almost incapable of expressing abstract ideas. All their notions are concrete. Though the book of Job is controversial, there is no argument in it. Each interlocutor contents himself with mere assertions and denials; and one assertion and one denial by the same speaker is often inconsistent with another. Job in general maintains that God treats impartially the wicked and the good, but from time to time he affirms that the wicked are always punished. He repeats over and over that there is no life beyond the grave; but in one passage he expresses a belief that God will descend on the earth to avenge him, and though death will have destroyed his flesh, yet that he, with his own eyes, will see Him. There is no such thing in any Semitic writing as a book, except a narrative. All their moral works are mere strings of sentences, without order and without consistency. Such is the book of Proverbs, such is the Koran, such is Job. The argument, if argument it can be called, is exhausted in the first speech of Job and the first speech of Eliphaz. The following speeches merely go over and over the same ground, turn and twist and pull at the same knot without loosening it.

I am wrong, indeed, when I say that their works are strings of sentences. For a real sentence, consisting of several members, qualifying and illustrating one other, such sentences as are found in Greek, in Latin, in German, in English, and, though less frequently, in French, are unknown to Semitic writers. A single proposition contained in half a dozen words is all that a Hebrew writer ventures on. He repeats this proposition with slight variations till he has done with it, and then passes abruptly to another. There is no discursus in his mind. It is apprehensive, not deductive.

Senior.—Do you suppose that the author of the book of Job was an Israelite?

Renan.—Certainly not. Every word attributed to Job expresses the pride, the impatience—the cold, severe, undevout religion of a Bedouin. That he should be quoted as an example of patience is a proof how little the books that are most talked of are read. He bears, it is true, his misfortunes at first with resignation, but it disappears at the end of the seven days during which he sits on the ground in silence.

'After this,' says the writer, 'Job opened his mouth and cursed his day.'

Senior.—Do you attribute the Song of Solomon to the same age?

Renan.—Its age is marked by the verse which compares the heroine to the cities of Tirzah and Jerusalem. Now from 975 before Christ to 923, Tirzah was the capital of Israel and Jerusalem of Judah. In 923, Omri, king of Israel, built Samaria, and Tirzah disappeared. The poem must therefore have been written during that interval. I am inclined to think that it was written by one of Jeroboam's adherents, not long after the death of Solomon. The reigns of Solomon and David, the only ones under which Palestine was united and powerful, seem gradually to have been invested with a legendary splendour of which their contemporaries knew nothing. Instead of the 700 wives and 300 concubines ascribed to Solomon in the book of Kings, Canticles gives him only sixty queens and eighty concubines. Instead of 400 chariots and 12,000 horsemen, he is accompanied by only sixty guards. His greatest magnificence seems to be a cedar chariot, the bottom plated with gold.

Senior.—Of all the books of the Old Testament, Canticles seems to me to be the one of which the scope is least intelligible, and the sacred character the least apparent. It reads to me like a collection of mere amatory songs.

Renan.—Of course the Christian interpretation in which Solomon is Christ, and the Shulamite is, according to Protestants, the Church; and according to Catholics, the Holy Virgin; and the Rabbinical interpretation, according to which the two lovers represent the human intellect in love with wisdom, are indescribably absurd. I believe with Ewald and Hitzig that it is a purely secular poem; but I also believe with them, that it is a moral drama, that it represents the resistance of a country girl taken from her lover into the harem of Solomon, and her triumph and return to her lover. I believe the principal *dramatis personæ* to be the Shulamite girl, the lover, and Solomon, with a chorus consisting sometimes of the women of the harem, sometimes of the inhabitants of Jerusalem, and sometimes of the villagers of Shulam.

In my book I have attempted to divide it into acts and scenes, and to assign his part to each character. It is without doubt most inartificial; the story is obscurely hinted at. The changes of scene are abrupt and incapable of actual representation. Sometimes the actor tells what he is supposed to be doing.

It seems to me that the poem is a libretto not intended to be read, but to be the framework of an entertainment consisting of song, dancing, declamation, and recitation. Perhaps to be acted at a marriage. With all its defects, however, it is one of most valuable specimens of Semitic poetry. Without it we should not have known that the stiff, austere, Jewish character was capable of tenderness. We should have had no picture of real love, founded on early intimacy, resisting the temptations of a court. We should have had no pictures of the village life and the village scenery of Palestine.

Senior.—We should have had Ruth.

Renan.—Ruth is charming; but it is not descriptive. It contains nothing equal to the beauty and feeling of the picture of early spring in Canticles.

' Lo, the winter is past,
The rain is over and gone,
The flowers appear on the earth,
The time of the singing of birds is come,

> The voice of the turtle is heard,
> The fig-tree putteth forth her green figs,
> The vines with their tender grapes give a good smell;
> Arise, my love, my fair one, and come away.'*

Even the Christian perversions of its real sense have borne fruit, and admirable fruit. It is the source of mystical religious poetry,—a poetry which has consoled the sorrows, and purified and exalted the devotion, of millions.

Since my last conversation with Renan I have been reading his version and arrangement of Canticles. The key to his interpretation is to be found in verses 11 and 12 of chapter 6. In our translation these verses are thus rendered:—

'11. I went down into the garden of nuts to see the fruits of the valley, to see whether the vine flourished, and the pomegranates budded.

'12. Or ever I was aware my soul made me like the chariots of Amminadib.'

---

* Shakespeare seems, in 'Cymbeline,' to have imitated this passage:—

> 'Hark, hark, the lark at heaven's gate sings
>   And Phœbus 'gins arise,
> His steeds to water at those springs
>   On chaliced flowers that lies:
> And winking Marybuds begin
>   To ope their golden eyes,
> With everything that pretty bin,
>   My lady sweet, arise.'

In the Vulgate the 12th verse is thus rendered:—

Nescivi; anima mea me conturbavit propter quadrigas Aminadab.

But Renan translates it:—

Imprudente; voilà que mon caprice m'a jetée parmi les chars d'une suite de Prince.

The English translation and the Vulgate are nonsense.

Renan believes these two verses to be the beginning of the story. That the Shulamite had been seized in her garden by the emissaries of Solomon, sent to collect beauties for his harem, and that the first act finds her in Solomon's harem; but after two conversations with Solomon she escapes to her village.

This act ends chap. ii. ver. 7.

In the next, ending chap. iii. ver. 5, the Shulamite describes a meeting with her lover.

In the third act, beginning chap. iii. ver. 6, and ending chap. v. ver. 1, the Shulamite is brought back to the harem in Solomon's chariot.

Renan supposes the 4th chapter to contain, up to the 7th verse, an address to the Shulamite from Solomon, and thence up to chap. v. ver. 1, an address to her from her lover.

The fourth act extends from chap. v. ver. 2, to chap. vi. ver. 3. The Shulamite hears the voice of her lover from without; she opens her window, but he is gone; she searches for him, and meets him in the garden.

The fifth act begins chap. vi. ver. 4, in the harem.

Solomon again addresses her with praises of her beauty, she rejects him, and entreats her lover to take her back to her village. He does so, chap. viii. ver. 5.

The chorus proclaims, chap. viii. ver. 7, the moral of the piece.

'Many waters cannot quench love. If a man would give all the substance of his house for love, it would utterly be contemned.'

This verse Renan supposes to be a sarcastic allusion to Solomon's failure to conquer the Shulamite.

I met this evening, at Mrs. Hollond's, Dufaure *

---

* Jules Armand Stanislas Dufaure was born December 4th, 1798, at Saujon, Charente-Inférieure, was educated for the bar, and practised at Bordeaux. He entered political life in 1834, and under the Guizot ministry became a Councillor of State, and afterwards Minister of Public Works. On the rejection of the law of dotation, he quitted the cabinet and joined the Liberal opposition. After the Revolution of February, 1848, he was elected for the Charente-Inférieure, and became Minister of the Interior, June 2nd, 1849. When the President resolved to usurp the whole power of the state, M. Dufaure was one of the few representatives who escaped seizure and imprisonment.

During the prosecution of the Count of Montalembert, in 1862, M. Dufaure defended the publisher of his pamphlet with great skill and eloquence. After the fall of the Empire, he was returned to the National Assembly by the department of Charente-Inférieure, and when Thiers formed his Government in February, 1871, he selected Dufaure as Minister of Justice. On the overthrow of Thiers in May, 1873, M. Dufaure went out of office. He again and Duvergier. I asked Dufaure about the bill, now before the Corps Législatif, for the amendment of the criminal law.

Dufaure.—It is a wicked bill; its great object is to subject to summary conviction by the court many offences now cognisable only by a jury. Among these offences are several, a conviction for which, under the atrocious law of *sûreté générale*, entails a liability to be sent, at any future time, at the will, or at the caprice, of the Minister of the Interior, to Algeria or to Cayenne. To ruin, indeed to kill, a man, all that will be necessary, will be to accuse him, before a judge who is a tool of the Government, of any of these offences. As soon as he has been convicted, and has gone through his imprisonment, he may be sent to die in Cayenne.

A M. de Flers was accused some time ago of having corresponded with the *Indépendence Belge*. His papers were seized, but no writing of his own was found among them. Some letters to him from the editors of the *Indépendence* were found, and on their evidence he was convicted and sentenced to three months' imprisonment. He was warned that Persigny intended, as soon as his imprisonment was

---

became Minister of Justice under M. Buffet's Administration in March, 1875, and Prime Minister in February, 1876; he resigned and was succeeded by Jules Simon in the following December. In December 1877 he again became Prime Minister.—ED.

over, to send him to Cayenne, under the law of *sûreté générale*. He avoided, therefore, returning home, and escaped to Belgium as soon as the prison door was open. It was well that he did so, for the gens-d'armes were waiting for him in his own house.

Duvergier.—I found, the other day, in my house, an old National Guard musket, of which I had forgotten the existence. The possession of military weapons without authorisation is an offence for which I could be summarily convicted under the new law, and should then become deportable under the *loi de sûreté générale*. So I took it and delivered it to the *Maire*.

Dufaure.—Another abominable clause in the new law, is one which declares to be libellous '*un écrit ou dessein non rendu public.*' If this law passes, Mr. Senior, you will be liable to be prosecuted, summarily convicted, imprisoned, and, when your imprisonment is over, sent to Cayenne for offensive remarks written in your journal, though shown by you to no one.

Senior.—And will this law pass?

Dufaure.—It has passed the Conseil d'Etat, and has been referred by the Corps Législatif to a committee. The Government may get frightened and withdraw it; but if the Minister of Justice persists, it must pass.

Thursday, April 10th.—I passed the early part of

the evening with the Duc de Broglie, and met there Dumon.

Duc de Broglie.—Here you see the beginning of a singular spectacle. A despotism apparently irresistible, which, without any formidable enemies or any assured successor, is gradually collapsing—like a building erected on a bad foundation or of bad materials.

Senior to Dumon.—Do you agree with the Duke?

Dumon.—Thoroughly. *Celui-ci* has no formidable enemies — except, perhaps, his own ministers.

Senior.—What say *you*, an 'ancien ministre des finances,' to Fould?

Dumon.—That he is one of the worst. His letter poisoned the empire. Instead of urging its publication, he ought to have insisted on its suppression. Living in the world he must have known the effect of such a revelation, after minister after minister had been congratulating the nation on the state of its finances. His vanity and love of display prevailed over his duty. The salt-tax can scarcely be carried, and his conversion of the four per cents into threes, is an operation against all the rules of finance. The holder of 1000 four per cents is to receive 1333 three per cents; the interest will not be diminished, and it will be incapable of future reduction. And a great part of the money which he has extorted from the holders of four per cents, as the price of the change, has been spent in purchases of three per cents in order to sustain their value in the market.

What is passing in the theatres shows Louis Napoleon's growing unpopularity. About's *Gaetano* was hissed, not for its own demerits, but because About is one of the Emperor's literary tools. An Imperialist piece, called, I think, *Les Mousquetaires*, was played and hissed at the Gymnase. A set of policemen in plain clothes scattered through the pit and the boxes, brutally attacked the hissers. One young man, a gentleman, was publicly handcuffed and taken to prison.

It was understood that the opponents would come the next day with *casse-tête* in their pockets. To prevent this, the whole theatre was taken by the police, filled by themselves, their families, and their friends; and so the piece was played for three days to an applauding audience, till the Government was ashamed, and withdrew it.

Another Imperialist piece is now in rehearsal, called the *Invasion*. It is to end with the cry of ' *Vive l'Empereur !*' The Republicans intend to answer by singing the ' Marseillaise.'

A mere trifle like this is sufficient in the existing state of the workpeople to produce an *émeute*. The Belgian revolution was brought on by the representation of *Masaniello*. It is said that the violence of the police at the Gymnase was occasioned by a complaint by the Emperor that they had not shown zeal.

Friday, April 11*th.*—Arrivabene* on his way from Brussels to take his seat in the Italian Senate, is with us. Guizot, Changarnier, and Circourt, breakfasted with us. We talked of the war in America.

Changarnier.—I do not think favourably of the cause of the North; either Beauregard is a better general than MacClellan, or his troops are better; for, after maintaining himself for six months in the face of a superior force, he fell back twice without leaving a gun or a man behind him. And I doubt whether the Federals can follow him, at least, as far as Richmond. The distance is 120 miles, through a devastated country covered with woods, intersected by rivers, and without roads. In a good country, and in good weather, a large army cannot march more than ten miles a-day. A French soldier, if he be accompanied by cattle, can carry seven days' provisions. If he be not so accompanied, only four. I do not think that the Federals will be so accompanied. Even if they were, they would have provisions for only half the distance. If they must carry their provisions on their backs, they cannot

---

* Count Giovanni Arrivabene was a native of Mantua, and was imprisoned at Venice, in 1821, for not having denounced Silvio Pellico. He was exiled, and during his exile condemned to death. He passed a good deal of time in London, in the house of Mr. Senior. He was naturalised a Belgian in 1840. Afterwards he was included in the amnesty, and became a member of the the Italian Parliament. He lived to a great age, and died only a few years ago.—ED.

have more than enough for four days, and they have twelve days' march before them. A day of rain will demoralise them. No one who has not tried it can tell what it is to march a mile, loaded as a soldier is, in mud up to the knees.

Guizot.—Montalembert has extracted from Lacordaire's *Conférences de Notre Dame*, a wonderful passage on the power of space.

The book was in the room, and he read it to us, as no one else can read.

'*Longtemps le dernier des capitaines avait rivé le sort à sa volonté. Les Alpes et les Pyrénées avaient tremblé sous lui; l'Europe en silence écoutait le bruit de sa pensée, lorsque las de ce domaine où la gloire avait épuisé toutes ses ressources pour lui complaire, il se précipita jusqu'aux confins de l'Asie. Là son regard se troubla, et ses aigles tournèrent la tête pour la première fois. Qu'avait il donc rencontré? Etait-ce un général plus habile que lui? Non. Une armée qui n'eut pas encore été vaincue? Non. Ou bien était-ce l'âge qui refroidissait déjà son génie? Non. Qu'avait-il donc rencontré? Il avait rencontré le protecteur des faibles, l'asile des peuples opprimés, le grand défenseur de la liberté humaine. Il avait rencontré l'espace; et toute sa puissance avait failli sous ses pieds.*

'*Car, si Dieu a créé de telles barrières au sein de la nature c'est qu'il a eu pitié de nous. Il savait tout ce que l'unité violente renferme de despotisme et de malheur pour la race humaine, et il nous a préparé dans les montagnes et les déserts des retraites inabordables. Ô montagnes inaccessibles, neiges éternelles, sables brûlants, marais empestés, climats destructifs, nous vous rendons grâce pour le passé, et nous espérons en vous pour l'avenir. Oui, vous nous conserverez de libres oasis, des sentiers perdus, vous ne permettrez pas à la chimie de prévaloir contre la nature, et de faire du globe, si bien pétri par la main de Dieu, une espèce d'horrible et étroit cachot, où le fer et le feu seront les premiers officiers d'une impitoyable autocratie.'*

We asked Arrivabene about the fortifications of Antwerp.

Arrivabene.—They are so extensive that they will require 80,000 men to man them. Antwerp is to be a fortified province, in which the Court and the Chambers may hold out against France for two months, until England, Holland, and Germany, relieve them.

Changarnier.—They tell *us* that they are intended to resist England until France can come to their assistance.

Arrivabene.—The fortifications are unpopular; they cost money; they take away valuable land, and they impede communications.

Guizot.—Our fortifications were among the causes which rendered the Thiers ministry unpopular; and, as his successor, I inherited their unpopularity. Had I foreseen that we should have a government which would arm itself with a revolver of 600,000 charges. I should, perhaps, have thought the fortifications unnecessary.

A fortification is like a hedge round a field. In many parts of France there are no hedges, and it is therefore necessary to have children in the fields to keep the cattle and sheep from straying. In Normandy we have hedges, and therefore we do not employ children. But our great man, though he has got his hedges, chooses to have the additional expense of as many children as if his fields were unhedged.

We talked of Naples.

Changarnier.—I know that Cavour offered Naples to Prince Napoleon, and I am told that he would have accepted it, if the Emperor had permitted him to do so.

Senior.—I believe that your information is incorrect; that you have reversed the facts, and that the truth is, that the Emperor was favourable, and that the Prince refused.

Changarnier.—It is a pity that he did not go thither; Naples would have ceased to be mischievous to the kingdom of Italy.

Arrivabene.—The Neapolitan element is a bad one, but its mischief is exaggerated. There is less brigandage than is supposed, and the brigands are generally foreigners, sent and supported by Rome. The Neapolitan troops amalgamate well with the general army.

Changarnier.—The power of military discipline is such, that armies composed of the most heterogeneous elements act well together; as we see in the Austrian army, drawn from populations bitterly hostile to one another.

Senior.—What will be the French force necessary for this Mexican war?

Changarnier.—Fifty thousand men, if the Mexicans resist us; but I hope they will not do so. The only people whom they hate are the Spaniards and the Americans.

Guizot.—When I was in office, I had a history of the relations between the United States and Mexico carefully drawn up. It is frightful. Never was a nation treated with such injustice, such insolence, such perfidy, or such cruelty, as Mexico was by the United States. It was evident to me that ever since Mexico became independent, the United States had endeavoured, with success, to render her weak, anarchical, and wretched, in order the more easily to rob her. They have occasioned many of her revolutions, and supported all of them; they have discouraged every attempt at good government, attacked her at first with fraud, and afterwards with violence, and succeeded in rendering and in keeping a country which nature intended to be one of the happiest in the world, one of the most miserable. They have no scruples, no public morality, and no fears. They are terrible neighbours. I am glad that the Atlantic is between us.

Senior.—I find in Paris a general wish for the success of the North, partly on the ground that the North is supposed to be fighting for liberty against slavery, but much more because the United States are supposed to be the enemies of England.

Circourt.—That the United States are the natural enemies of England is true; but they are also the enemies of all Europe. England without doubt is our rival; but she is pacific, she understands international law, and obeys it. Her ministers always act in the face of a powerful opposition, which pulls them up if they venture to behave fraudulently or unjustly. The Government of the United States does not consist, as a constitutional monarchy does, of an administration and an opposition, each watching and criticising the other. Neither the President nor his ministers are members of Congress. They have not to defend in public their acts. They cannot be turned out if Congress disapproves them. Formerly, when the President was re-eligible, his hopes and fears as to re-election were a check on him. Now, when re-election is practically at an end, almost all restraint is gone. If the nation is with him, as it always is, whenever his foreign policy is fraudulent or oppressive, he is omnipotent. And even if it be opposed to any of his acts he can be restrained only by the Senate; a body which seldom takes the trouble to interfere, except in some petty matter of patronage. Under the influence of the insolent, arrogant habits of fifty years of wonderful prosperity and unchecked ambition, the United States are always threatening war. They know little of the law of nations, and care about it still less. One of her naval officers writes to his Government to ask whether he ought to act legally or not, and the Government prints the despatch without remark. Mr. Seward apologises for giving up the Commissioners taken from the *Trent*, on the ground that their retention was useless. If the empire of the Seas is to belong either to England or to the United States, I had rather a hundred times see it in the hands of England. If the North can conquer the South and re-establish the United States, it will in twenty years be the most arrogant, the most rapacious, and the most unscrupulous power in the globe. All Europe, and still more all America, is interested in its disruption.

Guizot.—The most disagreeable country to negotiate with is the United States. The best is England. The English are proud, and obstinate, and touchy; ready to take offence, and not ready to accept an apology; but they never deceive you. You will not expect from me an eulogium on Lord Palmerston, but I always found him perfectly honest.

Senior.—You may have found honesty in Downing Street, you would not have found much in the House of Commons. Nobody there seems to speak his real opinions, or to avow his real motives.

Guizot.—Was not Peel honest?

Senior.—Peel wore two masks, one pasted over another.

Guizot.—But if everybody is known to be dishonest, nobody is deceived.

Senior.—That depends on the skill of the dishonesty. Peel deceived the whole world twice over, and each time for years.

General de Fénélon and Michel Chevalier * came in after the others had left us.

Senior.— Changarnier thinks ill of the Federal cause. What say you ?

Fénélon.—I do not think well of it. Their troops seem indeed to be better than they were when they fought at Bull's Run; but so are those of the Confederates. In fact, if the men in the Confederate army were not better than the Federal troops, they could not, unprovided as they are with material, have resisted as well as they have done.

---

* The following is an extract from the *Observer* :—' Paris, November 29th, 1879. The death of M. Michel Chevalier, the eminent political economist, is announced to-day.

'M. Chevalier was born at Limoges, on January 13th, 1806, and educated at the Polytechnic School, subsequently adopting the profession of an engineer. After having suffered imprisonment for his religious and moral opinions, which he publicly retracted, he became a Member of the Chamber of Deputies, and one of the most enthusiastic champions of Free Trade, endeavouring, but in vain, in conjunction with M. Bastiat, to organize a league similar to our Anti-Corn Law League. In 1860, M. Chevalier assisted Mr. Cobden in carrying into effect the Commercial Treaty between England and France, was president of the Social Science Conference at Dublin that year, and was created a Senator on March 14th. He was the prime mover in the proposal for a submarine tunnel between this country and his own, and the author of many works on " Political Economy," as well as other subjects.'

Chevalier.—It is impossible for any one who has not travelled, as I have done, in the South, to picture to himself the state of that country. In the first place, it is absolutely without roads, except railroads. There are tracks beaten out by cattle, or by foot-passengers, but no roads that can bear wheels, even in dry weather, and the first rain turns them into bogs. And, secondly, it is a country absolutely without manufactures. Growing cotton, picking cotton, and cleaning cotton; planting tobacco and packing tobacco; planting canes and making sugar, are the employments to which all classes are devoted. Everything that has to be made must be imported from the North or from Europe. There are scarcely any shops. The planter buys from the merchant, and feeds and clothes his slaves. Almost all the capital and labour which in Europe is employed in distribution is economised. If Adam Smith's proposition that the wealth of a country depends on the proportion of its productive to its unproductive inhabitants were true, the Gulf States would contain the richest population in the world; for almost every one there is a producer.

Fénélon.—Yes, but not for his own consumption. The Southern States are like one blade of what ought to be a pair of scissors. The North is the other blade. That the South has resisted so well shows wonderful tenacity and endurance.

Senior.—Until lately the South seems to have wasted its strength in uncombined distant operations.

Fénélon.—That is natural in a country with no powerful central authority, engaged in a defensive war. The governor of every state, nay, of every county in a state, and of every village in a county, thinks the defence of his own state, or county, or village, the great object. He will not sacrifice it to the general cause. This is less felt by the Federals, as they are the attacking party. If ever they are attacked, they too will feel it. New York would not sacrifice a warehouse to preserve Pennsylvania from ruin.

At the beginning, both armies being equally ignorant of war, the Southerners, as the most energetic and the most hardy, beat the Northerners. By this time they must be more nearly on a par, and the superior numbers and equipment of the Northerners would give them the advantage, if they could meet on the common frontier. But if the Confederates retire, if, as appears to be the case, they combine their movements, and act in a general and well-planned scheme, I think, as I said before, that they will be dangerous customers.

Senior.—Do you suppose MacClellan's army to be now a good one?

Fénélon.—Scarcely yet; it wants officers, it wants traditions. [What makes our troops so dangerous are their traditions.] Though one-sixth of the army is renewed every year, so that in six years the only old soldiers are the few who have re-enlisted, yet the tradition of victory remains. Algiers has in this respect been invaluable. Every regiment contains men who have served there, who know what fighting is, and are accustomed to success.

The effect of tradition was seen in the Italian War. The Austrian troops were good, but their traditions in a contest with the French were unfavourable. So it is with the armies of almost all the Continental states. If there were a war on the Rhine we should, at least at the beginning, beat the Belgians, and Dutch, and Prussians, as easily as we did the Austrians and Prussians in 1806 and 1807.

April 12*th.*—I called this morning on Guizot, who talked about the friends whom he made or found when Ambassador in London in 1840.

He mentioned only the dead—Hallam, Sydney Smith, John Austin, and Macaulay. As an original thinker, he seemed to put Austin above them all; as a man of learning, Hallam; as a companion, Sydney Smith; as a man of information, Macaulay.

Guizot.—I went over Westminster Abbey with Macaulay. He knew the biography of the tenant of every tomb. He could repeat the finest passages of the works of all those whose busts are in Poets' Corner.

Every one of these men might be considered as a candidate for pre-eminence in the literary world. They might have been expected to show the mutual jealousy of men of letters.

There was not a shadow of it. Austin's health kept him out of the great world, but the others lived in it as simply, as unpretendingly, and with as much mutual affection, as if the idea of rivalry had never occurred to them.

In the afternoon I called on Thiers. I found him in his garden.

Thiers.—Do you remember our walking up and down this garden with Lord Ashburton some years ago, and discussing the probable fortunes of the empire?

Senior.—Yes; and your prophesying that the amount of liberty contained in the imperial constitution would in time make it cease to be despotic.

Thiers.—Well, that time has come. Louis Napoleon has brought it on rather sooner than I expected.

He has irritated and alarmed and injured every class.

First, he has exasperated the most intolerant of all classes—the clergy; and, what is worse, all the laity who believe religion to be the most important element in human society.

France will not be Protestant. Napoleon, perhaps, might have made her so, for the clergy were then Gallican. Now they are Ultramontane; so are the believers among the laity. If France is not Catholic, she will be atheistic. By favouring the expulsion of the Pope from Rome, he is destroying Catholicism, for Catholicism cannot exist without the Pope.

Secondly, he has injured and alarmed the classes which, next to the clergy, are the most intolerant—

the manufacturers and the fund-holders; the former, by his absurd commercial treaty; the latter, by his deficit. He has alarmed all the lovers of peace and of prosperity by his senseless wars.

Senior.—You approved of his Russian war?

Thiers.—Yes; but not of his Italian war, or his Syrian war, or his two Chinese wars, or his Mexican war. The last four wars have merely wasted our money and our blood. The Italian war has given us a powerful rival—perhaps an enemy—on our south-western frontier, and has weakened irrevocably the power most useful to the European equilibrium— Austria.

When I was anxious to see Russia humbled, I relied on her place being taken by Austria. I hoped to substitute a pacific power for an aggressive one. Now that the influence of Austria is also destroyed, I begin to regret Russia.

All the politicians despise Louis Napoleon; all the friends of liberty hate him; all the Bourbonists hate him; all the Orleanists hate him; all the Republicans hate him. The whole of France is convinced that the imperial constitution is a failure, and a dangerous failure; and it is in these circumstances that he has unmuzzled the Chambers and given to them the most dangerous of all powers, the power to canvas and to blame the whole policy, foreign and domestic, of the Government. He must yield, indeed he has begun to yield. To yield even well is dangerous to a despot; to yield ill is fatal.

In the Palikao matter he has yielded ill. He has shown his ill temper by calling the French 'a degenerate nation,' and his obstinacy by threatening to ask for an uncontrolled power to pension his military favourites. The next concession that he will have to make is to give up his ministers. They are all bad, except Randon; but I should not advise him to change them all at once. When a hunter is pursued by a lioness whom he has robbed of her cubs, he does not throw them all to her at once; he gives up one, and when she returns he gives up another. One or two per session would perhaps do. He should begin by Persigny; then Baroche should go; then Walewski, then Thouvenel, then Fould.

Senior.—Might not Fould be kept?

Thiers.—By no means; he is the worst of all. He is a Jewish stockbroker, with no knowledge except of the tricks of the Bourse. Then he must abandon the absurdity of ministers *sans portefeuille*. A man who cannot defend his own measures before a Chamber is not fit to be a Minister. The Ministers *sans portefeuille* were invented in order to enable him to turn stupid, servile cherks and courtiers into ministers. His ministers must then enter the Chamber. They must then be chosen from among the men who possess the confidence of the Chambers. When that has been done, constitutional monarchy will be restored. I do not say that I expect all this, or even that I wish for it, for it might perpetuate, or rather, as nothing is perpetual in France, it might prolong, the Bonaparte dynasty, which I abhor. But it is the only mode by which that dynasty can be prolonged.

France is not dynastical. It has forgotten the *branche aînée*; it approves, but without enthusiasm, of the Orleans family; it fears the Bonapartes, but it dreads still more a Republic. If this dynasty fall, it will be succeeded in time by the Orleans family; but the interval may be a *bien mauvais quart d'heure*.

I see that Palmerston still believes in Italian unity, and tells us that such is the interest of France. Palmerston is an able man, but we must be permitted to be better judges of our interests than a foreigner can be; and fear and dislike of an united Italy are almost the only feelings in which all educated Frenchmen of every shade of opinion on other matters are united. I ought, perhaps, to say only dislike, for we have no fear of an event which we hold to be impossible.

Senior.—I know three or four Frenchmen who believe in an United Italy, and desire it.

Thiers.—Then you are fortunate enough to know all the Frenchmen, except the *ouvriers* of Paris, who hold that opinion or feel that wish.

Duvergier came in. We talked of Victor Hugo's *Misérables*.

Thiers.—It is detestable. The spirit is bad; the plan is bad; and the execution is bad.

Duvergier.—It contains some very fine passages.

Thiers.—You are a heretic. You have a taste for

strongly-seasoned meats. I believe that you could eat high venison. I am almost inclined to think that you read Michelet.

Duvergier.—Ought I to be burned if I do?

Thiers.—Perhaps not burned, only scorched. I reserve perfect burning for those who can read Victor Hugo.

April 12*th.*—I paid my visit of adieu to Prince Napoleon.

He, too, has been reading Lord Palmerston's speech, but not with the feelings of Thiers.

Prince Napoleon.—I am delighted to find a man who, with all his faults, is at the head of the statesmen in Europe, fully agreeing with me. The union of Rome to the rest of Italy is now only a question of time. I cannot believe that the time will be long, but while it lasts it is full of danger to the Emperor, to the Pope, to France, and to Italy. The Pope's death would be a great misfortune.

Senior.—Would he have a successor?

Prince Napoleon.—I have no doubt that his successor is already agreed on.

Senior.—Subject to the vetos of France, Austria, and Spain?

Prince Napoleon.—If the election be made *sur le corps du Pape*, that is, immediately after the death of the Pope, while his body is still on the bed in which he died, there is no veto. And such is the distrust of France in the College of Cardinals, that some one hostile to us will be named. Pio Nono is weak, and timid, and irresolute; but his successor may be a fool or a fanatic, still less accessible to reason than he is.

April 13*th*.—We left Paris.

1863.

[IN the summer of 1862 Garibaldi, who was disappointed with the slow progress of events, crossed over from Catania to Melito on the Calabrian coast, at the head of his army of volunteers, intending to march on Rome. The Italian Government sent troops to stop him, and a detachment under General Pallavicino came up with him at Aspromonte. An engagement took place on the 29th of August, in which Garibaldi was wounded and taken prisoner. On account of his brilliant services and excellent intentions he was pardoned ; and he retired to Caprera. Venice did not become free until 1866 when Austria gave it up to the French, and Louis Napoleon presented it to Victor Emmanuel, who made Rome his capital in 1870.

In Mexico the French were ultimately successful, and in 1863 the throne was offered to the candidate approved by Louis Napoleon, the Archduke Maximilian, who held it only until 1867, when a revolution broke out, and Maximilian was condemned and executed.

The Southern States of America appeared to be

gaining ground in the beginning of 1863. The fields which had formerly been sown with cotton were now cultivated with cereals, in order to supply the wants of the army; and the cotton famine and consequent distress in the manufacturing districts of England (from which they have never entirely recovered) at this time reached its climax. The States of America were not re-united until 1865.

Greece revolted in 1863 against her king, Otho of Bavaria. The crown was offered to Prince Alfred of England. It was refused by him and afterwards accepted by Prince George of Denmark, and England spontaneously ceded the Ionian Islands to form part of his kingdom.

The year 1863 saw the last struggle of Poland for independence. The Emperor Alexander was anxious to conciliate the Poles and to ameliorate their condition; he appointed as viceroy his brother, the Grand Duke Constantine, to carry these intentions into effect. But the Poles did not wish for any government except self-government; they thwarted the Grand Duke, upon whose life several attempts were made, and refused to serve in the army.

The Grand Duke revenged himself by a most cruel and arbitrary method of conscription. At midnight on the 14th of January, police agents and soldiers commenced the work at Warsaw. They surrounded the houses noted down in their list, and a detachment entered each dwelling to seize the men designated to serve, the parents being taken as guarantees in the case of the absence of the young men. During the first evening 2500 were carried off. Next day thousands took flight and commenced an organized resistance against Russia, which soon spread over the entire area of Russian Poland.

France sympathised strongly with Poland, and the numerous subjects of interest abroad diverted the French from too closely scrutinising their government at home. The Emperor was eager to establish his dynasty, and he tried to introduce gradually some appearance of constitutional liberty, as a means to this end. Nevertheless, and in spite of the highly commended zeal displayed by M. de Persigny in enlightening the people as to the way in which they should vote—Thiers, Jules Simon, and the other principal liberal candidates were triumphantly returned in the autumn of 1863 to be members of the Corps Législatif.

Seven years later the Empire fell with a crash, as violent and as sudden as had been anticipated by many of the speakers in these conversations.—ED.]

Hôtel Bedford, Rue de l'Arcade, Sunday, March 29th.—We reached Paris yesterday. This morning I called on Lavergne.

Lavergne.—Everything here is asleep. The people care nothing for liberty. Their predominant feelings—fear of revolution, and fear of the Rouges—though as strong as ever, are not active. They are content with their actual military predominance; and much as they would like to gain the Rhine, would not make any sacrifices for it. The higher classes retain their contempt and dislike of Louis Napoleon, keep aloof from his service and from his court, look with alarm at the increasing expenditure and debt, wonder at the folly of the Mexican and Cochin Chinese wars, but enjoy the public safety, and would not risk a revolution in order to obtain any amelioration of our institutions.

Louis Napoleon himself seems to be asleep. His pleasures, and his *Cæsar*, and his cigars, engross him. A month ago, when Mr. Home, the Spiritualist, was in Paris, he saw him fourteen or fifteen times, sometimes for hours together.

Senior.—Has he lost, or gained, since I was here last year?

Lavergne.—Relatively, he is where he was, for all his opponents have lost ground; positively, he also has lost ground. The Legitimists are forgotten, the Orleanists despair, and the Bonapartists, as a party, have ceased to exist. There are Imperialists,—that is to say, persons who hope to gain or to retain money and power from the Government for the time being, but there is no enthusiasm—no love for the Bonaparte dynasty. Fifteen years ago, it was something new; it was associated with grand, indistinct recollections and hopes; it was a defiance to Europe. Now, it has had all the success that it is likely to have, and it has purchased that success by an enormous and increasing debt. It has weakened

Austria, but only to create a power far more dangerous to us than Austria was, and at our very gates. It has beaten down our natural ally, Russia. And it has done all this wantonly. All its wars have been wars of aggression,—wars against nations, every one of whom was anxious to remain at peace with us.

This Mexican war is the crowning wickedness and folly. The mortality is frightful. Whenever the *Moniteur* tells us that the sanitary state of the army and of the fleet is satisfactory, we infer that our soldiers and sailors are dying of yellow fever or vomito. The survivors are furious. They call it ' Duke Jecker's war,' as they believe Morny to be the great holder of the Jecker bonds, and that the war is an act of brigandage on a gigantic scale ; that it is made in order to support fraud by violence. It seems to be an illustration, almost cynically exhibited, of the mischiefs of irresponsible power.

Senior.—The army used to complain of the slowness of promotion. They used to say that half ought to be killed off in order to open a *carrière* for the others.

Lavergne.—It was the officers who said that. All that the private sighs for is to get back to his cottage. And the officers are *désillusionnés*. They find that a campaign under the First Napoleon was a very different thing from one under Napoleon the Third, or even under Canrobert, or Pelissier, or Forey. They have no confidence in their leaders. Lord Wellington used to say that the presence of the

First Napoleon was equal to a reinforcement of 40,000 men. The presence of the Third Napoleon is as much dreaded as a diminution of the army by 40,000 men would be.

The Bonaparte prestige is gone. *Celui-ci* remains only because there is no one to take his place, and because we fear that in the gap made by his fall the Rouges might rush in.

Senior.—Will you be a candidate at the coming general election?

Lavergne.—I cannot afford to be so. It is easy to be a Government candidate. M. de Persigny and his subordinates take on themselves all the trouble and all the expense, but an opposition candidate cannot spend less than 500*l.*, and many have to spend 2000*l.* There are about three circonscriptions to a department, each returning one member, and each containing about 120,000 persons, and about as large as an English county. The different cantons are formed into circonscriptions, not on geographical, but on political grounds; the great objects being, first, to create everywhere an agricultural majority, which may swamp the seats of liberalism—the towns, and, secondly, by separating from one another the cantons suspected of liberalism in a circonscription, to make the canvassing and the distribution of bills and voting-papers as expensive as possible.

Senior.—I should have thought that the Government would have wished to ballast its ship by a small opposition.

Lavergne.—A decent Government would do so, but these miserable creatures know that their hired advocates—their *ministres sans portefeuille*, who can scarcely keep their ground before an opposition of five, would be driven out by one of twenty. Every opposition candidate will be opposed by fraud, by intimidation and by force. As public officers cannot be prosecuted without the assent of the Government, they are practically irresistible and irresponsible. The urns will be opened, voting-papers will be abstracted and inserted. Those who have abstained, and those who are known to have voted against the Government candidate, will be persecuted; those who are suspected of having done so, will scarcely fare better. Every circonscription in which the Government candidate has been beaten or endangered, will be for years teased, and troubled, and oppressed. Every circonscription, therefore, detests a contest, hates the candidate who disturbs it, and hates all his supporters.

I doubt whether the next election will give us a larger minority than the last did.

Thursday, April 2nd. — Lanjuinais passed the evening with us. He had been reading, in my article on 'Tronson du Coudray,'* the description of the present state of France.

---

* Published by Mr. Senior in the *Biographical Essays*. Longmans. 1862.

Lanjuinais.—You are not merciful to us, or even just. You say that we are bold, but not resolute; violent and impetuous, but not enthusiastic; that we are unfit for prolonged civil war; that we want combination and pertinacity. You attribute what you call our silent, abject submission, to our dread of deportation. It is produced by deeper and more generous motives than mere personal alarm. It is founded on the recollections of June, 1848, and on the histories of 1793. It is founded on the fear that, in the attempt to obtain liberty, we may endanger civilisation.

Louis Napoleon and his co-conspirators proclaim that rather than lose the means of gratifying, to its utmost degree, their ambition, their vanity, their luxury, and their hatreds, which their unrestrained power now showers on them, they will call to their aid all the evil passions of the uneducated masses. That they will treat France as the Austrians treated Gallicia, as Robespierre treated Paris. That they will raise the labourer against the proprietor, the workman against the master, the *peuple* against the well-born, the ignorant against the educated, and the poor against the rich. They threaten us with a general *sans-culotterie*. Many persons believe that these threats are of easy execution. I am not sure that they are incapable of execution.

The physical force of Paris is of three kinds:— the *prolétaires*, or mob, the bourgeoisie, and the army. I do not reckon the higher classes, because, though morally important, their number is contemptible. Any two of these bodies combined can crush the third. In 1789, the mob and the bourgeoisie conquered and drove out the army. From thence, until the *treize Vendémiaire*, the mob beat the bourgeoisie. On that day, and again on the 18th *Fructidor*, the army beat the bourgeoisie, the mob remaining inactive. In 1830, the mob and the bourgeoisie beat the army. In 1832, the bourgeoisie and the army beat the mob. In February, 1848, the mob beat the army, the bourgeoisie remaining inactive. In June, 1848, the army and the bourgeoisie beat the mob. In 1851, the army surprised Paris; neither the mob nor the bourgeoisie making any real resistance. It appears, therefore, that if the army can obtain the assistance of either of the two other forces, it is master of Paris.

Now, *la Ligne*, or *la Troupe*, as the army, excluding the *Garde*, is called, reflects France. It is proprietary and anti-revolutionist. But the *Garde* consists of about 50,000 men, and forms the garrison of Paris. When any regiments of the line enter Paris, they are confined to the Forts, made as uncomfortable as possible, and cut off from all intercourse with the mob. The *Garde* occupies all the barracks, all the best quarters, is highly paid, and as much favoured as discipline will allow. If you look at its officers, you will see that they are all elderly men, who entered the army many years ago, when there was little education, have remained in it ever since, and have forgotten all the feelings of citizens. I believe that Louis Napoleon can rely on them as blind instruments.

The *prolétaires* are not mere instruments. They have feelings and opinions of their own. But their feelings are Socialist. They believe that the present state of society is unjust to them. They believe that the Government can give to all classes equality; not, what is true, equality of suffering, but equality of enjoyment. They believe that, under the influence of the bourgeoisie and the higher classes, it refuses to do so. Their feeling, therefore, towards all above them, is a mixture of envy and resentment.

Now, if the Government flatters these feelings and hopes, if it offers to the mob the assistance of the army, and promises to gratify its envy, its resentment, and its love of excitement and of pillage, is it certain that these offers will be refused?

Those who believe, as I do, that Louis Napoleon, if pushed to extremities, will make these offers, and that a large proportion of the *prolétaires* will accept them, may be excused if they prefer what you call abject, silent submission to a contest which must be destructive and may be unsuccessful.

You must add the network of espionage and coercion, in which our dreadful centralisation has entangled us. This constitution was skilfully framed by the First Napoleon, and skilfully improved by *Celui-ci* for the purpose of tying us, as Gulliver was by the Lilliputians, flat on the ground. It is not to be touched. Merely to discuss it is a crime, for which a man, or even a woman, may be sent to die at Lambressa or Cayenne.

I believe that Louis Napoleon would gladly improve it. The birth of his son changed him. Till then he thought only of himself, and accepted the theory that the Bonapartes would go out—when he did. Now, he is anxious for his dynasty. He knows that only really constitutional dynasties are safe.

But between him and freedom rolls a sea of blood. The massacres of 1851, the deportations of 1852 and 1858, cannot be forgotten or pardoned. A real constitution implies liberty of speaking and of writing. Liberty of speaking exists in a few *salons* in Paris, and only there; liberty of writing is confined to large books, and even as to them it is imperfect. As respects periodicals and pamphlets, there is none. I believe that it would sweep him away in three months.

Senior.—Does the army read?

Lanjuinais.—No; but the people do. Socialism and Bonapartism prevail among them, because they are unopposed.

Senior.—Socialism is plausible.

Lanjuinais.—But Bonapartism is not. Still less is respect for the Bonaparte ministers. Freedom of discussion from the tribune and in the press would render them hateful and contemptible, and part of that odium and contempt would fall on him. As soon as that happened—as soon as the *peuple* joined the Bourgeoisie against him, the army would fight for him reluctantly the first day, negotiate on the second, and turn against him on the third.

Friday, April 3rd.—I breakfasted with Prince Napoleon. The only other guests were his aide-de-camps and secretary.

He asked me if there was much sympathy for the Poles in England.

Senior.—Our sympathies, at least our active sympathies, are only with the nations who have coasts. Besides, if a nation be regarded as one permanent individual, responsible for the acts of its previous generations, no nation has more deserved its fate than Poland. While it was independent it was the torment of Europe and of itself. It was always engaged in religious, civil wars; every party was constantly calling for foreign intervention, the nobles were petty tyrants, the people were slaves, they had no industry or literature, or toleration; they gave up their commerce to Jews, and then persecuted them; they were utterly without the forbearance, the candour, and the justice, which free institutions require. Since the partition they have been stirring up civil war throughout Europe. Every revolution has had Poles among its promoters, often among its exciters.

Prince Napoleon.—Well, we are less severe. We forget what Poland *was* in what she *is*, the victim of falsehood and systematic oppression. Poles have fought by our sides against foreign and against domestic enemies. They have assisted the *Peuple* of France in their struggles against the aristocrats. They have been one of the elements of the revolutionary leaven which saves us from the general torpidity of the Continent. But I recognise in your language the coldness, and, if you will pardon the word, the selfishness, of English policy. You will never, as we do, fight for an idea. Then you think yourselves bound by the treaties of 1815. We detest them, we repudiate them, we have torn them to pieces. They were fetters when we were weak, we threw them off as soon as we became strong. It was his submission to them that overthrew Louis Philippe. Your policy is founded on reasoning, ours on sentiment. It was sentiment, not reasoning, that made Louis Napoleon President, that made him Emperor.

But though you have no active sympathy for people without coasts, like Poland and Hungary, you must have a passive one, enough not to disturb you, but to make you look with pleasure on the active sympathy of less reasoning nations. You cannot but admire the self-devotion of the fathers and mothers who send out their children, or of the young men who after confession and absolution go out to die in battle against overwhelming numbers, or to be hunted down in the forests which are their only fortresses. You cannot but detest the barbarity of the Russians, who have turned the conscription, which our glorious revolution invented as the great security for national independence and liberty, into the most odious instrument of oppression.

If you will not fight for Poland, you will at least speak for her; and though speaking without acting is only a half measure, it is far better than silence.

[Prussia is at the bottom of the scale of baseness and degradation.] She joins the Czar in order to subjugate Poland for him, so as to leave him free to use his Russian soldiers to prevent his own subjects from insisting on a constitution. She has done still worse, she has violated the sacred right of asylum, the only resource of the oppressed. She has done what every civilised power in Europe would have refused, what indeed it would have been an insult to request from any civilised power — she has delivered the Polish refugees to Russia. She has delivered men of birth and education to be punished by the slow torture of the Siberian mines from having attempted to save their children from blows, degradation, and death in the snow and forests of the Caucasus. This the Prussian ministers have not only done, but avowed. With the light, graceful irony which may be expected from a German, they describe it by saying: 'We have not delivered the refugees to Russia, we have only removed them from Prussia by the Russian frontier.'

Austria comes next. She is merely silent; not from love of her enemy Russia, but because she fears to have to give up her share of the Polish robbery.

You, with your inactive sympathy, are the third accomplice. You say that the conduct of Russia is hateful, that of Prussia hateful and base, that of Poland heroic; and then you say, 'Poland has no coast,' and you fold your arms.

Senior.—And what use will you make of your active sympathy? Your ministers tell the Poles to rely on the generous and liberal feelings of the Czar.

Prince Napoleon.—That was a wicked insult, fit for a minister *sans portefeuille*, fit for such a renegade as Billault. Happily the policy of the Emperor does not depend upon that of his ministers. What we shall do I cannot tell. I am not in the Emperor's confidence; but that we shall do something, and something great, I am convinced. It may be a pacific intervention, it may be a warlike one. France does not wish for more wars. She has enough, much more than enough, on her hands already. She is not, like the Americans, carried away by the new excitement of having enormous armies and enormous debts. She knows that armies and debts are things to be kept as low as possible. But in a good cause, and there cannot be a better, France is always ready to sacrifice herself, or, rather, will insist on sacrificing herself; and certainly this is a case in which the Emperor will not resist the will of the people.

The conversation passed to English statesmen.

Prince Napoleon. — Derby, Ellenborough, and Gladstone, are your best speakers. Palmerston is your best party leader. He has, indeed, all the faults of a very young man. He threw away his first premiership by his presumption and impatience. But he has the tact and the experience of an old man. His foreign policy is thoroughly English, bold, almost defiant, in words; cautious, almost timid in conduct; except when no opposition is to be feared. He gratifies your vanity by his language to all and by his action against the weak; but he takes care to keep you at peace. Then his speeches gratify the national taste for triviality and platitudes. Every one can understand, every one can sympathise with them, for they express merely what has been thought from the days of Adam, and repeated from the time of Noah. He goes down to Glasgow, calls together the boys, and tells them that education is an excellent thing. Thereupon there is a *brouhaha*. Then he tells them that peace is an excellent thing—more applause. Then he reminds them that they have a dock which would receive the *Warrior*, and the enthusiasm *est à son comble*. A French minister who should talk such *banalité* would be pelted. You like to be governed *en plaisantant, quoique la plaisanterie soit quelquefois mauvaise*. Your great men chaff familiarly the *Peuple*, because the *Peuple* is powerless. All parties know that it is the familiarity of contempt. Here the familiarity is real, because the equality is real. Our servants are our equals. One of mine left me a year ago; he had been with me seven or eight years. He knew nothing when he came, but learned his business in my service.

Now he writes *pour me faire part*, that he has a son, and to hope to have an opportunity *de me serrer la main*. He will call on me, I shall shake hands with him, and perhaps in three or four months you will meet him dining with me.

Saturday, April 4th.—I called before breakfast on D. E. F.

We talked of the split in the Liberal party, between those who are resolved to combat this dynasty ' *à l'outrance,*' to accept no reconciliation, or even compromise, and those who, despairing to overturn it, seek to improve it, who are resolved to remain *des hommes possibles*, and if they cannot take the reins, at least to sit by the driver. At the head of this latter party is M. Ollivier.*

D. E. F.—Ollivier has done more harm than anyone calling himself a liberal. He and the young men who follow him maintain that instead of trying to obtain a liberal government by running the risks and undergoing the miseries of a revolution it would be be far better to try to liberalise what we have. That to do so we ought to accept office under it, and gradually alter its principles by altering its administration. This doctrine is so convenient a screen for timidity and inaction that it is adopted by many who would be ashamed to profess Imperialism. 'We would be Orleanists,' they say, 'if it would do any good. But what is the use of mere abstention?—of

---

* It will be remembered that M. Ollivier tried this experiment during his short-lived Ministry in 1870.—Ed.

refusing to be useful to the country or to ourselves, in order to keep up a sulky, inactive opposition?'

I tell those that hold this language that it is impossible to liberalise this Government, but that mere duration confirms it; that it is becoming *un fait accompli*, and that the mass of the people, who see only its exterior, naturally infer that it is liberal when they see that Liberals join it. I certainly see my own activity diminish with my hopes. First I thought that this tyranny would be broken to pieces in five or six months, then in four or five years, and now I think that it may last during Louis Napoleon's life.

Senior.—And what will follow his death?

D. E. F.—The immediate consequence will be the proclamation of the Imperial Prince, but, deceived as I have often been, I should feel convinced '*que ça ne peut pas durer.*' That is to say, unless the event is delayed fifteen or sixteen years. In that case, indeed a prince twenty-three years old, carefully educated, with strong natural talents, which this boy is said to have, may carry on a reign which will then have lasted for thirty years.

Sunday, April 5th.—Madame Cornu breakfasted with us.

Senior.—Every time that I return to Paris I expect to find you reconciled to the Emperor.

Madame Cornu.—At last you are right. On the fifth of last month he wrote to me to say that for twelve years I had refused to see him and that perhaps I should persist, but that he could not bear the thought that he might die before I had embraced his child; that the next day the boy would be seven years old; that Madame Walewska would call on me at one on that day, and that he could not avoid indulging a hope that I would allow her to take me to the Tuileries. I could not refuse.

The next day she came and took me thither. As we entered his cabinet the door was closed; and I found myself in the presence of the Emperor and the Empress. She was the nearest and took me by the hand. He stood still for an instant, then ran forward took me by the arm, threw himself on my neck, and kissed me. I kissed him, and we all of us, including the Empress and Madame Walewska, began to weep. 'Méchante femme,' exclaimed the Emperor, 'voilà douze ans que tu me tiens rigueur.' Then there was silence, which the Emperor broke by saying, 'Je crois que nous ferions mieux de nous asseoir.' He stood with his back to the fire, the Empress and I sitting on each side, and Madame Walewska behind the Empress. Then there again was silence and the child was sent for. I took him in my arms and kissed him. He looked astonished, the Emperor took him between his knees, and told him to repeat one of his fables. 'I have forgotten,' the boy said, 'the ends of them all.' 'Then tell us the beginning of one of them.' 'I have forgotten the beginnings.' 'Then let us have the middle.'

'*Mais, Papa, où commence un milieu?*'

It was clear that he would not show off, so he was allowed to go to his pony.

'*Cette dame,*' he said to his mother in the evening, '*doit avoir été très grande amie de Papa ou elle ne m'aurait pas embrassé.*' The child had broken the ice, though still there was some restraint; but it wore off, and we talked as familiarly as ever. As I went away, he said, '*J'espère que tu ne me quittes pas pour encore douze ans.*'

Since that time I see him or the Empress two or three times a-week. I find him in the evenings alone in his cabinet at work on his *Cæsar;* but he is glad to break it off, and to talk to me for hours on old times. He is quite unembarrassed, for his conscience does not reproach him; indeed, no Bonaparte ever has to complain of his conscience. I sometimes forget all that has passed since we saw one another for the last time before December 1851, when he was still an innocent man. But from time to time the destruction of our liberties, the massacres of 1851, the deportations of 1852, and the cruelties which revenged the *attentat,* rise to my mind, and I shrink from the embrace of a man stained with the blood of so many of my friends.

Senior.—Do you see the Empress and the child?

Mad. Cornu.—Constantly. The child flies into my arms, and the Empress is all kindness and graciousness. She is a Spaniard, she wants knowledge; in fact, she wants education; but she is very seductive. She is strict with the child, and manages him much better than the Emperor does, who, in fact, does not manage him at all.

Senior.—Francis Baring maintains that Prince Napoleon has more ability than his cousin.

Mad. Cornu.—Their talents are different. The Prince is by far the quickest. He acquires knowledge with wonderful ease; he decides rapidly; his conversation is brilliant; he can speak effectively with little premeditation. But he quickly forgets; he wants patience, both in meditation and in action. He works out no subject carefully; he rushes to action without having sufficiently considered his means; he is easily discouraged, and on the first opposition gives up his schemes, and forgets them.

Louis Napoleon is slow, both in conception and in execution. He meditates his plans long, thinks over every detail, waits for an opportunity which, when it comes, he does not always seize; he keeps often deferring and deferring execution until execution has become impossible or useless. But he forgets nothing that he has learned; he renounces nothing that he has planned. On the 29th of January, 1849, six weeks after he became President, he intended a *coup d'état*. He read his plan to Changarnier, and the instant Changarnier began to oppose it he folded up the paper and was silent. But he never abandoned it, and two years and a half afterwards he executed it.

Senior.—What are the relations now between him and Prince Napoleon?

Mad. Cornu.—They had a violent quarrel about the Prince's Polish speech. It was agreed between them that a speech should be made, but the Prince would not write, or even prepare himself; and his impetuosity, his want of early practice in public speaking, and the rudeness with which he was interrupted, deprived him of his presence of mind, and he went much farther than he ought to have done, or intended to do. The report is imperfect. Some of the worst parts of the speech, and of the interruptions, are omitted. When Billault said, '*J'ai servi fidèlement l'Empereur pour dix ans,*' the Prince answered, '*Oui, parceque nous étions les plus forts, si nous devenions faibles—on verrait.*' This is omitted. However, they have made it up since, and I do not believe that the Prince will persist in his journey to Syria, which was to have masked their quarrel.

Senior.—What are Louis Napoleon's habits now?

Mad. Cornu.—Worse than they used to be. He rides little, walks less, and is getting fat. He hates more and more the details of business, and yet is more and more afraid of trusting them to his ministers. But his *Cæsar* absorbs and consoles him. He said to the *bureau* of the Academy, when they came to announce the election of Feuillet, '*Je travaille à me rendre digne de vous.*' He thought at one time of offering himself for the vacancy made by Pasquier. He intended to be present at his own reception, and read, in the frightful Academic green coat, the *éloge* of his predecessor, and to characterise the nine different governments which Pasquier has served. But, with his habit of procrastination, he has delayed his candidature till the first two volumes of his *Cæsar* have been published. The first volume is ready, and he intended to publish it immediately; but the booksellers tell him that they will sell better in couples; and, as even emperors must submit to booksellers, he waits till the second is finished.

As Madame Cornu was leaving us, Corcelle came in.

Corcelle.—Vitet and Villemain were so astonished at the Emperor's announcement, that they went immediately to consult Guizot. 'There is nothing to be done,' said Guizot, 'but to receive him unanimously, and with acclamation.' And I agree with Guizot. Literary pursuits are not so common among sovereigns as to allow us to throw cold water on them. They will divert his time and attention and desires from worse things.

A curious adventure happened to me yesterday evening. I had an engagement in the Rue la Ville l'Évêque. My friend inhabits a low apartment at the bottom of the court, with a greenhouse before it. Lamartine's apartment is at the next door, and similarly arranged. Probably the two houses were built by one proprietor on the same plan. I was intimate with him before 1848, but I ceased to visit him when he became head of the Provisional Government, and we have not met since.

I entered, as I supposed, the court before my friend's apartment, rang at the door, was admitted, heard my name announced, and then discovered that I was at Lamartine's. There was not much time for thought, but it seemed to me that I could not suddenly, without previous explanation, present myself to a man whom I had once known familiarly, and had avoided for fifteen years. So I muttered something about a mistake, and ran back. But I must write to him.

Senior.—Well, here is paper, you can write your letter.

Corcelle.—No; such a letter as mine, and to such a man, cannot be extemporised. I must go home and write it at leisure.

Corcelle called on us in the afternoon.

Senior.—Have you written your letter?

Corcelle.—Yes, and I have got my answer. Here they are.

Senior.—May I copy them?

Corcelle.—Certainly.

And he gave the letters which I have copied below.

M. DE CORCELLE TO M. DE LAMARTINE.

'La crainte de vous étonner et de vous déplaire m'a seule empêché de m'excuser immédiatement, auprès de vous et de Mde. de Lamartine, de ma méprise d'hier soir.

'Après le premier moment d'embarras, me pardonnerez-vous un peu de superstition Chrétienne ?

'Je me figure que cette inadvertence qui m'a fait prendre votre demeure pour celle de votre voisin M. J. de Barthélemy m'est une occasion de vous exprimer les souvenirs qui ont survécu à nos divergences, mon admiration d'un noble écrit sur les affaires d'Italie, tous mes vœux pour vous, et mes respectueux et profonds hommages pour Madame de Lamartine.

(Signée)   'F. DE CORCELLE.'

'5 Avril, 1863.

M. DE LAMARTINE'S ANSWER.

'*Paris*, 5 *Avril*, 1863.

'MON CHER CORCELLE,

'Je suis bien sensible à votre charmante et délicate lettre. Je n'ai rien reçu de mieux dans ma vie, ni en acte ni en style. Soyez heureux du plaisir que vous m'avez fait.

'Je n'aurais point été étonné, mais j'aurais été charmé d'une rencontre à laquelle j'aurais pu prêter un souvenir d'ancienne amitié. Je vous remercie d'avoir écouté cette superstition Chrétienne, en m'envoyant une si aimable explication. Il n'y a point de superstition pour le cœur, il a toujours raison, car ce qui ne raisonne pas ne déraisonne jamais, écoutez le donc quand il vous parlera en ma faveur, et croyez que vous m'avez causé deux fois dans ma vie une impression durable et douce, une fois par votre amitié, et une autre fois par votre souvenir.

'Présentez je vous prie mes respects à Madame de Corcelle.

(Signée)   'AL. DE LAMARTINE.'

Senior.—Have you seen him since?

Corcelle.—Yes, I called on him yesterday. I found him of course much changed. His fine features remain, but he is emaciated, and rises and sits with difficulty.

I urged him to take some relaxation. 'It is impossible,' he answered. 'If I were to cease to work I should be ruined. I have paid three millions of debts. I have a million and a half more to pay. I shall go on working till I die, or am solvent.'

Senior.—How were those debts incurred? He has no children, and seems to live economically.

Corcelle.—Not in the country. There he keeps a sort of open house, and, what is worse, an open purse. He obeys literally the Scriptural precept to give to him that asks, and not to turn away from him that would borrow. Besides, he speculates. More than once he has bought up the wine of the Beaujolais district, and sold it at a loss.

Monday, April 6th.—I dined with Drouyn de Lhuys. It was a man's party; the majority of the guests were engaged in the sugar trade. I talked much to Herbet, formerly French Consul in London, and to Rouher, Minister of Commerce. He told me that the success of the Commercial Treaty was great and acknowledged, and that Protectionism was quickly becoming as obsolete a superstition as witchcraft.

Rouher.—We owe it altogether to the Emperor.

Senior.—I thought that you owed it to Michel Chevalier and Cobden?

Rouher.—Michel Chevalier would not have ventured to act, except under the orders of the Emperor.

Senior.—But did he not contribute to convince the Emperor?

Rouher.—I think not. No one has much influence with the Emperor, and certainly Chevalier is not likely to be an exception. I believe that the Emperor's own good sense made him a Free-trader.

Herbet is chief of the Commercial Department in the Affaires Étrangères. He complained bitterly of his work.

Herbet.—I have had only one day's holiday for three years. We are eminently a literary nation, for we transact everything by writing. I am kept writing from nine o'clock in the morning to six or seven in the evening. It is thus that we get worn out so soon. You oxygenate your blood by riding, by walking, and above all by your two months' holiday. We are the slaves of the desk, and the pen, and the lamp, from morning to night, and from January to December.

The rooms of the Hôtel des Affaires Étrangères

are such as Nebuchadnezzar might have built and Martin have imagined, but I regretted our meetings in the little dining-rooms of the Rue d'Anjou and Amblainvillers. Madame Drouyn de Lhuys sat on a gorgeous sofa, almost in solitary state, except when Rouher, or the Dutch Secretary of Legation, or I, approached her throne. I suspect that she knew little of any of the other guests. Of course, no politics were talked.

Friday, April 10th.—I went to Montalembert, who had given me an appointment at half-past one. I had scarcely entered when M. Carné was announced.

Montalembert.—I must let him in, for his is a canvassing visit.

The conversation soon went to Poland.

Montalembert.—Why are you English so cold?

Senior.—Because we expect no good. Nothing but a general war can re-establish Poland.

Montalembert.—Nothing but a war can re-establish Poland; but it need not be general, it will not reach you.

Carné.—I believe that it will, and that it will be disastrous to France. The old times of 1812 and 1813 will return. We shall have to fight Russia, Austria, Prussia, and England, and we shall be beaten.

Montalembert.—Why should England attack us? We shall not attack her.

Carné.—We must begin by Prussia. A war with Prussia will end by our taking the Rhine, and England will not stand that.

Montalembert.—I know that England will not allow us to seize Belgium; but would she fight for Mayence and Cologne? She did not fight for Savoy.

Senior.—Because your taking Savoy did not endanger us.

Montalembert.—It increased our force.

Senior.—Not greatly. It does not add to your population more than our natural increase adds every five years to ours. It would be different if you attempted to become masters of the Upper Rhine.

Montalembert.—But in order to succour Poland we need not cross the Rhine. Our military and naval arrangements are so near to perfection, that we could send 100,000 men round Jutland and attack Russia by the Baltic. Would you go to war to prevent that?

Senior.—Certainly not.

Carné.—We shall do it six months hence. We should have done it already if our hands had not been full of the Mexican war.

Montalembert.—The Mexican war has been a Godsend to Europe; indeed, a God-send to France. It is an enormous folly, but it has saved us from still greater follies. Such is our miserable state, that we thank a calamity for having prevented something worse. So long a time had passed since the apparition of a despot and a conqueror on the civilised portions of Europe, that until 1804 we had almost forgotten that there was such a thing as absolute power. The Bonapartes have shown it to us in all its deformity, and in all its splendour. It is a dangerous exhibition. It has proved that nothing is impossible, and that nothing is safe; that the wildest schemes may be carried into effect, and the oldest, the most useful, and the most sacred institutions swept away. It has infected even our literature. We are finding that the Roman Empire was an excellent form of government. Our master takes Cæsar for his idol, and Augustus for his model. One of your great literati, Mr. Merivale, is employed in *réhabilitant* Tiberius and Nero.

What is the state of your home politics?

Senior.—Tranquil. No one wishes to disturb Lord Palmerston.

Montalembert.—Does no one care about reform?

Senior.—No one, except to detest it.

Montalembert.—Universal suffrage *fera le tour du monde.* It is now the last court of appeal on all questions, international, among the rest. I have no doubt that the decree *appellant, dans l'argot dominant, la Nationalité Irlandaise dans ses comices* to decide whether it will remain connected with England, is already drawn up.

M. Carné now left us.

Montalembert.—He is a candidate for the chair now vacant in the Academy. We thought that all was settled, that M. Littré, a good man, and a good writer, member of the Académie des Inscriptions, author of the *History of the French Language*, would fill it. But, unhappily, somebody found out that Littré was an Atheist and a Positivist. It is supposed that he will retire or be rejected, and M. Carné is a candidate. We should prefer him to Littré, but I hope that some one with better pretensions will come forward.

I spent the evening at Thiers'. We talked of the elections.

Thiers.—They will be dangerous to *Celui-ci*, and, as he usually does, he keeps putting them off and putting them off. They were to take place in May, now, it is said, they are deferred to October. In the present state of men's minds, there would, I think, be an opposition of fifty in the new Chamber.

Senior.—Of fifty ? I never heard an estimate of more than twenty.

Thiers.—I do not say that fifty Opposition members would be returned. Perhaps twenty is the outside, but I expect that thirty who will start as Government candidates in order to get the help, or at least to avoid the enmity, of the Government, will afterwards join the Opposition. You know that it was decided at the Duc de Broglie's, that a candidate may swear allegiance to the Empire with a determination to destroy it. Still more, may he hoist its colours, though he must pull them down before he fires.

Senior.—Everyone tells me that you will be returned.

Thiers.—There are six or seven *arrondissements* for which I might come in without difficulty; but I have great doubts as to what I ought to do. Tell me your opinion.

Senior.—Mine would be interested advice, for I never heard you, and I have been longing for the last thirty years to do so. But it does seem to me that in your siege of this tyranny you have reached the counterscarp, that the time for sapping is over, and that you ought boldly to *battre en brèche.* Now there is no gun of your calibre.

Thiers.—Systematic opposition is not a business that I like. The worst government proposes much that is right. I prefer acting to speaking. When I speak, I like to be animated by the prospect of power. Now I am not likely to take office under this Government, or under that which will follow it. Again, though I think that the oath ought to be taken, I do not like to take it. They say that if a robber threatens to kill you, unless you swear not to prosecute him, it is your duty to swear and to prosecute. I admit this, but to make the parallel complete I must feel that it is my duty to enter the Chamber.

Senior.—That duty seems to me clear. It is necessary that there should be some Opposition members in the Chamber. It is the duty, therefore, of somebody to take the oath as the only means of entering it; and as no one would be so useful there as you would be, it seems to be peculiarly *your* duty. Is there any lassitude, any wish to devote yourself rather to literature than to public life, at the bottom of your objection?

Thiers.—Not the least lassitude. I like work as much as I ever did; but there may be something of the latter.

Senior.—I am told that all the Liberal members of this Chamber,—*Les cinq*, as they are called,—are to be returned without opposition; at least, from the Liberals.

Thiers.—Yes, it is unavoidable; but it is unfortunate. A better selection might have been made.

Saturday, April 11th.—We dined with Charles Jobez, and met the Archbishop of Rouen, Monseigneur Bonnechose. He began life as a lawyer, rose, by the age of thirty, to be a judge, and then took orders. He is a gentlemanlike, agreeable man, but a violent Protectionist. We talked of Rouen.

Bonnechose.—The commercial treaty and the American war have ruined us. The exasperation against you is furious. We accuse you of depriving us of cotton by preventing the Emperor from recognising the South and breaking the blockade, and we accuse you of having entrapped us into free trade. We were deeply wounded by the language in which you discussed the Treaty of Commerce. Lord

Palmerston said to the House of Commons : 'France is bound, but you are free. All that the Queen has done is to promise to use her best endeavours to obtain your consent; the Emperor consents on behalf of the nation.' It was not pleasant to have our impotence so cynically exposed. If the Emperor would only raise his little finger we should all rush to a war against you enthusiastically.

We went to a full-dress party given by Lady Cowley in honour of the marriage of the Prince of Wales. The large rooms were full, but we did not meet a French acquaintance except the Maréchale Randon and the Drouyn de Lhuys'. There were many French people, but none whom we knew.

Among the guests were Mr. Dayton, the minister of the Federals, and Mr. Corbyn from the South,—each confident of the justice of his cause, and of its success, and each angry with us for our partiality to the opposite side.

'If you had been really neutral,' said Dayton, 'and had not raised the rebel provinces into a nation, by allowing to them belligerent rights, we should have suppressed the rebellion in three months.'

'If you had been really neutral,' said Corbyn, 'and had not supplied the Federals with arms and ammunition, they would have given up in three months.'

Sunday, April 12*th.*—Circourt breakfasted with us.

It is the first time that he has gone out since the death of his wife, about six weeks ago. He was in better spirits than I expected. The constant spectacle of her sufferings for six years, cheered by little real hope—every day getting a little worse, must have so preyed on him, that I am not sure that their termination was not almost a relief to him. Incessant pain had injured every internal organ. All were found diseased; some extensively so. The prolongation of her life for so many years must have been owing to her great courage and patience, to very skilful treatment, and to Circourt's assiduous attention.

He stayed with us from ten to two. We talked principally of the subject which now most interests the French—Poland.

Circourt.—The enforcement of the conscription as a political measure directed against a particular class was an unjust act. But it was a Polish act. Wielopolski, the Governor of Warsaw, is a Pole; so are almost all the officials in the kingdom of Poland. The Russian army had not been recruited since the Crimean war; a new levy had become absolutely necessary. The proportion required from Poland was small, 15,000 men—not four per thousand. The only impartial mode of forced recruitments, the ballot, has never existed in the Russian empire; it is new indeed in Europe. Look at Shakespeare's description of Falstaff's proceedings. He requires from Justice Shallow four men. The Justice tenders to him six to choose from. He takes the four who do not bribe him to excuse them, and boasts that he has formed his company out of the worst *prolétaires* of the country.

The practice in Russia has always been to require from every *Seigneur* a certain number of recruits, and he chose whom he thought fit; those who had incurred his displeasure were sure to go; so were any who were generally unpopular.

Wielopolski recommended that, on this occasion, they should be taken, not, as was usual, from the agricultural population, but from the towns; and that, as there were no *Seigneurs* there, the officials (themselves Poles) should point them out. The Emperor objected that it was a new plan. Wielopolski persisted, and it was done. It is a mistake to suppose that he turned educated young men into soldiers. He took none of the upper classes, none even of the bourgeois. Those taken were just such as Falstaff took, except that they were taken only from the towns.

Montalembert tells us that the statement in the Russian papers, that the recruits had submitted to their fate, not only without resistance, but with pleasure, was the drop which made the waters of bitterness run over.

'Honour,' he says, 'to the people which can bear anything except official hypocrisy, except *le mensonge prodigué en son nom et pour son compte. Esclave soit; mais esclave reconnoissant et satisfait, non—esclave qui se laisse féliciter d'être libre et heureux, non, mille fois, non. La mort et la ruine, tous les désastres et toutes les tortures plutôt que l'adhésion silencieuse au mensonge couronné et impuni.'*

Now, I have no doubt that many of these recruits, the refuse of the town population, were really gainers by being turned into soldiers, and that some of them thought so. To suppose, as Montalembert does, that these expressions in the newspapers produced the insurrection, is childish.

What Wielopolski did was what Cavaignac did after the insurrection of June 1848, and what Louis Napoleon did in 1851 and 1852. Each of then seized and removed, without trial, some thousands of persons whose presence he thought dangerous. Such an expedient is revolutionary, that is to say, both illegal and unjust, even if done honestly; and capable, indeed certain, of being frightfully abused. But Wielopolski's use of it was less objectionable than Cavaignac's or Louis Napoleon's. They made exiles and prisoners of their victims,—he made soldiers of them. Every one of them supplied the place of an ordinary recruit, and they belonged to the same class as the ordinary recruits, except that they were townspeople instead of peasants. Most of them without doubt regretted the change; but so would have done the peasants whose places they filled. The Continental nations are not rich enough to make military service attractive. Their armies therefore do not consist, as yours does, of volunteers. Their recruits are always unwilling, and I doubt whether those taken on this recruitment were peculiarly so. It occasioned an insurrection, partly because the many years which had passed without a recruitment made it seem to be a new burden; partly because the people of the towns felt aggrieved at being exclusively subjected to it; partly because to be selected by the police was unusual, and more odious than to be designated by the *Seigneurs;* partly because the recollection of the waste of life in the last war made that selection seem a sentence of death; and partly because the Polish nobility is in a state of chronic disaffection, and the weakness of Russia, and the power and sympathy of France, made this appear to be a favourable occasion.

Senior.—But the peasants have joined in the insurrection.

Circourt.—Very few of them; only on the compulsion of the town insurgents, and when driven to it by the excesses of the Russian troops, who, like all semi-barbarians, often treat neutrals, or even friends, as if they were enemies. Scarcely any of the noble proprietors, or even of the *bonne* bourgeoisie, have risen. The bulk of the insurgents consists of the low townspeople, and of the poor nobles, the Szlachta,* about 85,000 families, without property or industry, who live principally as the retainers of the richer proprietors. They are the people who give to the Poles their national character. They have the vices

---

* *Note by M. de Circourt, who corrected this conversation:* '*Szlachta*' is the name of the class; '*Szlachty*' is the plural of the individuals.—A. DE C.

both of a conquering and of a conquered race : the *misero orgoglio d'un tempo che fù*, and the cunning dissimulation and perfidy produced by long oppression. They sigh—and as long as they are kept poor by their idleness, and idle by the want of education and by the prejudices of caste, they will sigh—for the good old times when they were the human beings of Poland, and the peasants mere domestic animals ; when any one of them had power to stop by a *liberum veto* the legislation and the policy of the kingdom. They hate the improvement which has followed the Russian Government.

Senior.—Who then are the Scythemen of whom we hear?

Circourt.—Szlachta and the poor townspeople. The bulk of the peasants are indifferent, or opposed to the insurrection. The Russian Government has not been a bad one to them. Even despotism is better for the lower classes than an ignorant aristocracy.

In 1848, Prussia resolved to give different institutions to the Germans, and to the Poles in the Duchy of Posen. I was employed to distinguish them. Every family wished to be registered as Germans. If I had blindly admitted their statements, I must have reported that there were no Poles in the Duchy of Posen.

Senior.—And how many are there?

Circourt.—780,000, in a population of 1,494,000. All the western frontier of the Duchy has been—to use a German expression—conquered by the plough. The Poles have been improved off the face of the earth. The superior diligence, thrift, and energy of the Germans, have enabled them to buy out the Poles.

Senior.—The Poles complain that the Prussian Government interferes, that it lends money to Germans below the market rate of interest to assist them in buying estates from Poles.

Circourt.—I dare say that it does so. But ought the Poles to complain of that? It is a most mild form of oppression, for it brings in new purchasers and increases the price of their estates. They are not forced to sell, though the Germans are tempted to buy.

Senior.—What is the whole Polish population?

Circourt.—6,792,000 : 3,872,100 in the kingdom of Poland, 1,100,000 in Gallicia, 1,046,000 in White and Little Russia, to the west of the Dneiper; to whom must be added 1,615,000 Roman Catholic Lithuanians, who, though not of Polish race, sympathise with the Poles as co-religionists. But of this total of 8,500,000, only the 3,872,100 of the kingdom of Poland are compact enough to form a separate State.

In the Russian provinces, to the west of the Dneiper, there are 5,950,000 Russians of the Greek Church, 1,140,000 Jews, and 115,000 Wallachs,—that is, 6,215,000, as against 2,661,000 Poles and Catholic Lithuanians.

In Gallicia, the Poles are only 1,100,000, the Ruthenes and others of Russian descent and religion are 3,100,000.

So that, in these outlying provinces, the portion of the population which is not Polish, or Catholic, is 9,315,000; that which is Polish, or Catholic, is only 3,661,000.

Senior.—How did the Poles penetrate into Western Russia?

Circourt.—The inhabitants gave themselves up to Poland in order to escape the attacks of more barbarous nations, the Magyars, or Huns, and the Tartars; that was the beginning of Russian serfdom. It was not a Russian institution. The Poles, that is to say, the Polish nobility, seized the land and gradually reduced the peasants to the state of serfs.

When the King of Lithuania, Jagellon, married the heiress of Poland, the Lithuanians and Poles gradually coalesced, the Lithuanian nobles adopted the Catholic religion, while the peasants remained Greek, and *they* also were reduced into serfdom. From Poland the malady of serfdom spread over Russia, but was not finally established in Russia proper, that is to say, in Muscovy, till about the year 1618.

On the whole, the Poles are the worst nation in civilised Europe; the most turbulent, the most unscrupulous, the least capable of doing good to themselves or to anybody else, and, after the French, the most capable of doing harm. And, as is the case with all weak, silly, ill-conditioned nations, they have always been ill-treated since the time when they were strong enough to ill-treat others. Nations are beasts who tear to pieces those who have not the wisdom or the strength to defend themselves.

Senior.—D. E. F. told me that a month ago he feared that this rebellion would produce an European war; that Louis Napoleon would be delighted to make it an excuse for escaping from Mexico, and rushing into another revolutionary struggle in support of Polish nationality; that public opinion in France would support him; that the common danger would create a new Holy Alliance between Russia, Austria, and Prussia; and that England would join them rather than see the First Empire renewed: but that his fears were abated when he saw the first effervescence in France cool, and when he saw reinforcements sent to Mexico.

Circourt.—It is certain that the Mexican affair, which we thought disastrous, has saved us—at least for a time—from a great danger. I begin to think, almost to wish, that we may keep Mexico. A military friend of mine, who has served long in Africa, said to me: 'Algeria has been a great financial burden, but it has given to us an excellent army. Now, however, it is almost worn out as a school. The Arabs have long submitted, the Cabyles are submitting. Soon there will be no fighting there. Mexico comes, happily, to supply its place. We shall bridge over the mortal district between Vera Cruz and Jalapa by a railway, and then our troops will be healthy. Their campaigns will be on mountainous plateaux : the long voyage will give experience to our sailors, and the treasures of Mexico will pay our expenses.'

Senior.—I do not believe in the last prophecy. Neither wars nor colonies pay their expenses ; but I have thought from the beginning that your occupation of Mexico was the only mode by which that fine country could be rescued from barbarism, the best mode by which the insolence and ambition of America could be subdued, and the safest outlet for your superabundant activity.

Do you accuse us of having occasioned the Mexican war?

Circourt.—I suppose so ; for we accuse you of having occasioned everything that we dislike. We accuse you of having produced the 24th of February, 1848, and the 2nd of December, 1851, of having created the kingdom of Italy, and of having robbed the Pope.

Senior.—Just as the Confederates accuse us of having armed the Federals, and the Federals of having made a nation of the Confederates.

Circourt.—It is the price that you pay for your power and your prosperity. You are the objects of general envy, and therefore of general dislike and general calumny. If you will only allow us to make MacMahon king of Ireland, Prince Napoleon king of Scotland, and restore the Heptarchy in England, we shall be your affectionate friends !

Senior.—Whence do you take your Polish figures?

Circourt.—Principally from Schmitzler's *L'Empire des Tsars*, Vol. II.; *La Population*, Paris, 1862; and from M. de Buschen's *Bevölkerung des Russischen Kaiserreichs*. They are both laborious and conscientious statisticians, and have made great use of Polish authorities.

Senior.—What will be the result if Europe does not interfere by force?

Circourt.—Ten thousand Russian soldiers could beat the whole Polish force, if it could catch them in a mass. They are about as formidable as the brigands of the Neapolitan dominions. Supported by French money, they may long keep up a guerilla war, destructive to the country and mischievous to Russia, but they must be worn out in time. Russia will fight to the knife rather than create an independent Poland. It would be a mere *avant-garde* of France in her next war against Russia.

Monday, April 13th.—Drouyn de Lhuys begged me to be with him this morning at ten. He was alone, and no other visitor was let in; but we had frequent interruptions.

Senior.—Do you find your work easier, or less easy, than it was when you left office nine years ago?

Drouyn de Lhuys.—I worked then from morning till night, and I work from morning to night now. At that time there were a few great questions; now there are questions everywhere. I cannot put my finger on the map without touching some burning coal.

Senior.—I suppose that the hottest coal is Poland.

Drouyn de Lhuys.—Certainly, as respects Europe; but it is one of the few subjects as to which France is unanimous. Every one feels that it is a matter in which we cannot be inactive. The course which *you* have taken has been to require Russia to execute the treaty of 1815, and to give to Poland a free Constitution and a national army. Russia has peremptorily refused, on the following grounds:—

First, she refuses to adopt your version of the treaty. It is an ambiguous instrument—I believe studiously so. The Western Powers would not allow it to contain words showing clearly that Poland was to be a province of Russia. Alexander objected to any which implied clearly that she was to be independent. There are expressions in it indicating each meaning vaguely, but neither meaning explicitly. 'The Poles,' it says, 'subjects of Russia, Austria, and Prussia, shall have a national representation and national institutions.'

This looks like independence under protectorates, such as your protectorate of the Ionian Islands; but it goes on to say that these institutions are to be *réglées d'après le mode d'existence politique que chacun des Gouvernements auxquels ils appartiennent jugera utile et convenable de leur accorder.'*

This is complete subservience. Russia would comply with it if she delegated the absolute power over Poland to a Polish Council and a Polish Governor, to be named by herself. She could call these the national representation and institutions, and the political existence which she thought it useful and proper to grant.

Secondly, she maintains that whatever may have been the rights of Poland under the treaty, they were destroyed by her rebellion in 1830 ; in fact, that their enforcement was thereby rendered impossible.

'How can I,' said the Czar, 'create a Polish army, which will immediately attack me? How can I give a constitution to rebels, while my faithful subjects are without one? And how can I, in the midst of the social revolution which the abolition of serfdom implies, prepare a constitution for sixty millions of people, differing in language, religion, and civilisation?'

We refused to join you in your demands ; first, because we do not admit the validity of the treaty of 1815 ; secondly, because Russia, having refused to obey *your* summons, must have refused to obey ours. She would have merely referred us to her answer to you. Thirdly, because we could not have the concurrence of Austria. She could not hold Cracow, in defiance of the treaty of 1815, and enforce its observance by Russia. What we have done, and what Austria has done, has been to send to Russia not a joint note, but a concurrent note, pointing out the danger of letting things take their present course; and you, after your first repulse, have done the same; and, in fact, the danger cannot be exaggerated.

A nation of eight millions of people, with a common language, a common religion, and a common history, has for ninety years opposed a perpetual moral resistance, and occasionally a physical one, to three out of the five great powers of Europe. It had defended its separate existence, or, what in bad French, is called its *nationalité*, against flattery, and bribes, and cruelty. It has been partitioned, it has been oppressed, its patriots have been attacked by seduction, exile, and murder. Its schools and its churches have been closed, its children have been taught a foreign tongue and a foreign religion, and to consider themselves members of a foreign Empire. Still it remains—exhausted—but unassimilated and unsubdued.

Is this contest between force and right to last for ninety years more?

We recollect the effect which the dragging twenty corpses through the streets of Paris produced in 1848. Poland is not a corpse, but what is worse, a bleeding victim held up before all the revolutionists of Europe. Is that safe? Is it safe for Russia, or for Austria, or for Prussia, or even for France? The foreign relations of all the Northern sovereignties are from time to time disturbed by the constant reappearance of the Polish question.

The Polish element in our population is always threatening our internal tranquillity. All this we have pointed out to Russia, and have urged her to put an end to it.

Senior.—How?

Drouyn de Lhuys.—As to the means, our notes are silent; we leave that to Russia.

Senior.—But what is your own opinion? You must have thought of some remedy. What is it?

Drouyn de Lhuys.—I know of none but to give Poland independence.

Senior.—Is she populous enough to form an independent kingdom?

Drouyn de Lhuys.—Eight millions of an energetic race are enough.

Senior.—But of those eight millions only one-half are to be found compact in the kingdom of Poland. The other half are scattered over vast territories, penned in by people who have no sympathy with them, whom they once conquered and oppressed. Circourt, to whom I go for statistical information, tells me that in the western provinces of Russia there are only 2,661,000 Poles and Catholic Lithuanians, and 6,215,000 Russians and Jews; that in Gallicia there are only 1,100,000 Poles and 3,100,000 persons of Russian race, and Greek religion; and that in the Grand Duchy of Posen, in which the proportion of Poles is the largest, there are only 780,000, out of a population of 1,494,000. It is obviously impossible to create into a Polish nation more than 4,000,000 of the kingdom of Poland.

Drouyn de Lhuys.—Circourt is well informed and honest, but you must not trust him implicitly on any matter in which his feelings are concerned. He is a strong Russian, a strong anti-Catholic, a weak Frenchman, and a fierce anti-Pole.

Senior.—I have consulted the *Bevölkerung des Russischen Kaiserreichs* of Buschen, and I find his figures agree with Circourt's. He gives (p. 62) for all the Russian Western Governments, Great Russia, Little Russia, and White Russia, only 1,046,947 Poles, not so many as the Jews, who are 1,139,633. He makes the Poles only 10·4 per cent of the population.

Drouyn de Lhuys.—The kingdom of Poland, with its four millions, will make a nation as large as many of the independent nations of Europe—as large as Holland, as Bavaria, as Denmark, as Hanover; and it might be supported by alliances, the Polish nobility contains between four and five hundred thousand of the bravest and most military race in the world. Every male among them will be a soldier. Such a race can maintain itself.

Senior.—I believe that it could maintain itself, but only on two conditions: first, that it was well governed; secondly, that it was neutralised and protected by its neighbours. Now the Poles have never governed themselves well, abroad or within. It is possible, however, that they have been improved by adversity. I earnestly hope that that may be the case, but I am not sanguine. Secondly, is it likely that Austria, Russia, and Prussia, will look favourably on their new neighbour?

Drouyn de Lhuys.—I think that Austria and Prussia will do so, if Poland keeps her hands off Posen and Gallicia. Independent Poland will be a less formidable neighbour than Poland, a province of Russia. Russia, of course, will be hostile, as she has always been; but the rest of Europe will keep her in order.

Senior.—Are we not counting the chickens before they are hatched? Poland cannot conquer her independence. I hear that few of the great nobles, or of the peasants, have joined in the insurrection.

Drouyn de Lhuys.—That is not what *we* hear. We are told that all the great nobles join, or at least favour, the insurrection, and also the bulk of the peasantry. Even the Jews are said to have risen against the Russians.

Senior.—It will require much evidence to convince me of that.

Drouyn de Lhuys.—It is certain that the insurgents have shown great courage and great fidelity to their cause. Their central committee is known to be sitting in Warsaw, in the midst of a Russian garrison; a single traitor would occasion its arrest; not one has been found.

Senior.—Do you think of a Congress?

Drouyn de Lhuys.—No, at least at present. *Un*

Congrès dance, mais ne marche pas. A Congress is a pleasant diplomatic holiday. You have agreeable colleagues, you breakfast together in the morning, talk for two or three hours, dine in good company, and dance every night. But for a policy of action, for circumstances in which boldness and decision are necessary, it is as bad as a council of war. When all the important points have been settled, we may have a Congress to work out the details, and to give authenticity and formality to pre-arranged results; but other and coarser means must be used to obtain those results.

Senior.—I am told, however, that there is already disunion among the insurgents. That Langiewicz fled, not because he was surrounded by the Russians, but because there was a party opposed to him in his own army.

Drouyn de Lhuys.—I fear that is true. Langiewicz had not importance enough for the position which he usurped; but his removal does not seem to have disheartened his countrymen.

April 15th.—Madame Cornu, the Corcelles, and Lady Ashburton, breakfasted with us. We had an agreeable conversation, but I do not recollect much of it. The Corcelles and Madame Cornu seemed delighted to meet again. They had not seen one another for years.

I remarked to Madame Cornu that I had not seen at Lady Cowley's great party in celebration of the Prince of Wales' marriage more than three French persons whom I had ever seen before.

Madame Cornu.—The Emperor cannot attract an aristocracy, so he is forced to make one. Persigny says, *nous autres des grandes maisons*, just as the Emperor considers himself as one of the sacred royal caste. If his aristocracy is not of the purest blood, it is at least rich.

Have you seen the house which Michel Chevalier is building in the Avenue de l'Impératrice? It is to cost a million. The Emperor's dentist—Evans—has become a millionaire. He had early information that the Avenue de l'Impératrice was to be created, and bought land at low prices, which is now worth 250,000 francs an acre. Persigny is building a palace at Chamarande.

Senior.—Not out of his savings, for his salary as Minister is not above 120,000 francs, and as a Senator, 35,000; and he must spend the whole.

Madame Cornu.—Nor does he do as most of the others do—steal, or take *pots de vin*. The Emperor gives him whatever he wants.

We spent a busy evening. Madame Drouyn de Lhuys had told us that she should have a few friends and a violin. We found the great Hôtel des Affaires Étrangères brilliantly illuminated; the violin was an orchestra, and the few friends about five hundred people. We knew few of them, and went on to Madame de Montalembert's. Here was a different sight. Instead of nothing but uniforms, we found only black coats. They were almost all strangers to us, and we left them for Madame d'Haussonville's. Almost all here were our friends or acquaintances. We had passed from Imperialism and Ultramontanism to Orleanism. We talked about rank in France and England.

Madame d'Haussonville.—Our rules are less precise than yours. Yours are governed almost exclusively by title. With one exception, we care little about title. Age, office, political or literary distinction, and, above all, birth, are far more important. With you the grandson of a duke may be a commoner, and would go out of a room after a City knight. The only exception is the title of duke—a duke is something apart.

Senior.—The fact which you mention, that hereditary nobility is with us confined to the eldest line, makes it impossible for us to recognise noble birth unless marked by a title. The late Jockey Duke of Norfolk proposed to give a dinner to all the Howards in the line of succession to the dukedom. He gave it up when he found that there were above a thousand of them. There are probably more than a thousand other Howards unconnected with the noble family. When a Mr. Howard comes into a room, no one but a genealogical antiquary knows whether he is a great-grandson of a Duke of Norfolk, or a great-grandson of a tailor. In France, if he belonged to the *noblesse*, his name would announce it—he would be M. de Howard.

Madame d'Haussonville.—And a great misfortune this is to us. It splits the nation into two castes—noble and *roturier*.

April 16*th.*—We dined with Duchâtel, and met there Dumon, the William Guizots, and some others whose names I did not catch.

Duchâtel and Dumon talked of Poland.

Dumon.—Public opinion has become less insane on the Polish question. We find that to reach Poland through Russia would be an enterprise of enormous expense and great danger, would probably involve a war against a coalition, and that the way by the Baltic would add to the dangers of the road the dangers of the sea. And what could we do when we got there? Are we stronger or better soldiers than the great Napoleon? Nature has kindly made every nation, especially every nation inhabiting a great, thinly peopled country, strong on the defensive. In our late war with Russia she was kind enough to spare us all the dangers and difficulties of a long march, by coming down to meet us at the very extremity of her empire. If she had abandoned the Crimea we could have done her no great harm, not nearly as much as we must have done to ourselves. We find too that a real Polish nation is a phantom. That if our war succeeded we might make a little Principality of the kingdoms, but that to add to it any considerable number of the neighbouring Poles would be impossible, unless we could have recourse to the arbitrary violence of the first Empire. A month ago such a war would have been popular, it would not be so now. I believe too that there are understandings between Russia and *Celui-ci* which make him unwilling seriously to injure or even to offend her. He is forced to speak big to please the French, but I suspect, and indeed I believe, that he has secretly informed her that his big words mean nothing.

Senior.—I hear that young Count Wielopolski has challenged Prince Napoleon for the attacks made by the Prince on his father.

Duchâtel.—He has; here is a copy of the challenge :—

Dans votre discours prononcé au Sénat le 17 courant, vous vous êtes exprimé à l'endroit de mon père d'une manière outrageante. Je viens comme fils, demander à votre A. I. pour cette indigne offense, la satisfaction qu'un homme d'honneur ne refuse jamais.

Toutefois, d'après vos antécédents si connus je n'ai pas grande chance de vous voir accueillir ma demande.

Il est des courages qui ne vont pas au-delà du ruisseau, et tel individu, sans-culotte effronté, quand il s'agit de déviser l'outrage, se refugie lâchement dans l'inviolabilité d'une condition privilégiée lorsqu'on lui demande raison de ses propos.

Votre A. I. voudra peut-être s'abriter derrière ceux

qui conspirent avec elle au Palais Royal et avec les chefs d'assassins dans les repaires de Varsovie.

Si dans ma patrie la bonne cause inaugurée par notre Roi Alexandre II., et à laquelle depuis deux ans mon père consacre ses efforts, ne finit pas par triompher des difficultés soulevées par des gens pervers ou malavisés, ce sera principalement aux soi-disants amis de notre cause, tel que vous, Monseigneur, et vos confrères revolutionnaires, qu'il faudra s'en prendre.

J'attendrai jusqu'au 2 Avril votre réponse, ainsi que la désignation de votre témoin ; si vous ne m'accordez pas la satisfaction demandée, souffrez, Monseigneur, que je livre cette lettre à la publicité.

Recevez, Monseigneur, l'assurance de tous les sentimens qui sont dus de ma parte à votre Altesse Impériale.

C. WIELOPOLSKI.

Varsovie, 24 Mars.

Senior.—This is the third time that the Prince has been challenged for words used in debate. Were I he I would put an end to such things by publicly declaring that I would never sacrifice to my own feelings the freedom of debate. This is what an English statesman would do, and public opinion would support him. Such a challenge as this would then be treated as an act of cowardice, like challenging a bishop. Sir James Stephen, when under-secretary for the Colonies, was challenged by a Colonial Governor whom he had reprimanded. He answered that his duty to the public made it impossible that he could accept such a challenge, and that Sir —— must have known *that* when he sent it.

Dumon.—Our old feudal notions of honour which required a gentleman to pretend to accept a duel as a pleasure would render such conduct disgraceful.

Senior.—At all events, the Senate ought to interfere and protect its own freedom of debate. A man who challenged a peer for words said in Parliament would be sent to Newgate for contempt until the end of the session, unless he previously purged, as it is called, his contempt by withdrawing the challenge, and asking pardon on his knees at the bar of the House.

Duchâtel.—Our Chambers have not the power of committing for contempt. They could not as yours have done assume it; and I do not believe that any government which we are likely to have would give it to them.

We talked of Madame Castiglione.

Madame Duchâtel.—There was a great exhibition of *tableaux vivans* the other day at Madame Meyendorf's house *pour œuvre de charité*. The tickets were thirty francs a-piece. Madame Castiglione promised to exhibit, and it was whispered about, as an excuse for the price, that she was to appear as *La Source*. After several *tableaux* the stage became a grotto, with a curtain in front. Now we expected *La Source*. The curtain was raised, and Madame appeared in a

Carmelite's dress, covered up to the neck, and a close fitting cap. After a minute it was lowered, and that was all we saw of her. The spectators were very angry. She had a right to be angry with those who had announced her as *La Source*, but she ought not to have punished us all by her rapid disappearance.

The conversation soon turned to politics.

Duchâtel.—My fears look rather towards America than towards Poland. Our sympathies were at the beginning, and indeed are now, with the North. We think that the victory of the South would perpetuate and extend slavery, and it is with grief and alarm that we see the North taking a course which seems intended to give the South that victory by forcing on a war with you. I cannot conceive a more unstatesmanlike, a more suicidal measure than the appointment of Admiral Wilkes to the Bahama Station. His titles to it in the eyes of the President, of his advisers, and of the northern people, were, that he committed against you a gross violation of international law, which nearly brought on a war, which probably *would* have done so if the indignation of Europe had not been so loudly expressed that the President was forced to disavow him. And for having done this he is placed in a position in which he has to exercise over British commerce rights, which even when exercised by a prudent man and a gentleman, are odious and vexatious, and when employed by a blustering ruffian may easily become intolerable. And he seems to be exercising them intolerably. He is stopping British vessels carrying on a lawful trade between one British port and another—vessels which have been previously examined by American cruisers and released. It is no excuse that the vessels are only sent to an American port for adjudication, and will be released. That will be no compensation to owners or shippers for the loss of time, expense, and vexation.

Senior.—I am told that the American prize court interposes wilful delay in order to keep the vessels and cargoes in its own hands.

Dumon.—At the same time Mr. Adams gives to a vessel loaded with arms to be used against us, a pass to enable her to proceed safely from one neutral port to another.

Duchâtel.—The North Americans seem to be mad, and when nations or individuals are in that unhappy state, their actions do not enable us to affirm their motives. But if sane persons acted as the government of the United States is acting, we should infer that, perceiving their chance of success desperate, they were endeavouring to obtain an excuse for their defeat by getting into a war with you, which will enable them to say we should have beaten the South if perfidious Albion had not interfered.

Senior.—If such be their wish of course they will obtain it. It is impossible to remain at peace with people who want to quarrel with you. We are the most pacific nation existing, but we are beginning to find that pacificness is not the means to preserve peace. The Russian war was brought on by Nicolas' confidence that nothing would provoke us to war. In the same confidence the United States, under the Government it is true of Southern Presidents, kept bullying us for years. When Mr. Seward in his memorable conversation with the Duke of Newcastle was reminded by the Duke that if he persisted in his avowed intention of insulting England it might bring on a war, he answered, 'I shall have to insult you, but there will be no war. You cannot go to war with us. There is as much British property in New York as there is American.' The *Trent* outrage and its consequences are the practical comment on that conversation.

Friday, April 17th.—Cieskowski, deputy for Posen to the Prussian parliament, called on me.

I repeated to him my doubts as to the possibility of creating a Polish kingdom of sufficient strength to stand alone.

Cieskowski.—Why there are twenty-two millions of people, and a territory much larger than any German state except Austria. We claim as our territory, besides the kingdom of Poland, Gallicia, Posnania, and all the Russian provinces to the west of the Dneiper.

Senior.—On what grounds?

Cieskowski.—Because we once had them, and were deprived of them by violent injustice.

Senior.—On that ground England may claim all the south of France and a great part of the north. On that ground Denmark has a right to Norway. Nothing could be more violent or unjust than the separation of Norway from Denmark.

Cieskowski.—That is the claim we put forward. We ought, perhaps, to restrict it to the countries inhabited by a population of Polish race, religion, or sympathy.

This would give us sixteen millions:
4 millions in the kingdom of Poland.
5 millions in Gallicia.
2 in Prussia.
5 in Western Russia.
—
16 millions.

Senior.—Of these twelve millions beyond the kingdom I doubt whether two millions are real Poles. The Lithuanians are Letts, only the higher orders speak Polish; the Gallicians are Ruthenes; the greater part of the population of Western Russia is Russian.

Cieskowski.—As for Lithuania there are two millions of Catholics. It is on that ground, and because the Lithuanians earnestly desire to be reunited to Poland, that we claim Lithuania. In fact, our great ground is the sympathy of the people. We are willing to let it be tried on any basis. Either by universal suffrage, or by the wishes of the higher classes, or by the constituted bodies of any of those countries.

Senior.—Are you sure that the peasants would vote for independence? They have not joined in the insurrection.

Cieskowski.—They have not; but there is much difference between voting for independence and fighting for it. They would be influenced, too, by their religious feelings.

Senior.—What is the difference intelligible to a peasant between the Greek and the Roman Catholic faith? What does he care about the procession of the Holy Spirit?

Cieskowski.—Nothing, but he cares about forms, though he does not care about doctrines. There are millions of Russians who have separated from the orthodox church on the question whether the sign of the Cross ought to be made with one finger or with two. The Roman Catholics put images into their churches; the Greeks put only pictures. That is quite enough for a schism. You see that the Lithuanian peasantry have been burning the Greek churches which Nicholas with his usual folly forced them to erect. The long fasts and the wearisome ceremonies of the Greeks are again obvious marks of the difference of the churches, and very disagreeable ones. Then the peasants are under the influence of the clergy, and the clergy *do* care about the 'procession,' and fancy they know what it means. I feel quite sure that in my own country, Posnania, the ballot-box would decide in favour of a Polish independent nationality.

Senior.—Of course it would among the nobles, to

whom it would restore the power of oppressing the people. But I suspect that if the question could be submitted to any court of international law you would take nothing by your claims except as respects the kingdom of Poland. The partitions were acts of detestable injustice and wickedness; but I believe as respects Posnania, Gallicia, and Western Russia, they could not now be set aside without new wickedness and injustice.

I dined with Kergorlay, and met Michel Chevalier and Count Uriski, a Pole, a native of Western Russia, but now domiciled in Paris.

I asked him what he thought of Cieskowski's views.

Uriski.—I could not tell any Pole or any Frenchman what I thought of them—I should be stoned; but to you I will say that his sixteen millions are nonsense. I do not believe that any Polish independent state could be created containing more at the outside than six millions, consisting of the Poles of the kingdom, and perhaps of a couple of millions more taken from those parts of the adjacent districts in which Poles largely predominate. Such a state could enjoy only a *quasi* independence. It must lean on Russia or on Germany. France is too distant to give it real support. To suppose that it would be a barrier to Russia is childish. It is much more likely that it would be her slave, and that she would keep it, as the neighbours of Poland did for the three centuries preceding its partition, poor, divided, and miserable, in order to keep it subservient. Whether it would be better governed than it is now is another question. The Poles have never shown any capacity for self-government. Their only chance of good government seems to be to form part of some wiser nation. But then they must accept their situation. They must try to make their government work well. No people can be well governed against their will. If I could decide by a wish the fortune of my brethren by race, it should be to become united to Prussia. The Prussian government is far better than any to which they have been subject, and better, above all, than their native government. Cieskowski, an inhabitant of Prussian Poland, enjoying himself one of the best governments of the Continent, is willing to run the risks and miseries of revolution and war in order to be a citizen of this reconstructed Polish nation. The only explanation that he can give is that he had rather be a Pole than a German. Why had he rather? Are the Poles a wiser or a better or a more civilised nation than the Germans? And if he clings to his race, would he lose that by cordially submitting to the Prussian government? This idolatry of nationality seems to me a return towards barbarism. It was the folly which induced the Ionians to wish to exchange the mild and wise protection of England for the fraudulent despotism of King Otho.

I congratulated Michel Chevalier on his nomination as administrator of the Crédit Mobilier.

Senior.—Did it come from the Government?

Chevalier.—No, from Péreire, as director of the company.

Senior.—I am told that it is worth 100,000 francs a-year.

Chevalier.—I hope that it will be worth more. A part of the income is derived from a percentage on profits.

Senior.—It is I suppose laborious?

Chevalier.—By no means, it does not require attendance for more than a couple of hours two or three times a-week.

Senior.—Your fabulous profits of forty per cent one year, and twenty another, scarcely can continue.

Chevalier.—No; they were exceptional. All that we now reckon on is from fourteen to fifteen per cent on our nominal capital of 500 francs a share; as the present price of the shares is about 1500, this gives to purchasers about five per cent.

We talked of the expense of living in Paris.

Chevalier.--It is scarcely less than it is in London; and as our incomes are smaller than yours, we are forced to economies, which you do not think of. Few families keep a really good cook. They have a *cuisinière*, who for low wages dresses the modest meals which are sufficient when they are alone;

and for great occasions they go to Chevet or some other *entrepreneur*, who provides them with a dinner at a fixed price, as low perhaps as ten francs a head, or as high as fifty. As soon as the soup and fish have gone round, I know from long and sometimes bitter experience who is my real host, what he is paid, and what will follow. I can tell a Chevet dinner, whether it is to be a ten-franc dinner or a fifty-franc dinner, at the first *entremets*. They give the key to the whole. The consequence is that the French *cuisine* is losing its fame. Chevet may have to provide 100, sometimes perhaps 200 dinners on the same day. He has a large staff of cooks and *marmitons;* but the minute attention to each dinner, indeed to each dish of each dinner, which a really good dinner requires, cannot be given. I have known true *gourmets*, after having dined with a minister, adjourn to a first-class *restaurateur* and there really dine — not that our *restaurateurs* are what they were. The public does not like to pay more than it used to do, though all the materials have doubled in price. The portions, therefore, become every day more elegantly small, and less and less exquisitely dressed. Democracy is the bane of refinement, in cookery, in apartments, in dress, and in manners. The manners of the *ancien régime* were as superior to ours as the old Sèvres china is to the heavy, gaudy crockery of either the first Empire or of the second.

April 18*th*.—We dined at the Embassy, and

met Arthur Russell, who had left Rome four days ago.

He brings little news. Antonelli remains and is likely to remain in power, but the state of the Pope's health is alarming. He is tolerably well now, but not likely, it is thought, to resist the heats of summer.

I was rather surprised to meet in the evening Countess Duchâtel.

This is the first time for some years that I have seen there an Orleanist, at least any one whom I knew to be an Orleanist.

Sunday, April 19th.—We dined with the Peyronnets, and spent the evening at Thiers. He asked me what Drouyn de Lhuys thought of the Polish question.

Senior.—He tells me that France, England, and Austria, have sent identical notes to Russia, pointing out the danger to Europe occasioned by the present state of Poland, but suggesting no remedy.

Thiers.—There can be no remedy until the Poles are civilised enough to submit to the fate which the crimes and follies of their ancestors, and of their neighbours, have inflicted on them—until they cease to try to make their government work ill. No people, whether Polish, or Irish, or Venetian, can be well governed against its will. It is cruelty to encourage the insurrection by holding out the hope of French assistance. There is not now in Europe a man who could lead an army of 250,000 six hundred miles from its frontier. The history of the world furnishes only half-a-dozen such men, Alexander, Hannibal, Genghis Khan, Timour, Fernando Cortez, and Napoleon, are all that occur to me. A general, good, or even first-rate, for ordinary war, loses his head as soon as he is two months', or even one month's march from his base of operations. Mad as *Celui-ci* is, I do not fear his making such an attempt.

My fears turn towards the Baltic. Sweden is arming. She could, if necessary, furnish three or four vessels, and 80,000 good troops. She is burning to recover Finland. She lost it by the wild, aggressive war which she made against Russia. She believes that when Russia is encumbered by her emancipation and by the Polish rebellion, the time is come for attacking her, on the pretence of assisting the Polish insurgents. This new doctrine of the right, or as it is now called the duty, of making war on a friendly sovereign, on the ground that you think that he misgoverns a portion of his subjects, puts one in mind of the worst proclamations of 1793. The Swedes count on the encouragement, and when they are beaten, as they will be, on the help, of France. I have no doubt that we shall encourage them, and if we do so, if will be difficult not to assist them.

Senior.—And could you assist them with success?

Thiers.—No; not even at the expense of a general war, for in such a war we should have all Europe against us, and *Celui-ci* is not the man to do what his uncle could not do. A French and Swedish fleet, and an army of 150,000 men, might burn Cronstadt, and perhaps St. Petersburg, but that would not bring Russia on her knees. Nothing but the exhaustion of a long war, an exhaustion worse than that produced by the Crimean campaign, will induce her to grant independence to even the kingdom of Poland; and if we were to engage in such an enterprise, we must ask for much more.

I am puzzled and alarmed by what I hear from America. What motive can the Federals have for forcing a war on you?

Senior.—The only motive that is suggested is that the Federal Government wishes to throw on us the blame of their eventual defeat.

Thiers.—Such a war would delight *Celui-ci*, who is burning with desire to recognise the South, to break the blockade, and to punish the Federals for their opposition to his Mexican expedition. But during the short time that it lasted it would do great damage to the whole civilised world, and it would give to the Confederates, that is, to the maintainers and propagators of slavery, whatever frontier they wished for. And the only real question now left us is, What shall be their frontier?

Monday, April 20th.—We breakfasted with Madame Cornu, and met there Renan, and Maury, librarian of the Institute, the Emperor's principal assistant in his *Life of Cæsar.* I asked Madame Cornu when she had last seen the Emperor.

Madame Cornu.—Yesterday. It is arranged that I go to him every Sunday at five and stay till a quarter to seven, when he has to dress for dinner; but often, as was the case yesterday, he keeps me much longer, and then has to run for it, that he may not exhaust the patience of the Empress and of the *chef*. He delights to talk to a person not bound by etiquette, who can question him, and contradict him, and talk over all his youth. I never conceal my republican opinions, and he treats them as the harmless follies of a woman.

Yesterday he was in very high spirits. I suspect that he has just made up his mind on some subject that has been teasing him. He dislikes coming to a decision, but, perhaps, for that very reason, when he has done so, he feels relieved and happy. He may have decided what to do about Poland, or what to write about some questionable anecdote of Cæsar, or when the elections shall be. I think that it may have been about Poland. I told him that in some classes of society I found an opinion that the forcible intervention of France alone in favour of Poland was impracticable. His answer was, '*Ey, ey.*'

Senior.—Seriously, or contemptuously?

Madame Cornu.—Laughingly, and contemptuously. His '*Ey, ey,*' may have meant nothing, but I think that it meant something. There certainly has been a great pressure on him to take up the cause of the Polish insurgents. There are the wildest ideas as to the political importance of Poland. The war party talks of a Poland twice as large as Prussia, and onethird more populous, which is to be the ally of France, and her citadel interposed between Russia, Austria, and Prussia—a check on them all. It affirms that it would be an easy thing to march on Poland by land, and that the sight of the first French uniform would raise up a Polish population of twenty millions. It associates Poland with the proudest times of the Empire. The *émeutiers* recollect that the Poles have always fought by their sides, have often been their leaders, and sometimes their exciters. The army is, as it always is, and perhaps ought to be, furious for war. The Catholic party hopes to make a religious war. It cares not what damage it may do to the country, if it can do good to the Pope, and harm to the Greek Church and to its schismatic head. Though the peasantry of the provinces is pacific, the low town population (and it is the population of towns, or rather of Paris, that governs France) is always warlike. It does not suffer—or does not know that it suffers—the miseries of war, and it delights in its excitement. If the insurrection be put down within a couple of months, or within three months, it will be a *fait accompli*, and be forgotten. But if it lasts, if it be carried on with heroic courage on the part of the Poles, and with barbarity on the part of the Russians, a force will be put on Louis Napoleon, which I doubt his being able to withstand. Again, if the new Chamber should be intolerable, and no one knows how it may act, he may dissolve it, appeal to the people in defence of Poland, and flatter them by promises of which war must be the result. It will be a very dangerous expedient, but he is accustomed to rush into dangerous enterprises, and to succeed in them.

There is one subject, however, on which he has not decided, and that is, the time of his candidature for the Academy. Pasquier's vacancy is to be filled up on Thursday next. His mind is still set on pronouncing Pasquier's *éloge*.

'I wish,' he said to me, 'that I could get some one to propose me as a candidate.'

'That is not the practice,' I said to him, 'the candidate presents himself.'

'I am shy,' he answered. 'If my *Cæsar*, or even the first volume of it, had appeared, I should feel that I had some claims; but I am not vain enough to think, that what I have published as yet entitles me to the honour of being a member of the first literary society in the world. I want somebody to say so for me. You may think that I ought to delay my candidature till the *Cæsar* has appeared; but I know now whom I should succeed, and whose *éloge* I should have to pronounce. If I delay, I may have to make a speech in praise of Feuillet or Victor Hugo.'

Senior.—You have read his *Cæsar* as far as it has gone; will it give him a claim to the Academy?

Maury.—I think that it will. It is a work of great and sagacious research, and contains passages admirably written. It is a wonderful improvement on the *Idées Napoléoniennes*.

Senior.—When Louis Napoleon wrote the *Idées Napoléoniennes* he was already a practised writer. He had been for years writing in the Pas du Calais journal, *Le Progrès*. It is seldom that a writer improves much after he is fifty. The only instance of an English writer that I recollect is that of Dr. Johnson, whose best written work, *The Lives of the Poets*, was written after he was seventy.

Maury.—That may be the case in England, where you enjoy a language freer from arbitrary restraints and idioms than ours is, and where you prefer the substance to the form. *La forme* is our idol. It resembles cookery. The best meat ill cooked is uneatable. Inferior meat well cooked may be delicious. We have been at work refining our style, introducing into it *des malices et des délicatesses*, until to write perfect French is the acquisition of only a long life. Our best writers—Voltaire, for instance—have gone on improving till they died. We spend much of what you would call useless labour on style. We omit ideas worth preserving, because we cannot express them with perfect elegance. We are sometimes in the state of a man speaking a foreign language, *qui ne dit pas ce qu'il veut, mais ce qu'il peut*, but we have created a literature which will live, for it is the style, not the matter, which preserves a book. Good matter ill expressed is taken possession of by a master of style, and reproduced in a readable form, and then the first writer is forgotten.

Tuesday, April 21st.—I called on Auguste Chevalier, and found him immersed in his business of editor of the *Constitutionnel* and *Pays.*

Senior.—How came you to undertake so troublesome and invidious an office?

A. Chevalier.—Of course, much against my wish; But the Government, especially my intimate friend Persigny, was in great difficulty. He had discovered that the late editor had been bribed by —— with 60,000 francs to oppose the Emperor's policy in Italy. That policy, you know, has changed, principally I suspect through the influence of the Empress. A violent paper, supposed to be written by Prince Napoleon, attacking the temporal power of the Pope, was to have appeared in the *Constitutionnel.* It had already been printed, when we found it out and stopped its distribution. It was necessary to dismiss the editor and supply a new one at a moment's notice. Persigny in his distress applied to me, and I could not refuse him. But it is a *métier de galérien.* I began to work at five this morning. I shall give it up as soon as we can find some honest hand to receive it. Honesty is rare among French political men, and the editor of a paper supposed to represent the feelings of the Government is peculiarly tempted. I wonder that my predecessor accepted anything so ignoble as 60,000 francs. He might have had 500,000.

Senior.—Who gave him to the Government?

A. Chevalier.—We inherited him from the Prince

de Polignac. Mirès had put him into the management of the *Pays* when he owned it.

Senior.—As you express the opinions of the Government, of course you know them. What is to be done with Rome?

A. Chevalier.—Nothing at present; our master, as you know, does not like to be hurried. I am not sure that in retarding the evacuation of Rome the Empress has not served the cause of the Italians. They are mad enough, if they were not restrained by our presence, to attack Austria, as they have done three times already; and it is not certain that we shall not leave them the next time to their fate.

Senior.—What are the relations between the Prince and the Emperor?

A. Chevalier.—Always changing, and never well understood. I believe that the Emperor is better disposed towards his cousin than his cousin is towards him. He is the elder; he educated the Prince; he has been his patron. Without him the Prince would never have been more than M. Bonaparte, with a great name and nothing to support it. The Emperor's affection for his family and for his old friends, even for his old acquaintances, is the redeeming part of his character.

Senior.—And what are you to do about Poland?

A. Chevalier.—Nothing, at least at present. We are treating the fever *avec la médecine expectative*. I was commissioned three days ago to administer a sedative in the *Pays*.

Senior.—I have not seen it.

A. Chevalier.—I have not the paper, but I can give you the proofs as they were settled by a great person.

He gave me a paper, of which I copy the end:

'Rien ne se ressemble moins que la situation actuelle et celle de 1859. Il s'agissait alors d'une question brûlante où la France n'était pas libre de ne pas agir. La guerre entre l'Autriche et le Piémont qui avait avec lui les populations Italiennes, était imminente. Il fallait ou consentir à voir l'Autriche dominer toute l'Italie jusqu'à nos frontières, ou parer à ce danger.

'Aujourd'hui, rien de pareil. Une question d'humanité, d'ordre européen, de sympathie pour un peuple brave et malheureux, mais aucun danger pour la France—voilà la situation.

'Dans ces circonstances, la France n'est ni plus ni moins engagée que les grandes puissances de l'Europe. Il n'y a pas de question française. Il n'y a qu'une question européenne.

'L'entente avec l'Angleterre, avec l'Autriche, et avec presque tous les états de l'Europe, ôte aux circonstances actuelles la gravité qu'on voudrait leur donner. L'union des grandes puissances suffit amplement pour amener une solution honorable, sans que la France ait à se jeter, seule, dans les aventures.

'Les journaux qui s'efforcent d'assimiler deux époques si différentes trompent donc le public, comme ils se trompent eux-mêmes.'

Senior.—And what will you do in the American affair?

A. Chevalier.—As much for the South as you will let us do. The Emperor is intensely Southern. If you did not urge him to be neutral, he would recognise the South, break the blockade, and be delighted if it occasioned a war; not that he loves the South, but that he hates the North. I believe that his disgust at their insolent Munroe doctrine was one of his motives for the Mexican expedition.

Senior.—Will you make Mexico an Algeria?

A. Chevalier.—I hope not; but when we are talking of what may be done by such a man as Louis Napoleon, and such a people as the French, no one can prophesy. We have qualities which Tocqueville attributed to the Americans, marvellous propensities to commit follies, and marvellous dexterity in escaping their worst effects.

I called on Buffet.

He has been reading my *Irish Journal*, and objects to Bishop Fitzgerald's statement that the Roman Catholic Church forbids inquiry.

Buffet.—Our doctrine is that the Church is infallible. If, therefore, a man professing to be a Roman Catholic were to tell his bishop that he doubted the truth of any doctrine, the bishop would have to prove to him that it was accepted or rejected by the Church, and require him to accept the decision of the Church as conclusive. Just as your Privy Council did not inquire whether Mr. Gorham's opinions were true or false, but simply whether they were or were not consistent with the Thirty-nine Articles. The syllogism would be this. What the Church says is true ; the Church says *this;* therefore this is true. But if, instead of denying or doubting the minor premiss, the inquirer doubted or denied the major, that is to say, the infallibility of the Church, the bishop would not only allow but enjoin him to inquire into it.

Senior.—And would he allow him to search for evidence on each side of the question? to read heretical books, and talk to heretics?

Buffet.—Certainly.

Senior.—And if he were unconvinced, would he be damned?

Buffet.—The Church affirms the damnation of only one man, Judas. As to all others, it admits the possibility that they may have sufficiently repented or believed, even *in articulo mortis.*

Senior.—And if they have died in unbelief?

Buffet.—The Church admits that those who have died in invincible ignorance, that is to say, who have never enjoyed an opportunity of hearing the truth, may be saved ; but if they have had that opportunity, and have neglected it, or rejected it, and have disbelieved until death, of course they must be damned. And you Protestants are no better. You accept the Athanasian creed, which affirms that unless a man holds, pure and undefiled, the true doctrine of the Trinity, without doubt he shall perish everlastingly.

Senior.—I asked the Bishop of Algiers whether it were necessary to salvation to believe in the Immaculate Conception.

'Certainly,' he answered, 'since the Pope has defined it. To deny it now is heresy, and heresy is a mortal sin. If ten of the bishops, I believe three or four hundred in number, whom the Pope consulted before he defined that doctrine had dissented from it, it would not have become a dogma, and might still have been denied without incurring the guilt and the eternal punishment of heresy.'

April 22nd.—Circourt breakfasted with us. I mentioned to him Thiers' fears of an attack on Russia by Sweden, which might draw France into war.

Circourt.—I have no such fears. The Swedes must know that Finland is irrecoverably lost to them. They ruled it oppressively. Not a Fin was allowed to take part in the management of his own country. It is now one of the best-governed countries in the world. The population consists of about 50,000 Russians, 250,000 Swedes, and 1,600,000 Fins. The Finnish population had doubled since Finland became Russian. They detest Sweden, and are loyal Russians.

Senior.—How do you account for the popularity of Russian rule in Finland, and its unpopularity in Poland?

Circourt.—The causes are religion and race. The Fins are Lutherans, enjoying the best form of Christianity. The Poles are Roman Catholics, subject to the worst. Lutherans are tolerant, and are satisfied with toleration. Roman Catholics require supremacy. In Russian and Prussian Poland, and in Lithuania, they are merely on a par with the other Christian sects.

Senior.—Are they on a par? We heard of persecution under Nicholas. We heard of outrages inflicted on the abbess and the nuns of a convent at Minsk to force them to apostatize to the Greek creed.

Circourt.—I do not believe a word of these stories. I do not believe that there ever was such an abbess, or such nuns, or such a convent. The lies of the Poles are beyond description or enumeration. Never believe a word a Pole tells you. He secretes and then pours out falsehood naturally, almost unconsciously. The Lutheran Fins are not merely unpersecuted: their clergy are paid by the State. Then they are an admirable race,—honest, diligent, quiet, and moral. They are among the happiest people in Europe, as the Poles are among the unhappiest. The Polish peasantry are less miserable than the nobles, or the townspeople, because they are better; but they are idle, dirty, and superstitious. The townspeople and the nobles have these faults, and all the others that belong to a subject race which has once been dominant.

All my information leads me to believe that the insurrection is subsiding. A friend who reached Paris a few days ago from Warsaw, tells me that he saw no signs of it. The letters come punctually in six days. The railways are untouched. The peasants have not joined in it. I do not believe that it is really much more important than the brigandage of Naples. I know that the Russian Government is anxious to do for the Poles all that can be done for them without injustice to its other subjects. It cannot surrender to Poland a population of 5,000,000 of Russians in its western provinces in order to please scarcely more than 1,000,000 of Poles. It is ready to execute the Treaty of Vienna, by giving to its Polish subjects a national representation and national institutions, *réglées d'après le mode d'existence politique qu'il jugera utile et convenable de leur accorder.* I believe that it would consent even to exempt the Poles of the kingdom from the conscription.

Senior.—Perhaps it would be better to make the conscription over the whole empire depend on ballot. The old mode of effecting it by the arbitrary designation of the local authorities seems inconsistent with the abolition of serfdom. Such proceedings as those which occasioned this insurrection would then be impossible.

Circourt.—I do not believe that the conscription was the cause of the insurrection, though it was the occasion on which it exploded. The mine had been long prepared.

Senior.—By whom?

Circourt.—By the great anarchical party,—by the party of which Mazzini is the type, perhaps the head.

It might have broken out in Hungary or in Venetia. No amount of good government short of the good government which makes a whole population loyal, would have prevented it. Bad government might have done so by crushing the spirit of the whole nation. But I have no doubt that what you suggest ought to be done, and will be done. The institutions of Russia are rapidly improving. The abolition of serfdom, a change which, for the number of the persons, and the importance of the interests, that it affects, and the rapidity with which it has been carried through, has not, and probably never will have, a parallel in history, is succeeding admirably. After a brief indecision, the peasants have set to work diligently and cordially to cultivate their own fields and to redeem their obligations to their former lords. In a short time Russia will be a comparatively well-governed country. The state of the Polish *petite noblesse* is hopeless. Their prejudices of cast, unsupported by property, must keep them, under any government, restless and miserable; but the rest of the nation has its destiny in its own hands. It may, if it will, be a prosperous part of a prosperous empire.

Senior.—There seems to be no chance of the leaders of this movement acquiescing in such a destiny. The Polish Provisional Government answers the Czar's amnesty by declaring that—' It was not with the intention of obtaining more or less liberal institutions that we took up arms, but to get rid of the detested yoke of a foreign government, and to reconquer our ancient and complete independence.'

Circourt.—In such language, I recognise the incurable folly of the Polish nobility. Independence means the right of 85,000 families to oppress four millions of their fellow-countrymen, and six or seven millions more of people who differ from them in race or in religion, and belong to them only because they inhabit countries which, two or three hundred years ago, went by the name of Poland.

April 23*rd.*—I spent the evening at the Duc de Broglie's. He talked to me, as every Frenchman does, about the dangerous relations of England to America.

Duc de Broglie.—I suspect that *Celui-ci* is trying to envenom them. He has been torpid for some time, and the usual result has come; our eyes, no longer fixed on foreign affairs, are looking to our own. This is always dangerous to him, but especially on the eve of an election. He wants a *coup de théâtre*. A war for Poland would be inconsistent with his secret engagement to Russia. The Mexican war goes on slowly, and neither its objects nor its causes are intelligible. He wishes to do something great, and quickly. Now, if he could engage you in a war with the Federals, or merely get you to recognise the Confederates, he would instantly follow your example. He would make an alliance with the South, obtain her toleration of his Mexican attempts, break the blockade, restore prosperity to our cotton manufactures, and establish French influence over all America, from the Potomac to Brazil. And it could be done in three months. He would gratify, too, his old grudge against the North; and against the French aristocracy, whose sympathies are generally Northern. I should regret it, because it would leave the South far stronger than I wish to see it.

Senior.—Or than I wish to see it. But it really seems as if the North meant to save him the trouble.

Duc de Broglie.—Their conduct is marvellous; it is incomprehensible. It shows how impossible it is to infer what will be the conduct of a nation, at least of a democratic nation, from its interests. If there be any nation in the world whom it is the interest of America to conciliate, it is England. The North thinks—I believe truly—that you do not sympathise with it.

Senior.—We did sympathise with it at first; but, of course, that sympathy was destroyed as soon as it openly threatened that, as soon as it had settled with the South, it would attack us.

Duc de Broglie.—Well, the more your sympathies were Southern, the more the North ought to have tried to avoid giving you just cause of complaint. Yet she has heaped, and is heaping on you, injuries and insults which I scarcely think you ought to bear. Sailors are not politicians. If your forbearance exceeds the limits by which the honour of a nation requires it to be confined—and you are very near those limits—you will discourage them. They will lose the courage—I had almost said the audacity—which ought to belong to their profession. Of this I feel certain, that a conduct towards us, even in the pacific government of Louis Philippe, one-tenth as offensive as the conduct of America towards you has been, and is, would have produced an immediate war.

April 24*th*.—Circourt called on us. The map of America was on the table.

Circourt.—I will show you what I expect to be the political map of America three or four years hence. It will consist of at least three Empires. The Western Empire, formed of Washington, Oregon, Nevada, California, Utah, Colorado, New Mexico, Anzona, Kansas, Nebraska, and Dakota. The Southern Empire, divided from the Northern by the Missouri River from its source down to its confluence with the Mississippi; then by the Mississippi down to its confluence with the Ohio; then by the Ohio up to the mouth of the Kankawa River; then by a line crossing the Virginia mountains, and running to the Potomac; and, lastly, by the Potomac itself, and the bay of Chesapeake. This would give to each empire a well-defined frontier.

Senior.—It would give the greater part of the Border States to the Confederates.

Circourt.—They will not be satisfied with less, and in a short time they will dictate their own terms.

The Federals seem to be bent on suicide, and it is by suicide that empires generally perish. Repeated defeats and disappointments may not break their spirit, but they disturb their reason; as the danger of irretrievable defeat grows nearer and nearer and looks larger and larger, they lose their presence of mind, and rush in to destruction, as if they were fascinated.

The terror of the Federals is foreign intervention, and they are right in believing that it would be fatal to them, but yet, as if, to repeat the word, they were fascinated, they are doing what will inevitably bring it on. They put me in mind of the bird that, in its extremity of alarm, runs into the serpent's jaws. Their insults and injuries must drive you into war.

Senior.—They may easily drive us into recognition of the South, but with more difficulty into war.

Circourt.—They tell the world that negotiations will be followed by war. I trust that you will take up the challenge which they have been offering to you for two years. It does not become a great and spirited nation to allow itself to be deterred by threats from an act of justice. We have been expecting you to do so for some months, and our master is eager to join you.

The next thing for you to do is to join us heartily in giving a good government to Mexico.

Mexico must either be a monarchy, untainted by slavery, and protected by France and England, or another Texas, a dependence of the Southern Anglo-American Empire, peopled by slaves and semi-barbarous whites. On the result of our interference depends the question whether it shall be a Brazil, a peaceful empire, representing in America European civilisation, and European respect for international law, or a portion of a great Anglo-American republic — anarchical and miserable within, and aggressive, unscrupulous, and mischievous without.

You committed a gross blunder when you withdrew from us last year. You were much more interested in rescuing Mexico from anarchy than we were. It was a God-send for you that we were Quixotic enough *pour tirer les marons du feu*. If we had not done so, you must have done so yourselves, or you would in a very few years have seen Mexico joined to the Southern Confederacy, and the largest and most powerful slave state in the world.

You may now repair your folly. I strongly urge you at the same time, if you can on the same day, to recognise the Confederates, and to go to the assistance of the well-intentioned and civilised party in Mexico — that which desires an European sovereign. You may perhaps thereby precipitate a war with the Federals, but in their frantic state of mind, I do not think that you can avoid one, and in that case the sooner it comes the better.*

---

* *Extract from the 'Times,' of November* 22, 1879.

'On the 17th inst., at his residence at La Celle, St. Cloud, near Paris, died, of apoplexy, Adolphe Comte de Circourt, at the age of upwards of seventy. Although from circumstances and from the modesty of his disposition, M. de Circourt played, with rare exceptions, no part in public life, and has left no important literary work behind him, few men of our time were more widely known in the most cultivated circles of France, England, Germany, Italy, Russia, and America. With a perfect command of the languages of all these nations, he corresponded with most of the distinguished men of his own generation. His knowledge of history and literature was inexhaustible, and his memory never at fault. To these qualities and attainments he added a highminded and chivalrous spirit, and a most affectionate disposition. Of his powers of conversation, Mr. Senior's volumes contain abundant evidence. Sprung from a noble family of Franche-Comté, and educated in the strictest principles of the Royalist party, M. de Circourt entered life with distinguished favour at the Court of Charles X., and was appointed private secretary to Prince Polignac. The Revolution of 1830 destroyed his political prospects, and he withdrew to Geneva, where he married one of the most accomplished women of her time, a Russian lady, Mdlle. de Klustyn. Although content to share the fate of his party, M. de Circourt renounced the intolerance and illiberality of their opinions, and his house in Paris became and remained for many years one of the most brilliant centres of culture and society. After the Revolution of 1848 he accepted from his friend, M. de Lamartine, the office of French Minister at Berlin, which he filled for some months. This was his only public appointment. His extraordinary attainments would have amply qualified him for a seat in more than one branch of the French Institute; but he disclaimed through life

April 27th.—Guizot, Changarnier, and Lady Ashburton, breakfasted with us.

Guizot.—Of the four great bodies now left in France,—the legal, the ecclesiastical, the administrative, and the military, the last is the only thoroughly good one. We have more than 6000 judges, at salaries rising from 105*l.* a-year to 1500*l.* Every appointment and every promotion depends on the favour of the Government. The life of every judge is a struggle, first for existence and afterwards for comfort; it is therefore one of servile subservience.

The Church is equally subservient, but to a foreign master—the Pope. The instant a boy enters a seminary, he ceases to be a Frenchman. He ceases indeed to belong to any country. He is not even an Italian : he is a Papist. His whole thoughts, his whole exertions, his whole opinions, are devoted to the predominance of the Papal power.

As to the administrative body, that is the blind instrument of the executive. Its 35,000 maires, its hundreds of *préfets* and *sous-préfets*, its thousands of *cantonniers* and *gardes champêtres*, in the provinces ;

---

all official distinctions and honours. His existence was devoted to his studies and his friends, and to a vast and ubiquitous correspondence which gratified at once his curiosity and his tastes. In the annals of Parisian society in the third and fourth decades of this century his name and that of his accomplished wife will retain a lasting place, and there are few parts of the globe in which these lines may not excite a feeling of regret at the loss of so large-hearted and upright a man.'

and in the towns its tens of thousands of *receveurs*, policemen, gendarmerie, and *employés* of different names and attributions, all appointed, promoted, and dismissed by the Government,—not one of whom, whatever be his misconduct, can be prosecuted without its consent,—form, with the judges, the chains with which France is pinned to the earth.

Senior.—I thought that the great chain was the army?

Guizot.—On the contrary; the army is the only body that has freedom, or that preserves any freedom for the others. Soldiers have leisure, they live together, many of them read—all talk; they have political opinions and convictions, they are drawn from the soundest portion of our population,—the small farmers, or, as we call them, peasants. They are proud of their profession, but not slaves to it; for everyone hopes that as soon as he has paid his debt to his country, he shall return to his cottage, and his parents, and his *fiancée*. They are beloved by the peasantry. You see, in the neighbourhood of their quarters crowds of women and children, to whom they distribute the remains of their rations.

Senior.—But is not the army the support of this despotism?

Guizot.—A portion of the army, brought from Africa, and corrupted for the purpose, surprised Paris, and enabled Louis Napoleon to turn out an unpopular Assembly and to overturn an absurd, unworkable constitution. And the whole army is the friend of order, and would rather retain the Empire than run the risk of a revolution.

Senior.—But is not the Emperor popular in the army?

Changarnier.—No. His military pretensions are -despised ; and, as a politician, he is accused of wasting his soldiers in wars in which France has no interest. The soldiers call the Mexican war 'Duke Jecker's war,' because it is supposed by them to be made for the purpose of enforcing Jecker's claims on the Mexican Government, in which the Duc de Morny is believed to have an interest.

Senior.—Considering what a thing it is to command 150,000 men, and that he made the experiment for the first time after he was fifty, he seems to me to have done well.

Changarnier.—I will not say that he did as ill as is possible,—for the Austrians did still worse; but his folly and incapacity were second only to theirs. He marched his 150,000 men in one long line, which any but the silliest imbeciles would have cut through in half-a-dozen places.

Only Hesse's stopping the Austrians for four hours on their march to Magenta, and the accident that the Austrian force that encountered MacMahon at Casale, retreated towards Magenta instead of towards Verona, and led MacMahon after them, saved him from utter ruin at Magenta. Only the inconceivable folly, or cowardice of Lichtenstein, who kept inactive 35,000 cavalry on our left, saved him from utter ruin at

Solferino. When he returned to Paris, at the foot of the Grand Staircase of the Tuileries, after he had kissed his child and the Empress, he turned back to the crowd of military men behind him and exclaimed, 'Never till I made this campaign had I the least idea of the genius of my Uncle.'

He was always surprised. He was surprised at Montebello, and at Magenta, and at Solferino. He always would believe that the enemy in front of them was a mere *reconnaissance*. Perhaps, however, that was an excuse for his quitting, as he always did, the field.

Senior.—I know that you doubt his courage.

Changarnier.—I remember telling you when we were together at Héry some years ago, that I thought the courage with which he forms his schemes very great. The chances that his Strasbourg and that his Boulogne attempts would terminate fatally were enormous. But that like many men of vivid imagination, he quails before the danger when it is actually present. His running into the sea at Boulogne was the act of a man who had lost his self-possession. During the whole of the Italian campaign he can scarcely be said to have been under fire, except that a spent ball once came near him.

During the battles of Magenta and Solferino he kept a couple of miles in the rear, and never gave an order. All that he did was to smoke. I know the great functionary whose duty it is to be the Imperial cigar-bearer. He keeps three or four boxes, each of which contains twenty-five cigars. Before the battle of Solferino was over two had been emptied, and three cigars had been taken from the third. It seems as if the intrepidity which once characterised the Bonaparte family was wearing out.

With regard to Prince Napoleon, it was unwise to put a man of his age, who had never heard a gun fired, in a responsible position. The feeling of responsibility at first disturbs a man; but it soon renders him insensible to danger, or to anything except his immediate duty. I have sometimes reflected with astonishment on what I had gone through. I remember breakfasting in a hut among the wounded and the dying. The remembrance of it some hours after nearly made me sick. I could not conceive how I could have eaten among such scenes; but I thought nothing of them at the time.

Senior.—To return to Louis Napoleon. Is he not popular with the Garde?

Changarnier.—Without doubt he is; but at an enormous sacrifice—at the sacrifice of popularity with the rest of the army. A Garde may be of two kinds. It may be what Napoleon's Garde was, a *corps d'élite* taken from the best men in the army, and employed on great occasions. Such was Napoleon's Garde. His army contained 800,000 men; his Garde did not contain more than 20,000; yet he says to King Joseph, 'The whole army of France is unable to furnish my Garde, without being somewhat enfeebled in spirit. Consider the harm that has been done to the armies of Holland and Naples, by the loss of the men who have been taken for the Gardes of those two countries. I could mention a regiment, once excellent, which the King of Holland has ruined for me. It is now worth nothing.

'You have withdrawn the best companies from some of my regiments for your Garde. This will disorganize them. Recollect that it takes six campaigns to form the character of a regiment, and that it can be destroyed in one moment.'*

Such a Garde is not unpopular, since every soldier may hope to be a member of it; and because it is the post of honour it is the post of danger. Napoleon employed his on every desperate service. The mischief of such a Garde is that it takes from the Ligne the four or five per cent of men who have real vigour and courage, whose example is necessary to leaven the rest.

The other kind of Garde is a mere privileged corps, selected not for good service, but for their stature, or by favour; such are your English Guards. They are of course unpopular. Such is Louis Napoleon's Garde. It has higher pay, better quarters, and greater indulgences than the rest of the army, and it is much less exposed to hardships and danger. It is therefore an object of jealousy and dislike to the Ligne. If a serious *émeute* should occur, the Ligne will give no cordial assistance to the Garde; and if that *émeute* were to extend to the bourgeoisie, and were the produce

---

* Letters of March 20th and May 4th, 1807.

of serious and widely extended discontent, the Ligne would parley with the *émeutiers*, and at last, perhaps, join them. It is from such an *émeute* that I expect the fall of *Celui-ci*.

I met yesterday at Drouyn de Lhuys Don Gutierrez de Estrada, whom Drouyn de Lhuys and Circourt, who both know him well, have described to me as the most intelligent and the most honest Mexican whom they know. I called on him this morning. I asked him to give me a sketch of his history.

Estrada.—I was born in 1800, became a member of the Mexican Senate in 1833, and Minister of Foreign Affairs in 1834. We were then under the Federal Republic. In 1836 we adopted a centralised Republic. I did not disapprove of the change, but I did not think it advisable to remain in office under a new constitution. I left America for Europe, and did not return until 1840.

I was then struck by the terrible changes which those four years had produced. They had been years of revolutions. Wealth, cultivation, almost civilisation, had disappeared. The Americans had driven us out of Texas; the French, tired out by the injustice and the robberies inflicted on them by the successive ephemeral governments, had seized the Castle of St. Jean d'Ulloa. Bastamente was President. I felt then, as I feel now, our utter unfitness for republican government, and I published a pamphlet, in which I urged the people to return to monarchy, the only government under which, bad as our monarchy had been, we had enjoyed anything resembling prosperity or tranquillity.

Of course I had to leave the country. I passed about a year in Cuba, and then went to Europe.

From that time until now I have been trying to realise my plan of a Mexican monarchy. It appeared to me that a Spanish prince was out of the question, Mexico would not accept him. The mutual jealousy of France and England was an insurmountable objection to a French or an English one: Prussia was too timid to give one, and a Russian would come from an unpopular stock. I resolved, therefore, to try Austria. Prince Metternich received me very kindly, and with his acquiescence I proposed the Mexican throne to Archduke Frederic. He was willing to accept it. I then talked the matter over with Lord Clarendon. He also approved of my plans, but urged the importance of avoiding raising the jealousy of the United States. The Munroe doctrine was then in vigour, and he would do nothing which might be construed as an attack upon it. I then consulted Louis Philippe. He embraced the plan cordially—almost eagerly. And I really think that it might have been effected if the unhappy Spanish marriages had not destroyed the alliance between France and England, and defeated any scheme requiring their co-operation. Then came 1848, and Europe was too agitated for any one to care about American affairs.

Mexico, however, was every day getting worse and

worse, and a large majority of the educated classes began to join in my opinions, or rather began to whisper them. Among them was Santa Anna, who, in March 1854, was, for the third or fourth time, proclaimed Dictator.

In July in that year he gave me a commission to obtain from France, England, Spain, or Austria, a sovereign for Mexico.

Here is a translation of it :—

'Antonio Lopez de Santa Anna, Général de division, Grand maître de l'ordre national de Guadalupe, Chevalier Grand Croix de l'ordre royal de Charles III. et Président de la République Mexicaine.

'A tous ceux qui liront ces présentes, Salut.

'Autorisé par la nation Mexicaine à la constituer sous la forme de gouvernement qui me semblera la plus convenable pour assurer l'intégrité de son territoire et son indépendance nationale d'une manière avantageuse et stable, en vertu des facultés discrétionnelles dont je suis investi;

'Considérant d'ailleurs, qu'aucun gouvernement ne saurait être mieux approprié à la nation que celui auquel il a été habitué pendant des siècles et qui a formé ses mœurs intimes;

'Par ces raisons et à cette fin ayant confiance dans le patriotisme, le mérite, et le dévouement de M. José Maria Gutierrez Estrada, je lui ai conféré par les présentes, pleins pouvoirs nécessaires, pour qu'il puisse entrer en pourparlers avec les cours de Paris, de Vienne, Londres, et Madrid, et faire les ouvertures indispensables, afin d'obtenir de ces divers gouvernements ou de quelques uns d'eux l'établissement d'une monarchie émanée d'une des maisons dynastiques de ces puissances, moyennant les dispositions et les clauses stipulées dans les instructions spéciales.

'En foi de quoi, j'ai fait expédier les présentes, signées de ma main et contresignées par le ministre des affaires étrangères avec la formule habituelle.

'Dans le Palais National de Mexico, le 1er Juillet, 1854.

'(Signé)   A. L. DE SANTA ANNA.'

Santa Anna's power did not last long. In August, 1855, alarmed by an insurrection of which Alvarez was at the head, he left Mexico. and took refuge in Cuba. Alvarez was driven out in 1856 by Comonfort.

In January, 1858, Comonfort was beaten by Zuloaga, in a battle in the streets of Mexico, which lasted for seven days.

Zuloaga of course became President. His government was opposed by a party at the head of which was Juarez. Zuloaga resigned, and took refuge in the British Embassy. Juarez declared himself President, and established himself at Vera Cruz. Miramon, who had been Zuloaga's best general, was declared President by the town of Mexico.

The war between Juarez and Miramon lasted until the end of 1860, supported on each side by confiscation and robbery of both natives and foreigners. Miramon seized 1,400,000 dollars belonging to British subjects, and deposited in the British Embassy. Juarez seized at Guanasuarto 180,000 dollars belonging principally to the English.

In February, 1860, this deplorable war seemed likely to end in favour of Miramon.

He was besieging Vera Cruz, in which Juarez had shut himself up. Two vessels, one under the Mexican flag, the other Spanish, laden with supplies for him, were captured, without the least pretence of right, by an American ship.

He was forced to give up the siege, retired on Mexico, fought a battle before the town, was deserted while it was going on by his cavalry, reached Mexico, and obtained the protection of the French consul.

Juarez entered Mexico, and, as his first act, ordered the Spanish minister to quit the country. He passed a law suspending for two years all the payments which had been secured to foreign governments by treaty. Then it was that England, France, and Spain resolved to obtain redress by the only means that were left to them.

When the allied fleets reached the Mexican coast, when their commanders, by their proclamation of the 10th of January, 1861, declared that 'besides obtaining satisfaction for the outrages inflicted on their nations, they had a higher interest, one of more general and beneficent consequence; that they came to stretch a friendly hand to a people on whom Providence had showered all its gifts, and whom they saw with grief wasting their strength and destroying their vitality under the violent action of civil war and perpetual convulsions,' I began, for the first time after many years, to hope for my country, I knew that its only chance of tranquillity was the obtaining a monarchical government; but the insolent refusal of the United States to allow it to adopt that form of government had led me to despair of it.

Senior.—When did they refuse?

Estrada.—General Scott, in his proclamation at Xalapa, peremptorily forbade it. 'There are among you,' he said, 'symptoms of a monarchical party. The United States will not allow such a party to establish itself or even to arise. They will not endure monarchy on American soil. I am here to put down any such party; I am here to annihilate it.' For years this proclamation lay like a weight on my breast. At length the civil war had broken up the tyranny of the United States, and restored freedom to the American Continent. At length the allied armies had given liberty of action and speech to Mexico. The long-repressed monarchical feeling could show itself. In the summer of 1861 I wrote to Rechberg, the Austrian minister, to repeat my wish to be allowed to propose an Austrian archduke for the Mexican throne. He answered cautiously, but not unfavourably. In the end of that year I visited the Archduke Maximilian himself. He did not throw cold water on my plans, but he required, as preliminaries, an unmistakable requisition from the Mexican people, and the support of the European powers. 'Austria,' he added, 'is too poor and too busy to take up your cause. Unless a French army will keep in check the anarchical party, we cannot commit ourselves.'

April 29*th.*—I received this morning from M. Drouyn de Lhuys the following note :—

'MON CHER MONSIEUR SENIOR,
 'Voulez-vous venir me voir demain Jeudi à 10h.
  'Tout à vous,
   'DROUYN DE LHUYS.'

April 30*th.*—I obeyed Drouyn de Lhuys' summons.

Drouyn de Lhuys.—The conduct of your Government in the Mexican business puzzles me. Your interests in Mexico are much more important than ours. You have more trade, more permanent establishments in the country, and you are more interested in putting an end to the Munroe doctrine and establishing in America a power sympathising with Europe, and a restraint on the ambition and the aggression of the Anglo-American states, whether united or separated. The strongest pictures of the state of Mexico at the time of our intervention, and of the hopelessness of obtaining redress or security from the usurpers, who successively seize its Presidential throne, are to be found in your correspondence on Mexican affairs. I have had a few passages cut out for you. Here they are:—

Sir C. Wyke to Lord J. Russell.

'*Mexico, June 27th*, 1861.

'It will be very difficult, if not impossible, to give your Lordship a correct idea of the present state of affairs in this unfortunate country, so utterly incomprehensible is the conduct of the Government, which, at present, presides over its destinies . . . The religious feelings of a fanatic population have been shocked by the destruction of churches and convents all over the country, and the disbanded monks and friars wandering about amongst the people fan the flame of discontent, which is kept alive by the women, who, as a body, are all in favour of the Church . . .

' In the meantime, Congress, instead of enabling the Government to put down the frightful disorder which reigns throughout the length and breadth of the land, is occupied in disputing about vain theories of so-called government on ultra-liberal principles, whilst the respectable part of the population is delivered up defenceless to the attacks of robbers and assassins, who swarm on the highroads and in the streets of the capital. The constitutional Government is unable to maintain its authority in the various

States of the Federation, which are becoming *de facto* perfectly independent; so that the same causes, which, under similar circumstances, broke up the Confederation of Central America into five separate republics, are now at work here, and will probably produce a like result. . . .

'Patriotism, in the common acceptation of the term, appears to be unknown, and no one man of any note is to be found in the ranks of either party. Contending factions struggle for the possession of power, only to gratify either their cupidity or their revenge; and in the meantime the country sinks lower and lower, whilst its population becomes brutalised and degraded to an extent frightful to contemplate.

'Such is the actual state of affairs in Mexico, and your Lordship will perceive, therefore, that there is little chance of justice or redress from such people, except by the employment of force to exact that which both persuasion and menaces have hitherto failed to obtain.'

SIR C. WYKE TO LORD J. RUSSELL.

'*Mexico, July* 28*th*, 1861.

'Since this day last month, when I had the honour of writing to your Lordship describing the state of affairs in this unfortunate country, matters here have only been going from bad to worse, and every day's experience only more clearly proves the imbecility and bad faith of a government now generally detested, and against which various conspiracies are on foot . . .

'Señor Comonfort, ex-President of the Republic, has arrived at Monterey, in Nuevo Leon, where it is said the Governor has made a *pronunciamento* in his favour, which will very likely be joined in by the neighbouring states, and probably aided by a party in this capital, who are thoroughly disgusted with the weak and tyrannical government of Señor Juarez.'

Sir C. Wyke to Lord J. Russell.

'*Mexico, August 27th*, 1861.

'During the past month the position of affairs has not materially changed in this country, where the hatred and contempt felt for the Government seem daily to increase . . .

'A more disgraceful state of things than that now existing here, it is impossible to conceive in any country pretending to call itself a civilised nation . . .

'The civil war now raging, and the weakness of the Government, have encouraged the Indian population to rise against the whites at Ixmiquilpana, about twenty leagues from here, where they have committed dreadful atrocities, thus adding a new element of discord and misery to those already existing. This movement, if not at once checked, may lead to terrible results, as the immense majority of the inhabitants of this Republic belong to the

Indian race, which is quite strong enough utterly to exterminate the degenerate and vitiated descendants of the old Spanish conquerors . . . All the respectable classes look forward with hope to a foreign intervention as the sole means of saving them from ruin, and preventing a dissolution of the Confederation, as well as a general rising of the Indians against the white population. If either Great Britain or France adopt coercive measures, the moderate party may take courage and be able to form a government which would afford some hope for the future; but without such support and assistance they are afraid to move, and will remain the victims of factions, whose dissensions have already caused so much misery and bloodshed.'

SIR C. WYKE TO EARL RUSSELL.

'*Mexico, Oct. 28th*, 1861.

. . . 'Every day's experience only tends to prove the utter absurdity of attempting to govern the country with the limited powers granted to the Executive by the present ultra-liberal Constitution, and I see no hope of improvement, unless it comes from a foreign intervention, or the formation of a rational government, composed of the leading men of the moderate party, who, however, at present, are void of moral courage, and afraid to move, unless with some material support from abroad.'

Sir C. Wyke to Earl Russell.

'*Vera Cruz, December* 29*th*, 1861.

... ' I am most anxious for the formation of a respectable government, who will understand that it is for their interest to receive the intervention in a friendly and not a hostile spirit, so as to aid them to re-establish order, and take the opinion of those who alone are entitled to have a voice in the matter. Hitherto, the men of property and intelligence have been completely silenced and domineered over by the rabble, who elected from their own class the members of a Congress, which, besides being a disgrace to the country, rendered anything like good government impossible.'

Drouyn de Lhuys.—You were the first to threaten the Mexican Government, to declare to it that your fleets were ready to enforce reparation. Our instructions to M. de Saligny were copied from yours to Sir Charles Wyke. It was you who drew up the Convention of November 1861, by which, after reciting in its preamble the necessity of seeking redress for the arbitrary and vexatious conduct of the Mexican authorities, England, France, and Spain, agreed to despatch to Mexico combined naval and military forces, to seize the several fortresses and military positions on the coast, and to execute the other operations which might be considered on the spot most suitable to effect the object specified in the preamble, and specifically to ensure the security of foreign residents. These opinions of Sir Charles Wyke were shared by the commanders of the joint expedition. Sir Charles thus announces them to Earl Russell:—

SIR C. WYKE TO EARL RUSSELL.

'*Vera Cruz, January* 16*th,* 1862.

' On the 8th inst. I received the official visits of General Prim and Rear-Admiral Jurien de la Gravière, and had long conversations with those officers as to the best means to be adopted for carrying out the intentions of the allies in our joint intervention in the affairs of Mexico.

' I found that they both agreed that our first duty was to aid and assist the Mexicans in obtaining such a government as was likely to afford more efficient protection to the lives and properties of foreigners resident in the Republic, before exacting from such a Government the execution of those engagements towards foreign powers which their present penury and hopeless state of disorganization does not permit them to fulfil.

'And they announced their intentions in the following proclamation to the Mexican people:—

' " The three nations which we come here to represent, and whose primary interest may seem to be satisfaction for the outrages inflicted upon them, have a higher interest, and one that has more general and beneficent consequences. They come to stretch a friendly hand to the people on whom Providence has showered all its gifts, and whom they see, with grief, wasting their strength and destroying their vitality, under the violent action of civil war and perpetual convulsions." '

Drouyn de Lhuys.—It was now that your jealousy began to show itself. It appeared to us to be obvious, and it appeared to be obvious to your own minister, Sir Charles Wyke, and to all the commanders on the spot, that no stipulations entered into with the usurping ephemeral Government of Juarez could be relied on, and that the real object of the expedition was to create in Mexico a stable government. Lord Russell, however, on the receipt of the proclamation disapproved it. He wrote to your Admiral to say that it must not be supposed that the British Government attempted the regeneration of Mexico: that its object was definite, and was limited to the protection of British persons and British property. The answer is, that it is only by the regeneration of Mexico that British persons and British property *can* be protected.

For this purpose we allowed General Almonte, the late Mexican Minister in Paris, and the head of the monarchical party in Mexico, to go to Vera Cruz, and our military men there permitted him to go on to our head-quarters. The Mexican Government required from us his expulsion, and murdered one of the most respectable men in Mexico, General Robles, on the suspicion that he was on his way to us. Thereupon Admiral Jurien determined to impose on the Mexican Government two conditions :—

I. A full and complete amnesty for all political refugees.

II. An invitation to the allied troops to go to the capital for the protection of the public peace, and an invitation to the Commissioners to deliberate and determine on the best mode of consulting the true and sincere wishes of the country.

And he proposed to the Commissioners to exact these conditions.

Then followed the Conference of the 9th of April, 1862, at Oribaza, in which the Spanish and English Commissioners refused to adopt the ultimatum proposed to them by Jurien. Jurien declared his determination, in that case, to march on Mexico, and the English and Spaniards declared that thereupon they would withdraw their troops. Each party has fulfilled its threats.

We are on our way to Mexico; you have retired, after having submitted to the indignity of treating with the ruffians who form the Juarez Government, and without having obtained either redress or even a promise of redress. If you had accepted Jurien's proposal, or if you had cordially adopted the proclamation issued, on your first landing, by your own Commissioners, I believe that all would have gone well. The infamous Juarez Government would have fallen to pieces; a French force, sufficient to enable the respectable and wise portion of the Mexican public to express its wishes, would have entered Mexico before the end of the summer of 1862, and a constitutional sovereign, probably the Archduke Maximilian, would now be reigning there.

Senior.—Under the protection of a French army?

Drouyn de Lhuys.—Certainly. We must have given him 25,000 men, and have kept them there for two or three years, until the Mexican sovereign had formed a native army.

Senior.—Officered by Frenchmen?

Drouyn de Lhuys.—Certainly. The Mexican soldier is good, or may be made good. The officer is detestable, and will remain detestable; he has no honour. Does your question imply any jealousy?

Senior.—Not in the least. Your presence and your influence in Mexico can do us nothing but good. I should be glad to see you make an Algeria of it.

Drouyn de Lhuys.—So should not I. We are mad, perhaps, in going thither at all; but we are not mad enough to wish for a dependency, four thousand miles off, with an unhealthy and stormy coast, which would cost us two or three millions sterling a-year, and would be lost the first time that we quarrelled with you, or with the Southern Anglo-American States. What we might do, and what it is your interest that we should do, is to establish there a constitutional monarchy with European sympathies. If you will cordially join us, we may do so now. But while we are doing your work you are grumbling in your beards, accusing us of ambition and of bad faith, and I know not what, as far as I can guess, out of sheer bad temper. You find from experience that your Convention of 1861 was an impracticable one; that it was inconsistent; that while it proposed to obtain indemnity for the past and security for the future, it forbade the use of the only means, the creation of a good government, by which those objects could be effected. If you continue to act thus, I foresee the result. We shall be tired of wasting our men and our money in the service of a grumbling, suspicious, dissatisfied ally. We shall easily enough force the Mexican Government to pay us the twenty or thirty millions that she owes us, and the Anglo-Americans, as soon as they see that we are in earnest, will advance it for them, at the price, perhaps, of a piece of territory twice as large as France. The rest of Mexico will soon follow the fate of that territory; and we, or our children, will have to submit to see all the Gulf of Mexico and Cuba a great slave-holding republic; and for all this you will be responsible.

Senior.—Have you had any further communication with Austria as to her Archduke?

Drouyn de Lhuys.—None since the actual war broke out. Unless you join us, we shall scarcely have any.

Senior.—Do your troops find the support which you expected from the Mexican population?

Drouyn de Lhuys.—They would have found it if we had begun our advance as soon as we had landed. The long delay and indecision occasioned by your opposition, and the presence of the Spanish troops, gave time and means to rouse against us a portion of the barbarous Indian population, which fifty years of civil war have inured to bloodshed and anarchy. But the whole Mexican people, and, above all, the Indians, are intensely Catholic. When the Juarez Government drove the monks and nuns out of their convents in Puebla, the populace kissed their footsteps in the streets, and opened every door to them. If we carry on the war seriously, if we do not abandon the country as soon as our military honour and our dignity have been satisfied, the religious resentment which this sacrilegious government is exciting will be our best auxiliary.

But, as I said before, if you persist in keeping aloof, I doubt whether we shall go further than our honour requires. The Mexican war is unpopular;—what I have said to you is what every Frenchman says to himself—'Why do we fight the battle of England without her gratitude, or even her goodwill?' If we want fields for the exercise of our superabundant activity, there are others much nearer home, from whence oppressed nations, far more deserving of our sympathies, call for us, in which we could render far greater services to humanity, and extend far more beneficially our influence. This Mexican war is producing in our finances a deficit of fifty millions a-year. Are we to impose new taxes, the most unpopular thing that a French Government can do, in order to carry on an unpopular war? Or are we to fill the deficit by loans, and lower the public funds by four or five per cent? Our late system has been to spread the *rente* over the whole country. We have succeeded in making it the most popular of investments. Every little farmer tries to have his share of it. A fall of four or five per cent will spread panic in the provinces among the classes on which this Government most relies. The next Corps Législatif will contain three or four times as many opposition members as this does. The present men—*Les Cinq*, as they are called— are not very formidable, intellectually or morally; yet they give the Government much trouble. What will twenty do, among whom will be first-rate speakers, such as Dufaure, Thiers, Montalembert, with such a subject as the Mexican war to dilate upon? You may be sure that unless you assist us to bring it to the end which *we* desire feebly, and *you* ought to desire warmly, it will terminate abruptly, and in the way which you will least like.

Senior.—The great difficulty will be to convince the English public that there really is a majority, or at least a majority of the educated portion, of the Mexican people in favour of monarchy, and in favour of any given monarch. We distrust universal suffrage under any circumstances, and still more when exercised in the presence of foreign bayonets. There are no constituted bodies in Mexico which can be trusted. I have no doubt that as soon as your troops are in Mexico they may obtain a *pronunciamento* in favour of the Archduke, or in favour of Admiral Jurien, or in favour of Prince Napoleon, or in favour of General Miramon, but what would be its value? I am inclined to think that the best plan would be to treat the Mexicans as children, who do not know what is good for them, and to take the matter into our own hands.

Drouyn de Lhuys.—I am inclined to agree with you; but what then becomes of the humbug of non-intervention? Can you afford to throw it over? It is it your pet humbug.

Senior.—I trust that we shall not let any humbug stand in the way of doing great good and preventing great harm.

Drouyn de Lhuys.—I wish that I felt that trust. With all your good sense, you are the people most governed by words, and the word 'non-interference' has a magic for you.

Guizot has often talked to me of Madame Viardot's 'Orpheus' as the finest acting that he ever saw. She is leaving the stage, and performed it yesterday for the last time. I thought her acting not quite equal to that of Mrs. Siddons in 'Lady Macbeth,' or to that of Jenny Lind in the 'Sonnambula,' but still exceedingly affecting.

The story in the Opera differs mischievously from that in Virgil. In the Opera Eurydice importunes Orpheus to look at her, and as he does so, falls dead at his feet. In Virgil Orpheus is the victim of his own passion and impatience :—

> 'Jamque pedem referens casus evaserat òmnis,
> Redditaque Eurydice superas veniebat ad auras,
> Pone sequens; namque hanc dederat Proserpina legem;
> Cum subita incautum dementia cepit amantem,
> Ignoscenda quidem, scirent si ignoscere Manes;
> Restitit, Eurydicenque suam jam luce sub ipsâ
> Immemor, heu! victusque animi respexit. Ibi omnis
> Effusus labor, atque inmitis rupta tyranni
> Fœdera, terque fragor stagnis auditus Avernis.
> Illa, Quis et me, inquit, miseram, et te perdidit, Orpheu,
> Quis tantus furor ? En iterum crudelia retro
> Fata vocant, conditque natantia lumina somnus.
> Jamque vale. Feror ingenti circumdata nocte,
> Invalidasque tibi tendens, heu non tua, palmas!'

Nothing visible could have given the idea of undefined, unlimited darkness suggested by the words *ingenti circumdata nocte*. But if, after the three bursts of infernal thunder, the stage could have been darkened, and Eurydice could have faded away, repeating those wonderful lines, the catastrophe would have been awful, instead of what it now is, rather commonplace. The scene which follows, in which Love sets all right, by reanimating Eurydice, and dismissing her to upper air, is a still worse innovation. It turns the Tragedy into a Farce.

May 1st.—I will throw together several long conversations which during the last ten days I have had with Renan, on the subject of his unpublished work, '*Histoire Critique des Origines du Christianisme.*'

Renan.—It is printed, but I do not intend to publish it until I have delivered my next course of lectures—perhaps not until I have delivered more than one course. It will scandalise the orthodox world. I reject totally the supposed inspiration of the compilers of the Gospels. It was an idea introduced by the schoolmen, in order to supply premisses for their disputations. The human mind was then the slave of authority. A text from Aristotle was conclusive in metaphysics; a text from the Bible was conclusive in theology. The skill of the disputer was shown by leading his adversary to an affirmation contradictory to one of the indisputable authorities.

Senior.—St. Hilaire, who is a considerable Orientalist, believes that the Gospels were not published in their present form until the second century.

Renan.—I disagree from him; I have no doubt that the Gospels assumed their present form in the first century, and I see no reason for disbelieving the uniform tradition that they were compiled by those whose names they bear. When I use the word 'compiled,' I exclude St. John, for his Gospel is obviously original, and its peculiarities are a strong proof that when it was written the other three Gospels existed. Not one of the miracles related by any of the earlier Evangelists is mentioned by St. John, except the feeding of the five thousand, and the walking of Jesus on the lake the following night.

St. John, indeed, scarcely mentions an event which is told by any one else. Such remarkable ones as the Transfiguration, the choosing the Apostles, and the institution of the Eucharist, at each of which he was present, are not even alluded to. There is not a single parable in the whole Gospel, nor any moral precept, except the 'New Commandment,' to love one another. The only condition on which eternal life is made to depend is faith in Himself. Strongly contrasted with the absence of moral teaching is the abundance of doctrinal teaching.

The union of Jesus with the Father, the necessity of a firm belief in this union, and the promise of eternal life to those who possess this belief, constitute nearly the whole Gospel.

This absence from the work of St. John of everything contained in the other Gospels could not have taken place by accident; and if it was intentional, he must have had all the other Gospels before him.

Again, it is impossible that the predictions ascribed to Christ three days before the passion could have been ascribed to Him by any one writing after the end of the first century; for that prophecy declares that, 'Immediately after the tribulation of those days, the sun shall be darkened, the stars shall fall from heaven, and the powers of the heavens shall be shaken; and then shall all the tribes of the earth mourn, and they shall see the Son of Man coming in the clouds of heaven with power and great glory. And he shall send forth his angels, and they shall gather together his elect from one end of the heaven to the other. When you see all these things, know that it is near, even at the door. Verily, I say unto you, that this generation shall not pass away until all these things be fulfilled. Heaven and earth shall pass away, but my words shall not pass away.'

Senior.—It seems clear that Matthew confounds two different events predicted by our Saviour in the same conversation. That conversation began by the remarks of the disciples on the vast substructions of the Temple. Jesus answered that the day was coming when one stone would not be left on another. Then Peter, James, John, and Andrew, asked him privately when this was to be, and what would be the previous tokens. He answers, according to Matthew and Mark, that the token would be the desecration of the sanctuary foretold by Daniel; * according to Luke, the surrounding of Jerusalem with hostile armies. 'There will then,' he adds, 'be misery such as never was endured before, and Jerusalem will be trodden down by the Gentiles.' Here the first prophecy, that of the fall of Jerusalem, seems to end. The second prophecy, which you have mentioned, and

---

* 'They shall pollute the sanctuary, and shall place there the abomination that maketh desolate.'—DAN. ii. 31.

which describes the end of the world, follows. Matthew connects the two by the word 'Immediately;' but as the events predicted in the second prophecy have not yet occurred, it is clear that Matthew, impressed with the then prevalent notion that the end of the world was at hand, confounded the two prophecies, and that Mark and Luke copied him. The second event, the destruction of the world, seems to be that of which Jesus says, 'Of that hour and day knoweth no man, no, not the angels which are in heaven, neither the Son, but the Father only.' But He *does* foretell the time of the first event, the destruction of Jerusalem, and fixes it within the lives of the existing generation, as He had previously fixed the arrival of the kingdom of Heaven before the deaths of some of those who then stood around him.* Luke seems to have perceived the inconsistency of these statements, and omits the affirmation that no one, not the angels, not the Son, but only the Father knew the time when the prediction would be fulfilled. John, as you remark, omits the whole conversation.

Renan.—Few things seem more remarkable than the scantiness of the memoranda of the teaching of Jesus. His disciples, indeed, did not belong to a writing class, they were illiterate artisans and fishermen. Nor was it a writing age. Much too is to be attributed to the prevailing expectation that the end of the world, or rather of this 'aion,' of this phase of

---

* Matt. xvi. 28.

the world's existence, was at hand and would be immediately succeeded by the kingdom of Heaven. It seemed unnecessary to record lessons which would soon cease to be applicable. I think it probable that the first record was that which Matthew made of the discourses of Jesus—the 'logia' as they are called. Then probably Mark added a narrative of some of the events of His ministry. Still later, probably after the destruction of Jerusalem, Luke published his collections, and the possessors of the different Gospels filled up their copies by extracts taken from the others; and thus the three first Gospels became chapter after chapter identical. Much later John wrote, and without adding anything to the moral lessons recorded by his predecessors, gave them a sanction by declaring the divinity and pre-existence of Jesus.

The general impression is that the teaching of Jesus was melancholy. Towards the latter part of His ministry, after He had warned His disciples that they would be objects of hatred and contempt, that they would all be persecuted and some destroyed, that He Himself would suffer an ignominious and cruel death, that Jerusalem would be trodden under foot, and that the whole Jewish nation would undergo calamities such as had never been endured before, of course the general character of His discourse became melancholy. But it does not seem to have been so at the beginning. The disciples believed that the kingdom of Heaven was at hand. What it was to be was not clearly indicated, but there can be little doubt that they expected the fulfilment of the prophecy of Daniel.

'I saw in the night visions, and behold one like the Son of Man came with the clouds of heaven, and came to the Ancient of days. And there was given to Him dominion and glory and a kingdom that all people, nations, and languages should serve Him: His dominion is an everlasting dominion, which shall not pass away, and His kingdom is that which shall not be destroyed. And the kingdom and dominion, and the greatness of the kingdom under the whole heaven shall be given to the people of the Saints of the Most High, whose kingdom is an everlasting kingdom, and all dominions shall serve and obey Him.'—Daniel, chap. vii.

The Pagan Golden Age was a painful recollection. They believed in the gradual deterioration of mankind.

'Ætas parentum pejor aris tulit
Nos nequiores, mox daturos
Progeniem vitiosiorem.'

The Jewish Golden Age was future, and it was believed to be now at hand.

Galilee even now, after the ravages of centuries of war and of Mussulman waste and tyranny, is one of the most delightful countries in the world, full of verdure, water, and shade. Nazareth itself is a charming little town, by far the most agreeable in Palestine. Its low square detached houses have no beauty within or without, but they are embosomed in vines, fig-trees, and oranges, and stand in gardens intersected by streams from the hills around. The fountain, which was the centre of the society of the ancient town, is ruined, as everything under Turkish rule gets ruined, but its ruins are still the resort of Nazarene women, whose beauty, a gift from the Virgin Mary, still makes them renowned in the East. The ridge, freshened by the sea-breeze, on the slope of which the town stands, commands a glorious prospect, extending from Carmel and the sea to the west to beyond the valley of Jordan to the east. It was in this delicious country that Jesus passed His youth and His adolescence, and He strayed little out of it during the wanderings which occupied His ministry. The villages of Magdala, Capernaum, Bethsaida, and Chorazin, were all in the small space of a few square leagues between Nazareth and the Lake. The trees, excepting the fruit trees which overshadow the gardens, have disappeared; but the waters of the lake are as clear and as blue as ever; its shores, free from mud, are covered with turf and flowers down to the water's edge, and are broken into little bays and capes, covered with thickets of arbutus, rose, and cactus. He does not appear to have travelled in Samaria more than once or twice, on His way to Jerusalem, and He seldom visited Jerusalem except to attend the annual feasts. The arid, naked plains of Judea probably offended His exquisite taste for the beauties of nature as much as the narrowness and hypocrisy of the Pharisees and Scribes disgusted His moral sense. He seems always to have returned with new delight to the verdure of Galilee and to the simplicity of the Galileans.

Senior.—And yet it was in Galilee that He said that a prophet had no honour in his own country.

Renan.—That must have been an ebullition of temporary disappointment. It was said, too, in the very beginning of His ministry, when His own brethren disbelieved in Him, and those who had known Him as a child, the son of humble parents, were slow to admit His Messianic pretensions. At a later period He was more reverenced in Galilee than in Jerusalem. Though His disciples were of the humblest, or the least respected classes—fishermen, artisans, tax-gatherers, and sinners, they were not unrefined. The coarseness of the European boor or working man is not to be found in the East. No man is more gentlemanlike than a Bedouin. Human nature requires little in such a country; the idea of comfort belongs to indoor life and cold climates. It was very rarely indeed that Jesus or His disciples were ill received. They had a common purse of which Judas Iscariot was the bearer, but he does not seem to have made much use of it. When the twelve, and afterwards the seventy, were sent out, they were desired to take with them no money, but they suffered no inconvenience for the want of it.

Senior.—Jesus complained that the Son of Man had not where to lay His head.

Renan.—I am not sure that that can be called a complaint. He had then a settled residence at

Capernaum. It was probably merely a statement that being on a journey He had for the time no fixed habitation.

There is no allusion in the Gospels to indigence among His disciples. Some of them, such as Zacchæus and Joseph of Arimathea, were rich, though He treated wealth as an obstacle to piety.

The peculiarities of His teaching were cheerful. Every previous religion had been ascetic. Even the disciples of John the Baptist had fasted. Every previous religion interposed between God and man a priesthood. Every previous religion was encumbered with ceremonies, long prayers, and observances.

Senior.—Not only every previous religion, but every subsequent one. There are no religions to which these qualities more belong than those of the Roman and of the Greek Church.

Renan.—Well, the religion taught by Jesus is utterly free from them. The scene of the first miracle attributed to him is a marriage-feast. No scruples as to the character of the master or of the guests prevented His acceptance of invitations. He came to call not the *just* but sinners to repentance. In the East a house which receives a stranger becomes for the time public. The inhabitants of the village, and above all the children, flock round it. Jesus would not allow them to be repulsed. The women showed their reverence and their love by offering to Him precious oils and perfumes. The disciples sometimes murmured at the waste or the interruption, but His affectionate heart sympathised with all testimonies of affection. He disapproved of all worldly cares, 'Sufficient,' he said, 'for the day is the evil thereof.' He reproved Martha for the elaborateness of her hospitality. The intercourse among the disciples was sometimes a little disturbed by questions as to their comparative rank in the future kingdom; but these were quickly ended by the interposition of their Master, and in general they seem to have lived together in perfect harmony. Their love and reverence of their Master were abundant, and so was His affection for them; though John had His peculiar love, and Peter was the one on whose vigour and devotion He most relied. The doctrine itself was called 'the good news.' The approach of the kingdom was the subject of constant expectation. It was one of the petitions of the only prayer which Jesus taught. I can conceive nothing more joyous than these early pilgrimages in Galilee, in a beautiful country, and a climate such as untravelled northerners cannot conceive; of a master speaking, as His enemies admitted, as no man ever spoke before, and of disciples young and enthusiastic, free from all worldly cares, and publishing everywhere the 'good news that the kingdom of Heaven is at hand.' That kingdom, according to the belief of the disciples, was to take place on this earth. It had a far greater influence on their imagination than the promises of happiness in a future world and in a future state of existence could have had.

Many of the expressions of Jesus seem to point to a terrestrial millennium.

'I appoint to you,' he said to His disciples on the eve of His passion, 'a kingdom as My Father hath appointed unto Me, that you may eat and drink at My table in My kingdom, and sit on thrones judging the twelve tribes of Israel.'

Now, enlightened by the events we know, that the kingdom of God foretold by Jesus was the improvement produced by Christianity. And when we compare the state of the Pagan world, with its slavery, its cruelty, its licentiousness, its injustice, its fraud, and its hopeless, unimproving corruption, with that of the countries in which Christianity in its purer form exists, we may well call the latter the kingdom of God.

April 26th.—I called on Mr. Dayton, the Federal minister.

I said to him that during the last five weeks I had conversed with many persons of political eminence on American affairs. That I found fears that the conduct towards us of the Federal Government would lead to war, universal; and an opinion that it was intended to produce war, prevalent; and that I thought it advisable that he should know the opinions, as to that conduct, of persons of political eminence, not merely impartial, but favourable to the cause of the Federals.

He answered that he should be grateful for the information.

I then read to him my conversations with Thiers, Circourt, A. Chevalier, Corcelle, Dumon, Duchâtel, and the Duc de Broglie.

Dayton.—I recognise in all that you have read to me, the *Times*. I believe that it is useless for a Northern American to state any facts, to contradict any falsehoods, or to use any arguments in England or in France. You—all of you, French as well as English—take all your opinions, all your premisses, and all your conclusions, blindly from the *Times*.

I have known men treat the *Times*, sometimes with contempt, sometimes with indignation; describe it as the unscrupulous organ of the English aristocracy and laugh at those under its influences, and immediately afterwards talk to me pure *Times*. The Government of the United States would be frantic if it did not do everything, and submit to everything, in order to avoid a war with you.

Senior.—That is precisely what *they* say; and the inference which they draw from your conduct, is that *you are* frantic. If, they say, the President and his advisers wish for a war with England, they are mad. If they do not wish for it, and yet do all they can to bring it on, then also they are mad. Take the appointment of Captain Wilkes.

Dayton.—I do not know what are the rules of your service. Captain Wilkes is the most popular man in our navy. He may have had claims which could not be refused.

Senior.—Captain Wilkes's popularity for having done all that he could to bring on a war with us, is a proof of the madness of the people. An English officer, who had so acted, would have disgusted everybody. What, then, do you think of Mr. Cassius Clay, and the motives which led his Government to publish his despatches, and afterwards to employ him?

Dayton.—I defend neither of those acts. They were great mistakes. But you give us great provocation by assisting the rebels. The *Alabama* is manned by English sailors.

Senior.—And is not your blockading fleet manned by English sailors? Can you tell me how to prevent a sailor from taking service where he likes?

Dayton.—You ought to have exerted greater vigilance to prevent her sailing. You ought not to have thrown on Mr. Adams the onus of proving her destination. When you complained, during the Crimean war, that we were building vessels for the Emperor of Russia, we did not throw on your minister the burden of proof; we examined ourselves, ascertained that it was so, and stopped the ships.

I admit that it is difficult to prevent the people, who are the greatest manufacturers of military supplies in the world, from supplying belligerents with arms. But if you cannot—as you say you cannot—prevent Nassau from being a base of operations to the Confederate armies, you should use the utmost toleration of our efforts to prevent this. If your sympathies are with those who are endeavouring to ruin us, you should not parade them. If you think that you will gain by the rupture of the Union, you are mistaken. Do you suppose that the Confederates sympathise with you, except so far as they believe that you hate us?

Senior.—No. I have no doubt that the Confederates hate us as much as you do; but they have the merit of keeping their secret better. If we knew all that they think and feel, we probably should feel towards them as you seem to be trying to make us feel towards you.

Dayton.—Well, I do not believe with your French friends that our public men are mad. I do not believe, therefore, that they wish for war. Nor do I believe that yours do. But each party is excited; each party is—whether voluntarily or not—doing great mischief to the other.

I see no remedy but patience, and an earnest attempt to repress the evil passions of the educated mobs in your country, and of the uneducated mobs in mine. Of one thing I am certain, that if you think that any interference on your part will stop the war, you are wrong. Not England, and France, and Russia—not all Europe, could influence us.

Senior.—Not by persuasion?

Dayton.—Not by force. What the South wants is food; and that you cannot give her. She has arms enough; she has men enough; but she is starving, and she will be starved out. My expectations of peace depend much on the manner in which you deal with the ironsides which the Confederates are now building in England. You excuse yourselves for not having stopped the *Alabama* on the ground that she was not obviously a ship of war. These ships are so. No merchant-vessel is plated. We maintain that they are intended for the Confederates, —intended to prey on the commerce of the Federals, your friends. You desire us to prove that intention. How can we prove it except by the facts which are already as obvious as they can be made? For what other purpose can they be intended? The builders alone have the documents by which the innocent destination of the ships can be shown. You should call on the builders to produce them. If they refuse, you may safely assume that they are intended to attack us. I do not ask you to confiscate them, or even to stop their progress, but merely to detain them until the builders prove—which they can do in a day —the innocence of their destination.

In the Crimean war, we did much more. We actually stopped the progress of the *Alexandra*, on the suspicion that she was intended for the Russians. Not an axe, or a hammer, was allowed to be lifted in her. We found our laws, as you have found yours, insufficient. We amended them. You merely fold your arms and allow proceedings opposed to your own municipal laws and to international law, to good feeling and to good faith, to go on, because your municipal law has not sufficient detective power. Then give it that power. You are not, as we are, bound by a constitution. Your Parliament is omnipotent. If it is not skilful enough to invent a law which shall enable such atrocities to be detected and prevented, let it copy the law which we passed for that purpose, and which was sufficient.

If you refuse to do this, and, in consequence of your negligence, or of your self-inflicted impotence, these ironsides escape and plunder us, the American people, irritated enough already, will be ungovernable. You have seen enough of them to know that their resentment is not under the control of their interests. They will really become as mad as your French friends call them. They will be quite ready to ruin themselves in order to ruin you.

May 2nd.—We left Paris.

[This was the last Journal that Mr. Senior wrote.]

THE END.

www.ingramcontent.com/pod-product-compliance
Lightning Source LLC
Chambersburg PA
CBHW030325240426
43673CB00040B/1278